John Greig was twice voted Scottish Player of the Year, and between 1961 and 1978 he played a total of 755 competitive games, and scored 120 goals. He won five league titles, six Scottish Cups, four League Cups and the European Cup-Winners' Cup in 1972. He also won 44 Scotland caps and was captain of his country for three consecutive years.

He was awarded the MBE in 1977 and became manager of Rangers in 1978, remaining in that post until he resigned in October 1983. He later returned to Rangers to work in public relations and was appointed to the Rangers Board. He lives in Glasgow with his wife Janette and has one son, Murray, married to Laura, and a granddaughter, Kaitlin.

Jim Black, who worked with John Greig on the writing of this book, began his career in journalism on leaving school in 1967. He joined the *Scottish Sun* as a sports writer in 1975 and spent 24 years with that newspaper before becoming a freelance writer on football, boxing and golf. He has reported on several World Cup and European Championship finals tournaments.

MY STORY

JOHN GREIG

WITH JIM BLACK

headline

First published in 2005
by HEADLINE BOOK PUBLISHING

First published in paperback in 2006
by HEADLINE BOOK PUBLISHING

1

0 7553 1355 0 (ISBN-10)
978 0 7553 1355 6 (ISBN-13)

Statistics compiled by Jack Rollin

Typeset in Garamond by Avon DataSet Ltd,
Bidford-on-Avon, Warwickshire

Printed and bound in Great Britain by
Clays Ltd, St Ives plc

HEADLINE BOOK PUBLISHING
A division of Hodder Headline
338 Euston Road
London NW1 3BH

www.headline.co.uk
www.hodderheadline.com

CONTENTS

ACKNOWLEDGEMENTS

In writing this book, I have the opportunity to give my thanks to a number of people.

To my lovely wife Janette, a big thank you for her love, support and understanding. Without her, I doubt if I could have achieved anything.

To my son Murray and his wife Laura, thank you for being there. Also to my little princess Kaitlin, who has made the last eighteen months so enjoyable for Janette and myself.

To Rangers Football Club and all who follow them for their support over a long number of years. It has been my privilege to serve them.

Finally to Jim Black, whose great work in helping me write this book is hugely appreciated.

CHAPTER 1

LEGEND

Those who have a statue erected in their honour don't normally have the opportunity to approve their likeness for the simple reason that they are already dead. So when I look up at the statue of yours truly that stands in Edmiston Drive, on the corner of the Main Stand and the Copland Road Stand, I do so almost with a sense of disbelief and certainly with a feeling that I am not worthy of such recognition.

They erected a statue to my former Scotland team-mate Billy Bremner at Elland Road and one to Sir Matt Busby at Old Trafford, but both had passed on by the time their contributions to Leeds and Manchester United had been recognised in such a manner. However, I should make it clear that the statue depicting John Greig in his playing days holds much greater significance. It is there primarily as a memorial to the sixty-six people who perished in the worst disaster in the history of British football and, as such, is a fitting tribute to those who lost their lives on 2 January 1971.

It is also a tribute to others who died in earlier tragedies. Ten years previously, on 16 September 1961, two fans were killed and sixty others injured when a stairway barrier broke at the end of an Old Firm game,

1

which finished in a 2–2 draw. There had been a much greater loss of life in 1902, when the west terracing at the ground collapsed during a Scotland-England international. A total of twenty-five fans died in that appalling accident, forcing Rangers to drastically reduce the capacity of the old Ibrox.

I had campaigned for years for a lasting memorial to be erected as near as possible to the site of the Ibrox Disaster. I didn't feel that the plaque, which stood close to the old Stairway 13, was any longer sufficient, as it didn't include the names of the dead. Over the years I had spoken to many relatives and friends of the deceased and I had gathered the impression that they were keen to see a more appropriate memorial; one which could be visited by the descendants of the victims of what was a truly awful accident.

I had favoured the erection of a small cairn bearing a plaque with the names of the sixty-six, but I was informed that would pose a problem in terms of security, as there was apparently no guarantee that such a monument could be made vandal-proof. Never for a moment, though, did I imagine that plans were in the pipeline for a statue of John Greig to be erected to commemorate the 30th anniversary of the tragedy in January 2001.

The first I knew of it was around the end of November 2000, when artist Senga Murray, who has worked closely with Rangers for a number of years, informed me that Campbell Ogilvie, who is Rangers' secretary and a director of the club, wanted to discuss something with me. You could have knocked me down with a feather when Campbell told me, in an almost matter of fact manner, 'By the way, John, we're putting up a statue at the end of Edmiston Drive and it's you.'

This was just five weeks before the planned unveiling and apparently those involved in the project were rather keen that I give it the once over, in particular the sculptor, Andy Scott. Heaven knows what their reaction would have been had I voiced my disapproval. Three days later, on the following Monday, my wife, Janette, and I drove to the Maryhill district of Glasgow to visit Andy's yard, to view the work in progress.

Perhaps it would have been more accurate to describe it as a work already completed, and it felt strange and more than a little unnerving to be going to catch my first glimpse of a replica of myself. I remember passing one of the windows in Andy's workshop and seeing this large shadow and wondering to myself, 'What the hell is that?'

My initial reaction was one of sheer disbelief. In fact, I was dumbstruck, to the extent that Andy became concerned by my silence, imagining that I wasn't happy with the finished article, but that was far from being the case. It was just the shock of looking at a bronze effigy of myself. Personally, I thought he had done a brilliant job. I was even more amazed when Andy explained that he had worked from a photograph he had seen in a book. Yet, the detail and the way he had captured various aspects of my personality were remarkable, in my opinion.

In addition to a feeling of overwhelming pride, I also felt deeply honoured and very, very humble, but I seriously questioned the decision, as it somehow didn't seem right to me that a statue to any one individual should be erected to commemorate such a dreadful waste of life. However, it was explained to me that those who had made the decision had done so on the grounds that I had been captain that day and had subsequently been directly involved with the relatives of many of those who had died.

So when I look at the statue I don't think of it as depicting me, but rather of what it represents. I got my wish for a fitting memorial plaque listing the names of the dead, even if the form it took was not quite what I'd had in mind. Believe me when I say that I feel immense pride to stand above the sixty-six names. That means much more than the undoubted honour of Rangers fans pointing to the statue and saying, 'Look, there's Greigy.'

I also consider myself fortunate to still enjoy a close relationship with the fans, more than a quarter of a century after I stopped playing, as was demonstrated in March 1999 when they voted me 'Greatest Ever Ranger'. Mind you, I have to disappoint those fans who ask me for my autograph and request that I write 'Greatest Ever Ranger' after my name. I refuse to do that because football is a team game and I was fortunate to play alongside great players. There have also been many other outstanding Rangers players, before and after me.

But while I don't consider it my place to broadcast the fact that I was given such a lofty accolade, it was a wonderful tribute nevertheless. Moreover, it was one that was bestowed on me by the fans, as they were the ones who did the voting. I have always maintained that while a player can con fans some of the time by kissing the badge on his jersey and declaring that he is playing for that jersey, you can't kid them all the time. They are the ones who judge a player's worth to the team and his feelings for the club and respond accordingly.

So receiving the highest number of votes in a poll featuring so many great players meant an awful lot to me, considering how easy it is for the younger and middle-aged fans to forget those players from the past whom they never saw play. After all, the game is more about today and tomorrow than past successes. I was in my late fifties when I was named 'Greatest Ever Ranger' in competition with the current stars and other worthy candidates who came before and after me, but maybe, in a sense, I shouldn't have been all that surprised.

I have never had anything other than the greatest respect for the Rangers fans and I think that respect has been reciprocated over the past forty-six years, bearing in mind that 70,000 turned out for my testimonial game in 1978 against a Scotland XI. No Rangers player had been granted the honour of a testimonial match before that. It was also the last occasion in which the old stadium was filled to capacity. In fact, the kickoff had to be delayed for thirty minutes to allow everyone access.

Graeme Souness, who later became manager of Rangers, was part of the international scene at that time. He was also responsible for landing me with the nickname 'Legend'. In 1990 I had not long returned to Rangers, in the role of public relations officer, when Graeme approached me one day and asked if I was busy. To be honest, there wasn't a great deal for me to do because the PR role had more or less been created for my benefit, so I told him the truth. 'In that case,' he said, 'go and get yourself some training gear and a pair of boots and join us for a kickabout.'

I had trained occasionally at lunchtime during the previous two years, but I hadn't kicked a ball for goodness knows how long, so I wondered what awaited me when I joined Graeme and the squad for training at Jordanhill. As the players did their warm-up exercises, I stood on the sidelines until they had finished. Then Graeme picked two teams and I found myself on the same side as Ally McCoist and Ian Durrant, who had been players during my time as manager.

Once the game kicked off, Coisty and Durrant began shouting for me to pass the ball to them with the instruction, 'Here, gaffer.' This went on for some time and I didn't pay any attention to the fact that they were addressing me as 'Gaffer'. But Graeme, who was in opposition, was clearly not amused and his anger eventually boiled over. Suddenly he stopped the game and turned to Coisty and Durrant. 'Right, let's get one thing straight,' he shouted. Then, pointing to me, he said, 'I'm the gaffer. He's the legend!' I was stuck with the tag, which was inevitably shortened to 'Ledge'.

But while others may perceive me as a Rangers legend, I still see myself as the wee lad from Edinburgh who kicked a tennis ball about the streets and dreamed of one day playing football for a living. I have been extremely fortunate to have achieved so much in my life through football. When I think of all the marvellous experiences I have had, how could I ever complain? Life has been wonderful to me in very many ways and, if I missed out by not chasing bigger money elsewhere, I have no regrets, because the satisfaction I've derived from my successes with Rangers and the happiness of my family have compensated for any material gain many times over.

CHAPTER 2
KICKING OFF

I can't claim to have been born to play football, but I was kicking a ball before I could even walk properly. In fact, I can't remember a time in my life when football hasn't played a huge part in it. My brother, Tam, was responsible for me developing such an early interest in the game. Tam, the third youngest of a family of six – four boys, Alfie, Alex, Tam and me, and two girls, Nessie and Margaret – was like a second father and he spent hours encouraging me to develop what skills I had been blessed with.

When I arrived on the scene on 11 September 1942 (tragically, the events of that day in 2001 have ensured that nine-eleven is now a date associated with infamy), Britain was at war. However, I have no memories of those dark days other than the air raid shelter that remained in our back garden for years after and which became a favourite play area for me and my pals.

We lived at No. 26 Clearburn Crescent, Prestonfield, almost in the shadow of Arthur's Seat, and it remained my home for the first twenty-five years of my life. My parents, Tom and Agnes, were already in their forties when I was born and there was a significant age gap between the bairn of the family and my elder siblings. Regrettably, there are only two of us left, me and my youngest sister, Margaret, who is ten years older. Being so much younger than the rest I was fussed over to an extent, but I can't claim that I was ever spoiled. My brothers and sisters ensured that I stayed in line, especially Tam.

My first ball was one my sisters knitted for me when I was two years old. Because it was soft, I was able to kick it around the house without doing any damage and I remember my first goal was my mother's sideboard. It was an old-fashioned piece of furniture and the space between the legs was the target.

When people ask me if I always wanted to be a footballer, I can honestly answer yes, because it never crossed my mind that I would do anything else. Although we lived in a tenement building we had a large hallway, which was covered with wax cloth, and Tam used to bring an old-fashioned leather football with lacing home with him, so I could practise my kicking. It was heavy for a wee lad and Tam made me take off my right shoe, so that if I kicked with that foot it would sting. The idea was to force me to kick the ball with my weaker left foot and by the time I was five or six I could kick equally well with either foot.

Tam also used to take me out to the back green or local park. He gave me a great deal of encouragement, yet later on, when he ran his own juvenile team, he refused to give me a game. One evening, when I went to watch his team play, I was allowed to join in, but that was it. Tam made it clear that was my first and last involvement with his team. I suppose it was his way of ensuring that my feet stayed firmly on the ground.

Apart from the back green, where I spent hours developing my skills with a tennis ball, I used to play a lot on a large area of ground directly behind my home. Our makeshift pitch was long and narrow and it wasn't unusual for teams of twenty players a side to be involved in games that lasted for hours on end. Jackets were used as goal posts and the pitch was so long that when the ball was at the opposite end there was time for the defenders to stop and have a drink.

Our next door neighbour's daughter married Frank Donlevy, who played for Partick Thistle, and Frank regularly had a kickabout with me on the back green. Jocky Robertson, the Third Lanark goalkeeper, stayed at No. 2 Clearburn Crescent and he used to give me sixpence (two and a half pence) every time I managed to score a goal against him. Wee Jocky had played junior football with my brother, Tam, and he was a good bit older than me, but I subsequently travelled with both Jocky and Frank Donlevy and played against them. Years later I had the satisfaction of scoring against Third Lanark in a league match and succeeded in bundling both the ball and Jocky into the back of the net. He was furious and chased me all the way back to the halfway line.

Although I had been kicking a ball about since I could walk, I didn't have my first competitive game until the age of nine, when Mr McLeod, one of the teachers at my school, Prestonfield Primary, asked if I would like to play in a schools match. He had obviously seen me taking part in impromptu games with my pals in the playground and reckoned I was a useful player.

I was dead keen to take the teacher up on his offer, but explained that I didn't own a pair of football boots. That wasn't a problem, though. He opened a cupboard containing a selection of old boots in various states of disrepair and eventually I found a pair that fitted me reasonably well. The boots were the type with wooden studs with the nails sticking out and Tam carried out the necessary repairs before polishing the boots ready for my introduction to the world of organised football. We ended up winning the Edinburgh Primary Schools Cup by beating Dalry in the final and I still have my first medal.

Tam played for Dalkeith Thistle and was good enough to attract the attention of a Hearts scout, but as luck would have it, the evening the scout came to our house to offer Tam signing terms my brother wasn't at home. My mother explained that he had gone to the pub. Hearts immediately lost interest, believing that my brother was a bit of a drinker, but Tam wasn't a big boozer. The reason he was a regular at various pubs in the area was because he was the east of Scotland darts champion and the competitions were held in pubs. Tam had done nothing wrong, but he regretted having thrown away the opportunity to become a professional and consequently made sure I toed the line.

Tam had been a fireman in the days of steam trains, before realising the dream that just about every youngster had then by becoming a diesel engine driver. In fact, I remember once getting off the train at Glasgow's Queen Street station and hearing someone shout to me. It was my brother, who had been driving the train that had brought us from Edinburgh. Tam died at the comparatively young age of forty-eight and I regret he didn't live long enough to see me complete my career, because he was so influential in my development as a kid.

At primary school I was actually quite bright and in exams always finished first or second in the class. My academic qualifications were sufficient to earn me a place at Boroughmuir. The trouble was that it's a rugby-playing school and I wasn't a fan of the oval ball game, so I cheated in a sense and completed the necessary forms to gain me entry to a junior secondary where football was the name of the game. This was unbeknown to my father, who went to his grave none the wiser.

On reflection, it might not have been such a bad idea to have aimed for higher academic achievements, but James Clark Junior Secondary suited my needs. The fact that I would have been able to sit A levels at Boroughmuir didn't seem terribly important at the time. When you're only eleven years old and hell-bent on becoming a professional foot-baller, those considerations don't matter a great deal.

I went straight into the school B team and there was also the bonus of being able to hire an old-style leather football for the weekend at the cost of one shilling (five pence). One of the teachers had come up with the idea and I couldn't get home quickly enough when school broke up on a Friday afternoon, because the most popular guy in the street was the one with a ball. I also used to plague the life out of my mother and sisters to buy me a plastic ball. The trouble was they burst easily if they came in contact with a sharp object.

As a young teenager I was small for my age, but the teachers insisted on me playing for the team the level above my year, so the opposition appeared like giants to me. On one occasion, when we played St Anthony's, I was threatened by a couple of guys dressed like Teddy Boys, complete with drainpipe trousers, beetle-crusher shoes and slicked-back hair. 'We're going to break your leg,' I was informed. 'But, why me? I'm just a wee lad,' I pleaded. But I wouldn't show my fear during the actual game, because Tam used to tell me never to let anyone see that they had got the better of me. 'If you get kicked don't go down,' he would say. 'Wait until the other person's back is turned before you rub your leg.'

In those days I was a ball-playing inside-forward with an eye for goal. I was also two-footed and got my share. Even though I spent most of my senior career playing in defence, I never lost the knack of scoring and I am ranked ninth in Rangers' top ten post-war goal-scorers with 140 to my credit.

In spite of my lack of inches and slight build I had a good pair of legs on me when I was a youngster. I had strong and powerful thighs developed during my early morning milk runs and the fact that I ran eight miles a day to and from school. My day began at 6.30 a.m. with my milk delivery, which took me two hours to complete. I received twenty-five shillings a week for my efforts, so when a rival dairy 'tapped' me and offered fifteen shillings for what amounted to just twenty minutes' work I jumped at the offer. When my dad found out he blew a fuse. My wages went to my mother, to help supplement her house-keeping money, and in addition to receiving a belt across the ear from my old man, I was told in no uncertain terms to make sure I got my old job back, because it paid ten bob more a week.

During my milk deliveries I also used to check out dustbins for discarded hard-backed books. The covers were used as improvised shin guards and to line the soles of my shoes, which were constantly worn out by all the running I did. I ran two miles, four times a day. It was two miles each way from my home to school and I also made the trip at lunch-time, racing the corporation buses up a big hill to try to increase my speed and endurance. I used to fantasise that the passengers were watching me, because my brother would say that you never knew who was taking note. In addition to the school runs and my milk deliveries, I also did a paper round in the evenings, so fitness wasn't a problem.

The old-fashioned gas lamps that used to adorn the streets of Britain also came into play as part of my training regime. I would run along the street with one foot on the pavement and the other in the gutter, to try to perfect my body swerve, and then jump up and try to touch the lamp posts in an effort to improve my ability in the air.

When I was fourteen I was put forward by my school for the Scotland schoolboys under-fifteen trials and I made it through to the final phase, along with the likes of Billy Bremner. The final trial to select the international squad was held at Dumbarton and I was chosen to play on the right wing, because of my height and build. However, I shouldn't have played after pulling a thigh muscle. The upshot was that when our side was awarded a corner, I was unable to take the kick and the right-half had to deputise for me. Unfortunately, with the right-half out of position, the opposition raced up the park and scored, and the teacher in charge gave me a verbal blast. Consequently, I never won the schoolboy cap I craved.

Around the same time I was approached by one of the teachers at Tynecastle School, which stands next to the Hearts ground. He explained that the team had reached the semi-finals of the Scottish Schools Cup and that if I was prepared to travel every day from Prestonfield he could arrange for me to change schools, so I could turn out for Tynecastle. I turned him down, though, largely on the grounds that it wouldn't have been fair to the lad who had played in the previous rounds of the cup to have suddenly been dropped to make way for me. Perhaps if I had been a bit more ruthless my life would have turned out differently, given the close proximity of the school to Tynecastle and my boyhood heroes, but fate decreed that I would never wear the maroon jersey of Hearts.

NEARER MY GOD TO THEE

Back in the 1950s it was every city dweller's dream to escape to the country. Leaving behind the smoke and grime for a few days of rural bliss had great appeal for those of us who spent the majority of our lives confronting the hustle and the bustle of an inner-city existence. Edinburgh is known as the Athens of the north, but when I was growing up, behind the capital's posh exterior lurked the grim reality of everyday life for many thousands of its inhabitants.

The tenement buildings are a sight rarely seen by the tourists who flock to Edinburgh in their tens of thousands every year, to visit world-famous landmarks such as the Castle and the Scott Monument and to walk the length of Princes Street. Don't get me wrong. I was more fortunate than many in that we lived in a house in the shadow of Arthur's Seat in one of the more desirable areas of the city. Not that we were rich, far from it, but my father and brothers were in employment, so there was always food on the table and my mother ensured that our home was kept spick-and-span. But like others of my generation, I jumped at the chance to venture out of my surroundings and sample another sort of living. So when the opportunity arose for me to attend a boys' camp in Perthshire, I badgered my parents to be allowed to go. It was a decision that very nearly cost me my life!

Perthshire, with its rolling hills, streams and rivers and spectacular scenery, is one of Scotland's most beautiful counties. Perth is known as the gateway to the Highlands and beyond the city, a twenty-minute drive away, lies the historic town of Dunkeld. Nearby is Birnham Wood, where one of the acts in Shakespeare's *Macbeth* is set, and the village of Dalguise, which has become a popular haunt for youth groups from all over Scotland. To a fourteen-year-old like me, my temporary surroundings represented a whole new world of adventure. Fresh air and freedom are a heady mix, but certain dangers lurk for the unwary and teenagers have a habit of ignoring sound advice once they are let loose. I was no different.

We had been well warned that the nearby River Tay was full of dangerous currents and even a whirlpool or two, potentially very threatening to non-swimmers, of which I was one. To this day I still can't swim to save myself, so what possessed me to venture into the waters of the Tay I do not know. It was probably a combination of foolhardiness, ignorance and not wanting to be the odd man out among my pals. It was even more ill-advised as we had been told that the particular area we had chosen to visit was an especially dangerous stretch of water.

However, the rest of the lads in the company were all accomplished swimmers and one by one they swam the short distance from the shore to a large stone in the middle of the river. I elected to follow their example and somehow made it, despite my inability to conjure up any sort of swimming stroke. Unfortunately, I discovered that I had left my towel behind on the bank, so I decided to swim back to retrieve it. Why, you are entitled to ask, did I bother when I was already soaking wet and had no chance of keeping the towel dry? Good question, but

I don't have a satisfactory answer, other than to say that it seemed like a good idea at the time.

I was soon in trouble. It was only a very short distance back to the shore and I was within touching distance of safety when my arms suddenly stopped moving. I didn't want to appear scared for fear of losing face, but I had every reason to be terrified, because I was suddenly being sucked under the water.

Just before I went under the first time I noticed this wee lad sitting on the bank throwing pebbles into the water and he was still there staring at me when I resurfaced. I don't know exactly how long I was under initially, but it seemed like an age. My first reaction was that I was in big trouble and that I had better start putting up a fight, but the more I struggled, the more water I swallowed. My next thought was that this couldn't be happening to me, because I was going to be a football player. That thought remains as clear as a bell in my memory, but it hadn't dawned on me that I was constantly being sucked under by the force of the small whirlpool I had swum into.

Gradually I started to feel very tired and I told myself to just relax and go to sleep and everything would be all right. I didn't see my life flash before me or anything like that. I had simply done the panic bit and it seemed easier to give into the force that was sucking the life out of me. I have no idea how long my ordeal lasted or how many times I was sucked under. It may have been only thirty seconds, but it could have been a couple of minutes for all I know. I do recall vividly the wee boy staring back at me each time I resurfaced, though.

I wasn't aware of anything else until I came to, lying on the bank with a guy called Peter Masterton sitting astride me and the leader of our party, Eric Gardner, urging a group of boys to stand well back, so that I had sufficient air. Later Eric told me that I had been unconscious for fully twenty minutes while they tried to resuscitate me. Peter, who must have been around twenty-two or twenty-three, had been the one who had dived in to pull me from the water and the pair of them had taken it in turns to apply artificial respiration. Years later, Peter told me that they had been just about to admit defeat and place a blanket over my face when a torrent of water suddenly gushed from my mouth and I returned to the land of the living.

Following my uncomfortably close brush with death, we walked slowly back to the camp and I was taken to the first aid tent, where I was given a couple of aspirins. After a few hours' sleep I was seemingly none the worse for my experience, though, because when I woke up I was ravenous. Fish and chips were on the menu for dinner and I scoffed down an extra helping.

However, I wasn't allowed to play football that evening and I remember being furious. I was lucky to be alive, but when you're only fourteen years old you recover quickly from such experiences and it didn't seem such a big deal to me. I am not so sure that my mother and sister shared that view when they visited me the following weekend and I informed them that I had very nearly drowned. It was my first time away from home and they were horrified.

I also recall that during that fortnight spent at Dalguise I constantly pestered the older lads to allow me to accompany them to the dancing in Aberfeldy. They weren't keen on the idea, but eventually gave into my pleading and I was transported there and back in the boot of an old Vauxhall car. Each of them took it in turn to stand with me outside the dance hall. Peter Masterton, who had rescued me from a watery grave, was one of those charged with the responsibility of looking after me and I have kept in touch with him over the years.

Peter emigrated to Vancouver and I met up with him during a Rangers tour to Canada in 1976. By then he had joined a local choir, which gave him the excuse to return to Scotland a couple of years ago, when the Mod, a Highland musical gathering, was held in Oban and we got together again then, too.

Coincidentally, I am not the only ex-footballer who has fallen victim to the Tay's treacherous currents. Former Manchester City and England star Francis Lee had a similar experience. Frannie is a keen fisherman and was caught out on the same stretch of the river, though thankfully in less dramatic circumstances.

Dalguise was definitely bad for my health. A year or two after I had been pulled out of the River Tay I was selected by Eric Gardner to return to that part of Perthshire for a week, as the representative of the boys' club he ran. I had by this time begun serving my apprenticeship as an engineer, but I clearly hadn't learned much more sense. On the Friday before I was due to travel to Dalguise I was injured at work, when a heavy steel plate caught me on the side of the face and knocked me clean out. A work colleague had pressed the wrong button and released the plate by accident.

I was probably quite fortunate not to be more seriously injured – or worse – but my face was full of red lead and there was no way that I should have gone ahead with the trip to Dalguise. I was in such a state that I couldn't even read the number on the corporation bus when it pulled up at my usual stop, but such was my respect for Eric that I wouldn't even entertain the idea of pulling out.

I was a sorry sight when I arrived at camp the following day to take part in commando-style training designed as a test of character, but worse was to follow. Part of the endurance course involved being pulled up a hill in a specially adapted chair, before being sent hurtling back down at great speed. Just before the chair reached the bottom the operator was supposed to pull on a rope that brought it to a sudden halt. However, the person operating the pulley system got it wrong and I continued my rapid descent, before crashing back-first into a large boulder, which left me battered and bruised.

Lying in bed that night I thought I was dying, but there was to be no respite for me. Early the next morning we were to be transported from the camp by jeep to a remote part of the Perthshire countryside and dumped! The idea was that we would eventually find our way back – somehow! To be fair, the organisers were keen to exclude me from the exercise after what I had already been through, but I wouldn't have it. I was determined to see the ordeal through and I insisted on going with the rest of the lads. Talk about a glutton for punishment!

Looking back, I think it was simply a case of me not wanting to let Eric down. He had chosen me to represent his club and I felt I had a duty to him. So the next thing I knew I was tramping over the hills near Pitlochry, aching from head to foot and I was happy to do so, because of Eric. He was quite simply the finest human being I have ever met and the person who influenced me most. He was one of those rare characters who devoted his time unpaid to helping hundreds of kids and never asked for, or received, a penny for his efforts.

Eric, who worked as a mechanic with the SMT bus group in Edinburgh, ran the United Crossroads Boys' Club, which operated from rooms in an old school just off the Royal Mile. My sister Nessie's husband was related to a fellow called George Thomson, who played left-back for Hearts and who was later transferred to Everton. As it happened, George's father ran a team called Tynecastle Athletic. They trained at Stenhouse and played in the Hearts strip, which was candy stripes in those days. Being a dyed-in-the-wool 'jambo', I jumped at the chance to train with them.

I was just fourteen at the time, but I ended up training with the under-seventeens. However, at the end of my first training session, this man approached me and said, 'Look, son, these other players are much bigger than you and three years older. You're too young to play for us, but I know of this club, United Crossroads, which is an under-fifteen team. Try them for a year and see how you get on.' It was one of the best things that ever happened to me, because it brought me into contact with Eric Gardner. Eric didn't just encourage my development as a footballer, he taught me certain standards and gave me values that I try to adhere to in my daily life.

I never did return to Tynecastle Athletic. Instead, I played for United Crossroads under-fifteens and the under-sixteens in turn. We were so good that we beat most other teams out of sight, but there was one occasion when we wiped the floor with the opposition and ended up being given a tongue-lashing by Eric. We were winning 11–0 at half-time and I had scored five of our goals, so at the interval we decided to switch the entire attack into defence and vice versa. Eric wasn't at the game, but when he learned the next day what we had done he gave us a right rollicking. He told us in no uncertain terms that we should never try to belittle the opposition in such a way. He got his message over, because we felt ashamed at what we had done and embarrassed at letting him down.

I trained two evenings a week with United Crossroads and often after training Eric would keep me back so he could give me extra coaching. This involved setting up two small nets in the gym and the pair of us playing one on one.

It wasn't all fun and games, though. Our task on a Sunday afternoon involved scrubbing floors and generally tidying up the club rooms. Once that had been done to Eric's satisfaction, we were allowed to go out and play football. It was character-building and many hundreds of boys passed through Eric's hands over the years, including Ken Buchanan, the boxer who went on to become world lightweight champion. Others who played for United Crossroads included Alan

Anderson and Pat Stanton, which meant that the captains of Hearts, Hibs and Rangers had all been members at one time or another.

Although I thoroughly enjoyed playing for United Crossroads, after a couple of years I felt that I was in danger of being left behind. So towards the end of my second season, when I was approached by an official from the amateur side, Edina Hearts, and offered the chance to play for them, I leapt at it – but I left without bothering to tell Eric.

Edina Hearts were involved in several cup competitions at under-seventeen level. More importantly, the previous year Hearts had signed nine of their players, so I viewed it as a short cut to Tynecastle.

I ended up winning several cup medals and played in the final of the Scottish Amateur Cup, when I scored direct from a corner to earn a replay against Gairdoch Amateurs, but eventually I was forced to summon up the courage to visit Eric. I explained to Eric my reason for joining Edina Hearts, but I needn't have worried. Eric said he understood and pointed out that Hearts were going to sign me anyway, so it hadn't mattered. When I asked him if it would be all right if I returned to train with United Crossroads, he didn't hesitate in saying yes, which was typical of the man.

Eric died some years ago, but he left behind a rich legacy of young men who might otherwise have failed to make much of their lives without his influence and guidance. I, for one, have many reasons for being grateful to a man who helped shape my future.

LITTLE BOY BLUE

Signing for Rangers reduced me to tears, but I simply wasn't allowed to refuse Al Capone! The Al Capone in question was a Scot by the name of Bob McAuley. Apparently, he had earned his nickname because he was living in America when Rangers signed him during a close-season tour to the States. I had no idea that we were to have such a distinguished visitor. All my brother, Tam, had told me was that someone was coming to our home to see me on a Sunday morning in August 1959.

Usually, my father enjoyed a lie-in and a leisurely read of the papers, but on this particular Sunday, when I appeared for breakfast the old man was sitting by the fireside, fully dressed. As a consequence of problems with his circulation, my dad had taken to sleeping on a bed settee in the living room, so he could be near the fire, in the hope that the heat would help his blood flow, but he had forgone his usual breakfast in bed. When the door bell sounded a short time later, I was ordered to take a seat and in walked the stranger who was about to change my life.

Once I had been introduced to our visitor we sat round the dining room table and I was given a speech all about Rangers. I was informed that I would travel to Ibrox twice a week – on a Tuesday and Thursday – for training. I was also told that I would continue to play for my club side, Edina Hearts, in the meantime and, if everything went according to plan, I would eventually be called up by Rangers.

Bob McAuley then produced a set of papers from his jacket pocket and said, 'Sign here, son.' As it turned out, they were provisional forms, but I was having none of it. 'I'm not signing anything,' I declared. My elder brother was adamant and he ordered me to put pen to paper, but still I refused. Eventually my father intervened. He had been sitting quietly in the corner, pretending to read his newspaper, but clearly listening to every word that was being said. Lowering his paper sufficiently for his eyes to be seen peering over the top of the page, my dad issued the same instruction – 'Sign!'

My father was only around five feet five inches tall and slightly built, but I was scared stiff of him. He was as hard as nails and his word was law, so I took my first step to becoming a Rangers player. I never had cause to regret my action, but if you'd seen my face at the time you wouldn't have known it.

Bob McAuley also explained that he had not made contact with any of the Edina Hearts officials, because he didn't get on well with them. However, he added that when it came time for me to travel to Ibrox to complete the formalities, he would ensure that someone from my club was present. However, as the situation stood, he was effectively making me a provisional signing without the permission of my club.

Before he took his leave, Bob McAuley assured me that I wouldn't regret my decision to commit myself to Rangers, but I thought differently. By the time Tam came back into the room I had burst into tears. 'I'll never forgive you,' I informed my brother, but again my father had his say. 'Listen,' he said, 'Tam knows more about football than you and I put together, so if he thinks you should sign for Rangers, that's it.'

I was still one month short of my seventeenth birthday and I had been promised £1 a week plus travelling expenses, but it wouldn't have mattered had it been ten times as much. I had dreamed of playing for Hearts and the dream had just been shattered, but eventually I dried my eyes and resigned myself to my fate.

There was nothing else for it, so I decided to go for a kickabout with one of my pals, John Meechan. When I met John at the entrance to our close I told him that a guy had been to see me and that I had signed for Rangers. 'Glasgow Rangers?' asked John. 'Aye,' I replied, and he informed me that Rangers were playing Hibs at Easter Road the following Saturday, so we agreed to go to the game.

Having paid our way in to join a crowd of more than 44,000, we watched Rangers beat a decent Hibs side, including Joe Baker, who was to go on to win eight England caps, 6–1. Perhaps not surprisingly, my reaction was that this was some team I had signed for. Ralph Brand scored four of the Rangers goals, with Andy Matthew and Jimmy Millar getting the others, and from that day on I was a Rangers fan. Not once in the past forty-six years has my loyalty ever wavered.

If the truth be told, I was very disillusioned with Hearts. A short time before I had played for Edina Hearts against Loanhead Juniors, in the expectation that Hearts were about to make a move to sign me. That belief grew when I chased a long pass that ran out of play behind the goal line. As I made to retrieve the ball, I spotted someone leaning against the side of the goal and he kicked it back to me. That person was Tommy Walker, the legendary Hearts manager.

As it happened, Eric Stevenson and I were the only survivors of the team from the previous season and as nine of the current lot had already signed for Hearts and Eric had committed himself to Hibs, I was convinced that my time had also come. But I never heard a word. Maybe Tommy Walker was put off by my size.

I was still slightly built for a sixteen-year-old and perhaps he thought I would be too easily brushed aside in the senior game. Whatever his thinking, Mr Walker clearly wasn't impressed by yours truly. Bob McAuley was more astute. He took note of the size of my brothers and sisters and decided that there was a very good chance that I would eventually grow taller and fill out accordingly. Thank goodness for that.

I didn't know it at the time, but there was one other club besides Rangers interested in signing me. Years later Tam showed me a letter he had received from Bill Shankly, inviting me to Huddersfield for trials. Denis Law was there at the time and Shanks was keen to add to his Scottish contingent, but Tam explained that he hadn't wanted me to go to England.

So I was destined to become a Rangers player instead and two or three months later I paid my first visit to the stadium where I have spent so much of the past forty-six years. I was not disappointed. First impressions are important and when I looked up and saw the vastness of the place I was gobsmacked. I was also shaking as I made my way up the marble staircase for my first meeting with Scot Symon. The Rangers manager was an imposing figure and a man who was to achieve incredible levels of success during his fourteen seasons in charge.

As a player, Scot Symon was an accomplished wing-half with Dundee, Portsmouth and Rangers. He also demonstrated his versatility by playing cricket for Scotland. After hanging up his boots at the age of thirty-five, he had entered the precarious world of football management with East Fife.

His success in guiding the Methil club to promotion in his first season in charge, and his subsequent achievements in taking what was an unfashionable club to two Cup finals, inevitably brought his talents to the attention of bigger clubs and Preston North End moved to secure his services in 1953. But Scot Symon's stay in Lancashire was short-lived. Little more than a year later he was on the move again, this time to Ibrox, but not before he had also fashioned a Cup final appearance for Preston. Regrettably, in spite of the presence of Tom Finney, Preston failed to lift the FA Cup when West Bromwich Albion rather surprisingly beat them at Wembley.

Scot Symon was the chosen successor to William Struth at Rangers and there could not have been a harder act to follow. In the thirty-four years he was at the helm, Bill Struth had turned Rangers into the dominant force in Scottish football and created several outstanding teams in the process. But by the time I arrived on the scene in 1959, Scot Symon had made his mark and Rangers had won the championship three times in four seasons.

Not that I was thinking about league titles as I made my way into Scot Symon's oak-panelled office. I was too nervous to think! In addition to the great man himself, there was my brother, Tam, and two representatives from Edina Hearts, who were still none the wiser that I had already signed provisional forms, so we went through the procedure again – this time officially. Once the formalities were complete it was explained to me that I would be called up by Rangers at the end of that season, 1959–60. In the meantime, I had to complete additional forms to enable me to return to junior football if I failed to make it in the senior grade. It was also confirmed that I would train at Ibrox two evenings a week.

I later joked that Rangers couldn't have had that much faith in my ability if they were making me sign for a junior club, but it was a form of protection and I became a registered player with Whitburn Juniors. However, despite stories to the contrary, I never played for Whitburn. In fact, I couldn't have even told you the exact location of their ground at that time. When Whitburn reached the final of the Scottish Junior Cup in 1966, the club invited me as their guest and, when I was instructed to meet up with the main party, I had to ask for directions.

By then I was captain of Rangers, but when Scot Symon reached for his cash box, which was stuffed with bank notes, and extracted two tenners, I was a long way from being a player on the big stage. I don't think I had even seen a £10 note before and the manager had two in his hand. He informed me that this was my signing fee. However, instead of handing me both notes he gave one to me and the other to Tam, explaining that he was aware that my brother had been instrumental in persuading me to sign for Rangers in the face of interest from other clubs. Tam, I recall, was also given a little extra to compensate him for missing a shift at work. Meanwhile, I was informed by the manager that if I turned out to be the player he thought I would become, he would ensure that I made up the financial shortfall many times over in the coming years. As things turned out, he was true to his word.

So I had a foot in the door at Rangers, but there was no instant passport to the first team and a lot of hard work and uncertainty lay ahead. Fortunately, though, I had the security of my apprenticeship as an engineer to fall back on if things didn't work out as I hoped at Rangers. I had been lucky enough to secure employment on leaving school at sixteen, but it hadn't been a case of picking and choosing.

Back in the 1950s great store was placed on securing an apprenticeship and my father stressed the importance of getting a trade of some sort. So, each evening he would come home from work and study the jobs page in the local evening newspaper. This took the form of a process of elimination. First he scanned the list for apprentice electricians and the following day I had to trudge round Edinburgh, calling at the various outlets to offer myself as a potential candidate for employment. When I drew a blank my father then dispatched me to enquire at the city's printers, and so on and so forth.

These job-finding exercises usually involved walking miles, but I eventually found employment by chance. My mother, who sadly died in August 1988, worked as a cleaner and her client was the widow of a sea captain, whose son was a local councillor and JP who just happened to have a friend who ran a small engineering company. When my mother mentioned to the lady that I was looking for work, she arranged, through her son, for me to be given an interview and I was duly taken on. Heaven knows how I managed it, because I was hopeless with my hands, unlike my brother, Tam, who could turn his hand to any sort of repair.

I recall on one occasion bringing home a standard lamp that I had made in woodwork class at school and my mother hid it away in a corner in my bedroom. She would never have said it to my face, of course, for fear of hurting my feelings, but it was a truly hopeless effort on my part, even though I had enlisted the help of my pals to put the finishing touches to my pathetic attempt at creating a lasting memorial to my schooldays.

The truth is I hadn't wanted to leave school in the first place. While I had been one of the brighter pupils in primary school, once I made the move up to secondary education I was an underachiever academically. The reason, quite simply, was that my mind was more on football than lessons, because I realised that I had a real chance of making it as a player. But I was in no rush to leave. Having stayed on at school to complete fourth year in the forlorn hope that I might win schoolboy international honours, when the time came to leave I had a tear in my eye.

I had been appointed head prefect, not because of my educational achievements, but rather as a result of my attainments on the football pitch. I was also responsible for taking the class register and that presented me with the opportunity to pull the odd stroke. On one occasion, when Hearts were playing Raith Rovers in a midweek Scottish Cup tie, which was being played in the afternoon in the days before floodlights, I arranged for the time off by erasing a classmate's name from the note his parents had given him to be excused lessons and substituted my own instead. I have often wished that I had paid more attention to education. You are lucky if your career as a footballer lasts fifteen years, but you require knowledge to guide you through the remainder of your life.

Football was already the be-all and end-all for me, though, and I had no other hobbies as such. I didn't own a bicycle, for example, and on the one occasion when I borrowed my brother's I very nearly killed myself. It was Sunday afternoon and I went careering down a steep hill before realising that the bike had no brakes. I ended up shooting out into the middle of a main road and only avoided being mown down by a car because there was a lot less traffic in those days and, being the Sabbath, the roads were pretty much deserted.

My other sporting interest was boxing and I used to listen to the big fights, involving the likes of Rocky Marciano, Don Cockell and Randolph Turpin, on the radio. Years later I actually met Marciano's brother on a business trip to Chicago, but most things involved football in some shape or form. When I was in my early teens both Hearts and Hibs were a match for the Old Firm and I remember cutting out photographs of the big-name players which appeared in the now defunct *Green Dispatch* and *Pink News* and pasting them into scrapbooks. It was also around the same time that I began to develop an interest in how the game was played. I had a box of buttons and I would spend hours setting them out on the living room carpet in various formations.

We were not a rich family be any means and we had to make our own amusement. Very few people in our neighbourhood owned a TV set, but I do remember the Saturday afternoon in 1953 when I saw one for the first time. I had been kicking a ball about in the street when a neighbour called to me to ask if I wanted to watch a match that was being shown 'live' on TV. The game in question was the FA Cup final between Blackpool and Bolton Wanderers and I sat transfixed as Stanley Matthews engineered one of the greatest comebacks of all time. I could hardly have wished for a more memorable introduction to the small screen.

My introduction to the real world of the workplace was a lot less pleasant. I wasn't a week into my apprenticeship with J&R Slack when I managed to incur the wrath of my foreman, a fellow by the name of George. My gaffer had assigned me to the task of drilling holes in metal bars shaped like Toblerone chocolate bars and each time I finished one I stacked it against a wall. What I hadn't realised was that the vibration from the machinery I was using was causing the bars to move and, as luck would have it, at the precise moment my gaffer had chosen to enquire how I was getting on, the whole lot came crashing down on his foot. George suffered the misfortune of a broken big toe and ended up in plaster for several weeks. From that point on he hated me and he used to tell me to try to throw myself under a passing bus on my way home from work. However, a couple of years later, once I had grown several inches and filled out, I returned to visit some of my former workmates and said to George that I bet he wouldn't tell me to throw myself under a bus now. He agreed!

Although by then I had become reasonably well known, I felt it important to maintain contact with the guys I had known before I became John Greig of Rangers. They were genuine people, working five days a week doing a job I would have hated, and I have always believed that it is more important to be liked for what you are rather than who you are.

I had also been fortunate to be assigned a job in Glasgow early on in my apprenticeship. I was still a provisional signing with Rangers, training two evenings a week, so it suited me down to the ground to be working in a city I still knew very little about. The job, at Tennents Brewery in Duke Street, involved a six-week stint. My journeyman and I were supposed to stay at digs near to the brewery, but they were so bad that we decided to travel daily from Edinburgh, catching the train from Waverley Station at 6.15 a.m.

Word quickly got out that I was training with Rangers and one of the electricians invited me to join him and his workmates in a lunch-time kickabout on a piece of waste ground opposite the brewery. I soon got a taste of Glasgow humour, though, when one of them turned to me and asked, 'Is it true that you've signed for Rangers?' 'Yes,' I replied and quick as a flash he hit me with the comment that I was 'F***ing hopeless.'

But these fellows were great to me and the six weeks I spent in their company turned out to be a huge learning curve. Up to that point I think I had been to Glasgow only twice before, once to visit my sister who was living in army barracks in Maryhill and on another occasion to play against Glasgow Schools at Cathkin Park. In truth, I had been frightened by the thought of coming to work in Glasgow, because of the reputation the city had and the fact that I hadn't been away from home before, other than to boys' camp.

But I need not have worried, even though the cultural and social differences between Edinburgh and Glasgow are considerable and west of Scotland humour takes a bit of getting used to. Regrettably, the deep religious divisions that prevail in Scotland as a whole and the west in particular are still a fact of life. Thankfully, the vast majority of people aren't tarred with the same brush and there is a humorous side to the divide as well, but, back then, I hadn't much idea about the

Catholic-Protestant thing. So, when I ordered fish and chips for lunch on a Friday I quickly discovered that it wasn't the done thing, according to my new workmates. Tradition dictated that fish is eaten by Catholics on a Friday and I was a Rangers player!

At first I thought I was the victim of a wind-up. I had deposited my lunch on a table in the canteen to go in search of cutlery, but when I returned my meal had disappeared. 'Where's my lunch?' I asked. 'Bobby Dickson's taken it,' came the reply. I was in a panic, because I didn't have enough money to buy another meal, but a couple of minutes later the said Bobby Dickson appeared carrying a plate of steak pie and potatoes and instructed me to tuck in. I'd had my first lesson in the ways of the west of Scotland.

Meantime, I was starting to grow. Between the ages of sixteen and eighteen I shot up five inches in height and put on a couple of stone in weight. I also became stronger and better able to cope with the physical demands of being a footballer. Rangers were also apparently pleased with my development. I had progressed to playing several games for the second and third teams when the manager summoned me to his office. Again, I made my way up the marble staircase quaking in my shoes, expecting to be given a row, but Scot Symon wanted to speak to me about the offer of a full-time contract.

I was both surprised and delighted, but I told him that I would have to discuss the matter with my father first. As it was a Thursday I knew it was safe to speak to my old man, because he wouldn't have been to the pub. Friday was payday, so he was always skint approaching the end of the week. Dad said it was up to me to decide, but he pointed out that, with so many youngsters looking for work, how difficult it had been for me to find a job as an apprentice engineer and added that the competition among football players was even more intense. He didn't try to change my mind, however.

So, the following Tuesday, I again reported to the manager's office and told Scot Symon I was accepting his offer of a full-time contract. He asked me how much I earned as an apprentice and I told him I was on three pounds ten shillings a week. He also asked how much I earned as a part-timer. I told him that he paid me £6 a week and he replied that he would increase my wage to £10. Considering that my combined earnings from engineering and football amounted to £9.50, a week he was effectively giving me an increase of 50p!

Others of my generation, like wee Willie Henderson, were given substantial fees to sign for Rangers, but Willie was a schoolboy international and had the pick of any number of clubs. Scot Symon was a gentleman, though, and he looked after me when it came time to sign a new contract, but I would have jumped at the chance even if the manager had kept me on my existing football wage, because I was being given the opportunity to live my dream.

Many people perceived Scot Symon as a difficult person, aloof even. Others saw him as a quiet and reserved man, but once the subject turned to football he was in his element. He was happy to sit for hours talking about the game. I didn't always agree with his point of view, but I had the utmost respect for him, because his knowledge was extensive.

Scot Symon didn't spend a great deal of time on the training ground, preferring to concentrate on the administrative duties associated with managing a club of the magnitude of Rangers. However, while he left it to others to oversee training, he was the one who picked the team and dictated the tactics, and considering the number of trophies Rangers won during his time in charge he clearly didn't do a bad job. True, Scot Symon failed to win a European trophy, but he twice guided the club to the Cup-Winners' Cup final – in 1961 and 1967 – and that constituted a sizeable achievement.

Perhaps he was a little too conservative in his views and, while he recognised the need to keep pace with an ever-changing game and was capable of handling the new developments, he never really embraced modern philosophy with any enthusiasm, preferring to stick to the ways he had always known. I suppose, almost inevitably, Scot Symon eventually became the victim of modern trends, but when he left the club suddenly, in 1967, to be replaced by his assistant, Davie White, it came as a shock to all the players. Under his managership, Rangers won the championship six times, the Scottish Cup five times and the League Cup on four occasions. It's a record that stands comparison with the achievements of those who went before and others who came afterwards. The arrival of Jock Stein at Celtic also impacted on Scot Symon and Rangers, but that's another story.

EARLY DAYS

I quickly learned that simply signing for Rangers didn't earn me the automatic right to regard myself as an equal. As far as the established stars were concerned, I was a wet-behind-the-ears kid from Edinburgh with a lot to learn. You didn't speak to first-team players unless they spoke to you first and I soon realised that I had to earn certain rights. The point was brought home to me rather forcibly one evening at training while I was still a part-timer.

Players like Ian McMillan, Max Murray and Willie Telfer had elected to remain part-time to enable them to pursue alternative careers. As a result, they trained in the evening with the youngsters. During one of these sessions we were training behind one of the goals at Ibrox when the ball was kicked on to the terracing. I went to retrieve it and threw it back, before jumping over the wall to rejoin my colleagues, but I received a hefty slap across the back of the head for my troubles. It was administered by Willie Telfer, who told me, 'Listen, son, you're no longer a schoolboy. Next time wait until you return before giving the ball back, because when you're off the pitch we're effectively a man short.'

Willie was a bear of a man. He worked in a slaughterhouse

and was as tough as old boots. I recall one evening he turned up for training clutching his thumb to his hand. He had to do this, because his thumb was hanging by a few shards of skin following an accident at work. Most people would have passed out, but not big Willie. He turned to our trainer, Davie Kinnear, and asked him if he was any use with a needle and thread. When Davie replied that he was, Willie instructed him to stitch his thumb back on – without anaesthetic!

When I eventually did go full-time, in 1960, there was no shortage of big names at Ibrox, but the club's training facilities were virtually non-existent. In those days we trained at Benburb Juniors' ground, which was nearby, until Rangers eventually purchased the derelict White City race track opposite the stadium. On my first day at training I was paired with Ian McColl. Little did I know then that he would be the man who would give me my first Scotland cap four years later. I also learned pretty quickly that I was expected to display a degree of versatility when the manager, Scot Symon, instructed me to play on the right wing in a practice game, because the regular outside-right, Alex Scott, was injured.

I was still travelling daily from my home in Edinburgh, of course, and that enabled me to further my education in the company of established first-team players like Ralph Brand, Jimmy Millar and Billy Stevenson. Along with Bobby King and Bobby Grant, they commuted by train from the capital and I loved sitting with them in the buffet car listening to their stories. I was very fortunate that these guys looked after me and nurtured me in the early days and I will always be grateful to them.

Players from other clubs were also regular travellers. There was the Third Lanark trio of wee Jocky Robertson, Junior McGillivray and Jimmy Goodfellow, who later went on to play for Leicester

City, appearing in the 1961 FA Cup final against Spurs, and Frank Donlevy and Sandy Brown of Partick Thistle. Travelling in the opposite direction, from Glasgow to Edinburgh, was a sizeable contingent of Hearts and Hibs players. Somehow I can't imagine trainloads of football players commuting by train between Scotland's two major cities nowadays, but the rivalry was good-natured and there were also plenty of laughs.

I remember one New Year's Day, Jocky Robertson arrived at Waverley Station very much the worse for wear. In fact, he was still drunk from the night before. Third Lanark were playing Falkirk at Brockville and when Jocky got off the train at Falkirk High Station he had difficulty walking in a straight line. Imagine our surprise when Scot Symon read out the half-time scores and announced that Thirds were winning 3–0, but the second half was a different story. Falkirk mounted a remarkable counter-offensive after the restart to win 5–3. When Jocky joined the train on the return journey we asked him what had happened. 'I sobered up,' explained Jocky. 'They plunged me into a cold bath and forced me to drink several cups of coffee at half-time and it all went wrong after that.' I don't know exactly how many thousands of miles I clocked up travelling between Edinburgh and Glasgow, but my parents didn't get rid of me until I was twenty-five, when I married Janette.

My progress at Rangers was pretty steady and after playing several times for the third team I was promoted to the reserve side, largely on the strength of scoring five goals against Maryhill Juniors. I was an inside-forward in those days and got my fair share of goals. The Rangers second team at that time was: Billy Ritchie or George Niven; Bobby King and Davie Provan; Ronnie McKinnon, Doug Baillie and Billy Stevenson; Willie Henderson, Greig, Jim Christie, Willie Penman and Bobby Hume. We were good enough to win the reserve league championship in 1960–61 and I reckon we would have beaten most of the current SPL sides.

The following season I made my first-team debut in a League Cup tie against Airdrie on 2 September 1961. I had been earmarked to play in a Glasgow Cup tie to break me in a little more gently, but I damaged knee ligaments and was out for five weeks. I was still only eighteen when I pulled on a Rangers jersey as a first-team player for the first time and I was a nervous wreck beforehand – so much so that in an effort to relax me Jim Baxter suggested we have a game of head tennis. It was a very astute move – especially because Jim wasn't very much older than me. He had rigged up a makeshift court by placing a broom handle between two chairs and he told me to imagine that there was a six foot high net. We must have looked quite a sight standing in our jock straps heading the ball back and forward. In those days the players weren't allowed to put on their shirts and shorts until just before kickoff because we always had to look immaculate when we went onto the pitch.

But it turned out to be a dream start. Rangers won, 4–1, and I scored our opening goal just ten minutes into my debut in front of a crowd of 32,000 at Ibrox. I'm not sure Jim's plan to help me unwind worked after all! Jim Christie and Ralph Brand, with two, got our other goals after Jim Storrie, who went on to play for Leeds United, had equalised for Airdrie. The League Cup was played in sections of four teams in those days and Rangers were unbeaten, topping our section with eleven points from five wins and a draw. I also played against East Fife in the quarter-final first leg at Ibrox when we beat them, 3–1, but that was the end of my involvement in the competition that season, although Rangers went on to beat Hearts in the final.

I had grown up a Hearts fan, but they had failed to make my dream of playing for them come true, while Rangers had given me my big break, so I suppose I was quite pleased deep down when Rangers won the midweek replay, 3–1, after being held to a 1–1 draw the previous Saturday at Hampden. One of the Hearts players that day was a fellow by the name of Billy Higgins. It just so happened that Billy had played against me when I played in my first cup final, for Prestonfield Primary as a nine-year-old in borrowed boots, when we beat Dalry.

I suppose if I had also become a Hearts player they would eventually have transferred me anyway, as they did with so many others, but although Hearts were certainly no longer the force they had been in the 1950s, they still had one or two exceptional players, notably defender Johnny Cumming and winger Johnny Hamilton. However, compared to the team that boasted the likes of Alfie Conn, Willie Bauld, Jimmy Wardhaugh, Dave Mackay and Alex Young, the 1961 side was up against it.

My three brothers were Hearts fans so I suppose it was only natural that I would follow in the family tradition, but the closest I came to fulfilling my boyhood dream was playing at Tynecastle for Edinburgh schoolboys on two or three occasions. I remember another time playing against Leith Schools at Easter Road. I think we won, 5–1, and I scored a hat-trick. The following day the local paper, the *Evening News*, carried a photograph of me scoring one of my goals. The article also compared me to Bobby Johnstone, the Hibs inside-forward and one of the 'Famous Five' of Gordon Smith, Johnstone, Lawrie Reilly, Eddie Turnbull and Willie Ormond. That was a compliment indeed, but I hated it because the newspaper had likened me to a Hibs player.

Around the same time I was selected to represent Edinburgh against Glasgow Schools at Cathkin Park, home of the now long defunct Third Lanark. The Glasgow side included a young Alex Ferguson and most of their players were older than me. The fact that they wore a strip similar to Queen's Park's black and white stripes made them look even bigger. Glasgow proved too strong for us, but I was singled out in at least one of the following day's newspapers. The late Alex Cameron, writing, I think, in the *Scottish Daily Mail*, commented that, in his opinion, the little rosy-cheeked boy at inside-forward for Edinburgh had a big future.

If Hearts were ever going to sign me I suppose it would have been then, when I was being mentioned in the press, but it never happened and, on reflection, maybe that was just as well. Somehow I don't think I would ever have had the opportunity to lead Hearts in a European final, but I was Hearts daft at one time and my hero was the great Willie Bauld of Conn, Bauld and Wardhaugh fame. The so-called 'Terrible Trio' were something else. I remember the late Willie Woodburn of Rangers and Scotland fame picking me as his player of the decade in his column for the *News of the World* and granting me one wish. My wish was to meet Willie Bauld and Woodburn arranged for it to happen. I must have had Bauld's autograph a hundred times, but I was still thrilled to have the opportunity to talk to my hero face to face.

Yet, if there was one player I would have modelled myself on it was Dave Mackay, a truly outstanding individual in an exceptional team. I loved watching Mackay and I was heartbroken when he was transferred to Spurs, where he went on to become one of the legends of the game. Mackay had the lot; he was fearless and aggressive, had two good feet and the heart of a lion. In addition to these attributes, he could pass the ball with tremendous accuracy, take long throw-ins and he tackled like a tank. It's not often that you get a player who can tackle so effectively and also pass the ball with precision. With Mackay on one side and Cumming on other, the opposition must have squirmed at the sight of the Hearts half-backs, but, of course, the game was much more physical in the 1950s.

One of my proudest moments was playing in the same Scotland team as Mackay. I was winning my tenth cap and Davie was making what turned out to be the last of his twenty-two appearances for his country against Northern Ireland at Belfast's Windsor Park on 2 October 1965. Regrettably we lost, 3–2. But for serious injury and the intense competition for places, Mackay would have played many more times for Scotland.

In addition to Mackay, Scotland was blessed with players of the talents of Jim Baxter, Pat Crerand, Jimmy Gabriel, Frank McLintock and later on the likes of Billy Bremner. Alex Young – christened 'The Golden Vision' by Everton fans – was another favourite of mine. Alex, who went on to become a huge star at Goodison, had, as his nickname suggests, tremendous vision. He wasn't big for a centre-forward, but like so many naturally gifted players he had the ability to make time for himself. I could never understand why he played so few times for Scotland. Eight caps seemed ridiculous, but perhaps Young was ahead of his time.

Such was my love of Hearts at one point that when I played juvenile football for Saughton I used to rush to get changed as soon as the final whistle sounded and set off running down Gorgie Road in the hope of catching the second half at Tynecastle. They used to open the gates fifteen minutes from the end of games to allow spectators to exit the ground early and I would sometimes try to talk my way in. More often than not, though, I would knock on the doors of the surrounding tenement buildings, which overlooked the ground, in the hope that someone would let me in to watch the game from their living room window.

A month after the 1961 League Cup final, on 18 November, I made my league debut for Rangers against Falkirk at Ibrox, when Jimmy Millar scored a hat-trick as we swept to a 4–0 win. The following week

I scored in a 3–2 win over Dundee United at Tannadice, the first of seven league goals I scored in my debut season.

We were playing four-four-two in those days, before anyone had heard of the system, and I was fortunate to be surrounded by outstanding players. Jim Baxter and Ian McMillan were wonderful ball players and read the game superbly. Willie Henderson or Alex Scott supplied pace and drive on the right wing and Davie Wilson was equally effective on the left side. Up front, Millar and Ralphy Brand – known as M&B – formed a lethal combination of strength, speed and finishing. Between them they scored a phenomenal sixty-seven goals that season in all competitions.

I managed eight goals in a total of nineteen appearances, which included my European baptism in the Champions Cup quarter-final first leg against Standard Liege of Belgium. I wore the No. 8 shirt in a forward line of Henderson, Greig, Millar, Brand and Wilson. Liege were considered to be one of the leading sides in Europe and they emphasised the point by beating us, 4–1. I didn't play in the return at Ibrox, which we won, 2–0, but that wasn't enough to take us through. I also recall that wee Willie Henderson missed the second leg after being held up in traffic. Can you imagine the same thing happening nowadays?

Rangers finished runner-up to Dundee in the championship, but achieved a Cup double. I only played a small part in our Scottish Cup success, with my sole appearance coming in the third round, when we drew, 2–2, with Aberdeen at Pittodrie. Eric Caldow also missed a penalty. Rangers thumped the Dons, 5–1, in the replay, before going on to beat Kilmarnock and then Motherwell in the semi-final. In the final itself Brand and Wilson scored to secure a two-goal victory over our near neighbours, St Mirren.

My big break came in the summer of 1962, when the club undertook a close-season tour of Russia. Jim Baxter was prevented from going because of National Service and Billy Stevenson had walked out on the club, so the chance was there for me to stake a claim for a regular place. In the event, we beat Lokomotiv Moscow and Tblisi and drew with the Russian champions, Kiev. Incredibly, 10,000 fans turned up at Glasgow Airport to greet the team on our arrival back. I had played left-half in Russia to accommodate Ian McMillan at inside-right and the newspaper reports were complimentary. I think, too, Scot Symon had decided that my future lay as a defender rather than a midfield player.

Immediately following the trip to Russia we travelled to Monchengladbach to play Borussia in a game to commemorate the opening of their new stadium and Scot Symon played me at left-half in place of Baxter, who was still on army duty. Near the end of the game I ran to take a throw-in and a group of British soldiers who were based in Germany shouted, 'Come on, Jim, give us a goal.' They were under the mistaken belief that I was Jim Baxter because I was wearing the No. 6 jersey, so for the next ten minutes I tried to do everything with my left foot!

My success in Russia and Germany didn't win me an automatic first-team place at the start of the following season, but eventually I earned a regular spot at right-half, at the expense of Harry Davis, who was in the latter stages of his distinguished career.

I had reverted to inside-right by the time football was forced to close down for a six-week period in the winter of 1962–63, due to the terrible weather. There was no under-soil heating in those days and even training was difficult in such atrocious conditions. We trained on a red ash pitch just behind where the Rangers' Pools office is now situated and a thaw had set in making the surface wet and greasy. Harry suffered the misfortune of pulling a calf muscle during the practice game and I replaced him at right-half the following Saturday at

Dunfermline. I think Harry played only one more game after that, but he was great to me. Because Harry had played directly behind me for a time, he looked after me and I remain friendly with him to this day. That same season, I scored the only hat-trick of my career in a League Cup tie against St Mirren at Ibrox on 1 September 1962, when Rangers won 4–0.

I made my Old Firm debut at Ibrox on 1 January 1963, but I didn't know I was playing until a couple of hours before the game and when Scot Symon gave me the news I wasn't sure whether I should laugh or cry. My problem was that I had been up half the night celebrating Hogmanay. For once I broke my self-imposed rule about never going out socially on the eve of a game, because I had been sidelined with a back injury and hadn't expected to be involved.

Janette and I were courting at the time and she persuaded me to go first-footing with her. Fortunately, I'd had very little to drink, no more than a couple of shandies, so it wasn't as if I was hung-over. However, the manager certainly bowled me over when he walked along a line of young players who were sitting in the foyer, wishing each of us a Happy New Year. When he got to me he said, 'Happy New Year, John – you're wearing the No. 8 jersey!'

I overcame my initial surprise to score the third of our four goals in a 4–0 victory, but I have often wondered how the Rangers fans we met at a party at 4 a.m. in a house in Edinburgh reacted when they heard my name being announced. Most of them were going to the game and I dread to think what the ramifications might have been for me had the score been reversed. Even though we were still a few years away from tabloid headlines condemning the behaviour of certain players, I'm sure I would have been a candidate for exposure in the press, despite my relative abstinence.

We didn't play again until early March, because of the big freeze, but I ended up appearing in twenty-seven of our thirty-four league games and also featured in five League Cup ties, as well as all seven Scottish Cup matches. In the process I scored ten goals – five in the league and the same number in the League Cup. I also won my first league championship medal when we finished nine points in front of second-placed Kilmarnock, but the highlight of my second season was probably beating Celtic in the Scottish Cup final.

The first game finished all-square, thanks largely to Celtic goal-keeper, Frank Haffey. He had been pilloried by the critics for his part in Scotland's 9–3 humiliation by England at Wembley two years earlier, but he hardly put a foot wrong against us. Haffey was beaten only once, by Brand, in the forty-third minute. Bobby Murdoch equalised for Celtic almost on the stroke of half-time and it finished 1–1. However, we were disadvantaged by the fact that George McLean, who had been signed the previous year on the strength of his display for St Mirren in the Scottish Cup final, was injured early in the second half and was a virtual passenger on the left wing, with Wilson moving to centre-forward as there were no substitutes then.

The replay eleven days later was a somewhat different story. McMillan, who replaced the injured McLean, and Henderson ran the show and from the moment Brand scored after seven minutes Rangers dominated the match. Wilson added a second goal close to half-time and Brand made it 3–0, nineteen minutes from the end. The Old Firm has always had remarkable drawing power, but even by Rangers-Celtic standards the attendance for those two games was nothing short of remarkable. The combined figure was just a couple of hundred short of 250,000.

Photographs of Rangers' Cup-winners show me with bits of cotton wool stuffed up both nostrils to staunch the flow of blood. I also ended up minus a couple of teeth after I was accidentally kicked in the face by

John McNamee, as I went to head the ball. Mind you, you should have seen the state of McNamee's boot!

Rangers' involvement in Europe lasted just two rounds, but it was a valuable learning experience for me, especially the second leg of our first round tie against Seville in Spain. We had thrashed them, 4–0, at Ibrox, thanks largely to a Jimmy Millar hat-trick, and the Spaniards reckoned that it was payback time. Seville grabbed a lifeline by scoring twice in the first ten minutes, but when we regrouped and managed to repel their other efforts to score, the Seville players lost their discipline completely.

Trouble kicked off near the end of the game when Canario, who had been a member of the outstanding Real Madrid side, head-butted me for no good reason and laid me out cold. By the time I regained consciousness, it was a madhouse. It seemed that every player was involved in the battle. Davie Wilson was also butted, Ronnie McKinnon was bitten and Jim Baxter was the victim of a vicious, two-footed assault when one of their players launched himself at Jim studs up and raked them down his chest and stomach. Wee Willie Henderson, meanwhile, threw a punch at someone and then ran to hide behind Bobby Shearer for protection. When I looked across at the dug-out, all I could see was Harry Davis, who had fought in the Korean War, laying out the opposition one by one. Harry, as hard as nails, required just one punch per opponent!

I had never seen anything like it in my life and the fans began to hurl hundreds of cushions on to the pitch. Eventually, the Portuguese referee blew for time at least two minutes early. As it happens, I got my own back on Canario in another game a few years later, but we were so concerned about a fresh outbreak of hostilities at the post-match banquet that every Rangers player turned up with an empty San Miguel beer bottle in his pocket – just in case!

After disposing of Seville, 4–2, on aggregate, we were drawn against the mighty Spurs side that were to go on to win the Cup-Winners' Cup against Atletico Madrid in Rotterdam by a margin of five goals to one. I played in both games against the Spaniards, but missed out in the following round when I was deprived of the opportunity of facing the man I had tried to model myself on – Dave Mackay. Considering that Spurs walloped us, 5–2, in London and followed up that success with a 3–2 win at Ibrox, that was perhaps no bad thing.

CHAPTER 6
SIMPLY THE BEST?

I am loath to describe the 1964 treble-winning Rangers team as the best I played in, but a lot of fans still talk about that side and reel off the names of the players who lost only six of the fifty-two competitive games we played, so I'll leave it for others to judge.

Along with goalkeeper Billy Ritchie, I was fortunate to play in every one of those games. We were beaten by Hearts, St Johnstone (twice) and St Mirren in the league and hammered, 6–0, by Real Madrid in the second leg of the preliminary round of the European Cup, after losing, 1–0, at Ibrox. The defeat in the magnificent Bernabeu Stadium was the only real black spot in a season when we dominated the domestic scene, including chalking up no less than five Old Firm wins. We beat Celtic, 2–1 and 1–0, in the league; 3–0, home and away in the League Cup; and sent our arch rivals crashing out of the Scottish Cup with a 2–0 win at Ibrox in the fourth round.

A total of twenty-one players contributed to our success in being crowned champions and double Cup-winners, but much of the time we lined up as follows: Ritchie; Bobby Shearer and Davie Provan; Greig, Ronnie McKinnon and Jim Baxter; Willie Henderson, George McLean or Ian McMillan, Jim Forrest or Jimmy Millar, Ralph Brand and Davie

Wilson. I don't like to compare players from different generations, because the game continues to evolve, but it was testimony to the skills of the 1964 side that the entire half-back line of Greig, McKinnon and Baxter were Scotland regulars, along with the wingers Henderson and Wilson. Provan was also involved in the international scene on a couple of occasions.

So, what made the 1963–64 side so good? Basically, it was all about balance. We were strong in every department of the team and had prolific goal-scorers in Forrest, Brand, Millar and McLean. Between them, the strikers notched up a total of ninety-four goals. In addition to creating many of those goals by crossing the ball with such accuracy, Wilson and Henderson weighed in with sizeable contributions. Wilson, who also had the knack of being able to cut inside and shoot with either foot, actually out-scored Millar and McLean with sixteen, despite being injured for a time, while wee Willie got six.

We were also mean at the back, conceding an average of just slightly less than a goal a game. Ritchie was a sound shot-stopper and he could also kick the ball almost the length of the pitch, so his clearances often set up an attack that resulted in a goal being scored. But, like all goalkeepers, Billy had his moments and I remember one day at Kilmarnock he was beaten by a shot from Bertie Black. Bertie hadn't connected properly with the ball and it bobbled awkwardly, before finding the net. Billy was furious and reacted by throwing the bonnet he nearly always wore at the ball.

Shearer was a full-back who didn't believe in taking prisoners and his regular partner, Provan was tall and commanding and could be relied on to make key interceptions. Eric Caldow, who had suffered the misfortune of breaking his leg playing against England at Wembley at the end of the previous season, was never the same player after that and played only a handful of games in the subsequent campaign.

However, Shearer and Caldow had been the full-backs when England hammered Scotland, 9–3, at Wembley in 1961 and the joke did the rounds that because the ball was orange, Frank Haffey, the Celtic goalkeeper, refused to handle it and the two Rangers players refused to kick it. Those versed in the ways of the west of Scotland will not require any further explanation!

I have already alluded to the fact that the half-back line also represented Scotland and you need a solid mid-division, which we had, yet McKinnon and I were two of the three youngsters in the side. Henderson was the other. It was a very experienced team, apart from we three. I had replaced Harry Davis, McKinnon had taken over from Bill Paterson and Henderson had been considered good enough for Rangers to feel confident about selling Alex Scott to Everton, in the belief that they had a readymade replacement waiting in the wings.

The three newcomers were fortunate in as much that we were able to benefit from having so many experienced players around us to offer guidance and support. In fact, the 1978 side I finished in was not dissimilar to the team of 1964 in terms of having two or three youngsters blending with older, more experienced players.

Tactics were not the big deal back then that they have become in the modern game and most teams expected the opposition to play in a set manner. But we were already playing a form of four-two-four and Millar's habit of dropping deep behind the other strikers and leaving Brand to burst through the middle often confused the opposition and worked to our advantage.

The first part of the treble was completed on 26 October 1963 in front of a crowd of 105,907 at Hampden, when we hammered Morton, 5–0, in the League Cup final. Forrest scored four and his cousin, Alex Willoughby, claimed the other. Mind you, it wasn't quite as one-sided as the score line would suggest. Morton were a decent side. They had a goal-scorer in Allan McGraw who was up there with the best of them and ensured that the score line remained blank until the fifty-second minute, but once the floodgates opened there was no stopping us.

The calibre of the opposition from the quarter-finals onwards was perhaps not considered top drawer and we had most of the play against East Fife and Berwick Rangers to reach the final. But we'd had to beat Celtic and Kilmarnock in the section stage of the competition, so we considered that we had earned the right to play on the big stage.

Just a little over there weeks earlier Real Madrid had given us their bit of a lesson. Puskas and company had been fortunate to come out on top in the first leg, when the little Hungarian snatched a late winner, but luck had nothing to do with it in the return when the 'Galloping Major' mowed us down with ruthless efficiency. Mercifully, although the humiliation of a six-goal thrashing dented our pride, it did not have a lasting effect in terms of impacting on our league form.

We bounced back with a win over St Mirren at Love Street and followed up with another couple of victories against East Stirling and Queen of the South either side of the League Cup final, but at halfway we trailed Kilmarnock and that made the New Year Old Firm derby crucially important. Celtic had home advantage, but we had Jimmy Millar, and my pal scored the winner midway through the second half. The next day we rattled in four goals against Partick Thistle.

The only blip in the next three months came in the form of a 3–2 home defeat by St Mirren in early February. After that we remained unbeaten until the final game of the season, when St Johnstone snatched a single goal victory at Perth on 29 April – our first away defeat of the season in the league. Not that it mattered. The title was already ours. In the days when it was two points for a win we were already six in front of Kilmarnock, who had completed their programme.

The reason for the delay was our involvement in the Scottish Cup final five days earlier. With the League Cup and the League Championship already in the bag, only Dundee stood between us and the domestic grand slam. I say only Dundee, but the fact is they were an outstanding team in their own right and just two seasons before had been crowned champions. Moreover, the following season, Bob Shankly's Dark Blues had made it to the last four in the European Cup before going out to the eventual winners, AC Milan.

Two of the Dundee team, right-back Alex Hamilton and centre-forward Alan Gilzean, were international team-mates of mine and Gilzean had scored the winner when I made my debut against England just a fortnight earlier. So, there was no way we dared underestimate the size of our task. In addition to Hamilton and Gilzean, there were five other survivors from the 1962 championship side: captain Bobby Cox, wing-half Bobby Seith and forwards Andy Penman, who was later to become a Rangers player, Alan Cousin and Hugh Robertson.

On the day of the game we met up as usual at the St Enoch Hotel in the centre of Glasgow for our pre-match meal. In those days teams didn't spend three or four days at a secret hideaway prior to a Cup final. Part the way through lunch a porter arrived from, I think, the Buchanan Street hotel where the Dundee squad were based prior to making their way to Hampden. He handed our captain, Bobby Shearer, a small package and when Bobby opened it he lifted out a plain white tea cup bearing a message written in lipstick. 'This is the only cup you'll win today,' it said. One of the Dundee players – I'm pretty sure it was Alex Hamilton because 'Hammy' was a real joker and a great character – had decided on the wind-up.

Hammy and his mates ended up bitterly disappointed when we lifted the trophy on the back of a 3–1 victory in front of a crowd just short of 121,000. Shearer handed the real Cup to me and the spoof one was duly given back to the Dundee prankster, but the score line doesn't even begin to tell the full story of one of the most exciting finals Hampden has ever witnessed. There were times when we threatened to overrun Dundee, with Henderson and Wilson a constant threat down the flanks, but no matter that Brand and Millar hammered away at Dundee's rearguard, we just could not find a way through. And when Millar eventually broke the deadlock after seventy-one minutes, Dundee immediately hit back on the break and Kenny Cameron equalised just sixty seconds later.

The barrage continued, but to no avail. The reason for this was the outstanding form of the Dundee keeper, Bert Slater. He frustrated us time and again with some truly remarkable saves. The Dundee fans – there were at least 25,000 of them – must have been gearing up for a midweek replay when the game moved into the final minute, but in a breathtaking finale Rangers scored twice.

With time rapidly running out, Baxter sent Henderson scurrying down the left touchline, after he had switched wings, and he beat Hamilton, before his cross was directed precisely onto the head of Millar, who was completely unmarked, and Jimmy's header floated into the net. There was hardly time to re-centre the ball, but there was sufficient time for Henderson to revert to his usual position on the right and go past Cox this time. Henderson's cross was struck by Wilson and turned away by Slater, but Brand was ideally placed to convert the rebound via a goal post.

Slater had no chance with either goal and the game was rightly daubed, 'The Slater Final'. I recall attending a party at my sister's home the following New Year's Day night and Bert was there. He was wearing a leather jacket and he refused to take it off, because he had a hole in his shirt – from all the pats on the back he had received!

The 1960s was a great time to play football because there were so many outstanding players and great teams. Significantly, perhaps, there were very few foreigners in our game then. Morton and Dundee United had begun the influx to an extent, with the arrival of several Scandinavians, and we had Kai Johansen at Rangers, but by and large they were something of a novelty.

I look back on those days with a great deal of fondness, because there were so many exciting games. We played against high calibre players most weeks and just about every fan could reel off the names of the opposition team.

There were no substitutes either. They were introduced with the intention of giving both teams an equal number of players if someone was badly hurt, and the idea made complete sense, but the system soon started to be abused. However, it was one thing a manager making a tactical substitution when there was only one substitute. Nowadays, spectators must be driven crazy at times, especially in challenge games, by the sight of players being changed constantly. I cannot believe that FIFA actually wants to increase the number of permitted substitutes as the situation is already farcical, in my view.

However, back to Rangers' Class of 1964 and considering what we achieved in terms of a clean sweep of Scottish honours, you won't be too surprised by my claim that we were capable of beating anybody – Real Madrid apart! The next twelve months didn't turn out as expected, though. What a difference a year makes. Rangers went from treble-winners to only League Cup-winners, despite the team showing little change of personnel. The bulk of the 1963–64 team was still in place, yet we managed to win only one of our opening seven league games. A home draw with Dunfermline on the opening day of the league season was soon followed by a 3–1 defeat by Celtic at Parkhead on 5 September.

There was a degree of respite in the League Cup, when we topped our qualifying section with five wins and a draw, but our title defence was in tatters by the end of September, with Dundee taking revenge for their Cup final defeat by a 4–1 margin at Dens Park. By the time we were two-thirds of the way through the season, Rangers trailed Hearts, Dunfermline, Hibs and Kilmarnock and were in fifth place in the championship table. Come April 1965 we remained there, with the same four teams above us. The only difference was that Kilmarnock had assumed top spot, following a dramatic two-goal win over Hearts in the final round of fixtures to snatch the title on goal difference.

The European Cup involved us in a first round play-off against Red Star Belgrade at Highbury. The sides had finished all-square at 5–5 on aggregate, thanks largely to the goal-scoring exploits of Forrest and Brand, although I did make a significant contribution when I claimed one of our two goals in the second leg in Yugoslavia. We won the play-off, 3–1, after establishing a three-goal lead. Jim Baxter was outstanding and the principal architect of our success, but tragedy struck in the next round when Baxter suffered a broken leg in the dying seconds of the second leg of our tie against Rapid Vienna in Austria. By the time Jim was stretchered off, Rangers were three goals to the good. A 1–0 home win and a 2–0 result in Vienna earned us the reward of a third round clash with Inter Milan, but, despite a Jim Forrest goal giving us victory in the return, the Italians progressed at our expense on the strength of having won, 3–1, at the San Siro.

The Scottish Cup campaign also lasted three rounds. Having begun with a 3–0 win over Hamilton, we followed that up by beating Dundee, 2–0, at Dens Park, but Hibs ended our aspirations of retaining the trophy for a fourth successive season by dint of a 2–1 victory at Easter Road. However, at least we had something to show for our efforts. Having qualified from our section we beat Dunfermline and Dundee United in turn to clinch our place in the League Cup final, where Celtic were the opposition, on 24 October 1964.

Baxter, by now captain in succession to Shearer and Caldow, chose that particular Saturday afternoon to have one of his most inspired games for the club – and there were many. In a match full of skill, flair and constant excitement, the crowd of 91,423 roared themselves hoarse. The game was finely balanced in the first-half, but Forrest gave us the lead seven minutes after the restart and then added a second ten minutes later. Jimmy Johnstone pulled one back for Celtic in the sixty-ninth minute to set up a grandstand finish, but we held out to claim the silverware.

It was in that final that Baxter showed his extensive knowledge of the game. When Celtic switched John Hughes and Johnstone, Jim countered the move by doing likewise with Provan and Caldow. The season was a personal triumph for Jim Forrest, who scored an amazing fifty-seven goals, and, on a personal note, I had the satisfaction of playing in every game and scoring five. There were certainly mitigating circumstances for our failure to win more than one trophy, the most significant being Baxter's broken leg, which kept him out of action for four months, but Henderson also missed much of the season with bunion trouble. However, there was further disappointment in May 1965 in the shape of Baxter's transfer to Sunderland. Rangers received £72,500 for his services, but the money in no way compensated for Jim's loss and the effect his departure had on the team's longer-term prospects.

With Baxter gone, Scot Symon appointed me captain, a role I was to fill for the next thirteen years under three other managers – Davie White, Willie Waddell and Jock Wallace. But when Mr Symon approached me one day after training with the news that I was to follow in the footsteps of such Rangers legends as David Meikeljohn, Jock 'Tiger' Shaw and George Young, there was no fanfare of trumpets. He said simply, 'I want you to be captain.' That was it. The manager clearly didn't feel that any other words were necessary when bestowing such an honour on me.

There was also another highly significant development in Scottish football around the same time as Jim Baxter was on his way to Roker Park and John Greig was assuming the captaincy of Rangers – Jock Stein had taken up residency just a few miles away at Parkhead. Jock's appointment as Celtic manager in March 1965 had far-reaching consequences for Rangers and, as it turned out, for both Scot Symon and his successor, Davie White. Celtic had not won a trophy for eight years, but that was all about to change in the most dramatic fashion possible.

Within weeks of Jock's arrival, Celtic fans had something to cheer about. Celtic won the Scottish Cup, beating Stein's former club, Dunfermline, in the final, but a wind of change was also blowing through Ibrox. Shearer and McMillan left at the end of the season and Brand followed Baxter south in August, when he was sold to Manchester City for £30,000. On the plus side, defender Kai Johansen was signed from Morton. The Dane's arrival was to prove highly significant in the course of the following season.

In stark contrast to the previous campaign, when we had got off to such a disastrous start in the league, we lost only one of our first seventeen matches and we had the added satisfaction of beating Celtic, 2–1, at Ibrox on 18 September. The New Year game at Parkhead on 3 January turned out to be somewhat different, however. We must have made Celtic angry when Davie Wilson gave us the lead after just ninety seconds, for we ended up on the receiving end of a painful 5–1 defeat. Stevie Chalmers scored a hat-trick on one of the worst days of my career. The second-half went from bad to worse after Chalmers began the ball-rolling in the forty-ninth minute. His third goal on the stroke of full-time was the final straw.

For all that we suffered at the hands of our old rivals, though, Rangers led the championship on goal average at the end of February. However, we were unable to sustain our fine run of form and March turned into a nightmare month following defeats by Falkirk and Dundee United and draws with Hearts and Kilmarnock. That run handed the initiative to Celtic and although we finished the season with seven straight wins, the title was bound for Parkhead. In the end only two points separated the teams, but perhaps if I had known then that it was the first of nine in a row for Celtic, I would have elected to leave the country.

Celtic had also beaten us in the League Cup final on 23 October. John Hughes did the damage with two first-half goals, both from the penalty spot, after McKinnon had handled a free kick, followed by Provan bringing down Johnstone from behind. These goals had come against the run of play, after Forrest had missed a couple of chances, but we were nothing if not persistent and we put Celtic under considerable pressure in an effort to retrieve the situation. All we had to show for our efforts, though, was Ian Young's own goal six minutes from the end.

At least we finished the season on a high. Celtic were slight favourites to beat us in the Scottish Cup final, but we upset the odds in a replay after the first game on 23 April ended goal-less. In truth, it was a pretty drab affair, with both sides lacking real spark and imagination. The replay, the following Wednesday, was thankfully a much livelier encounter. Johansen confirmed our superiority when he struck to claim the winner in the seventieth minute and at least half the Hampden crowd of 96,862 went home happy. It was the last time they would have cause to smile for four long years.

Our victory over Celtic gave us entry into the European Cup-Winners' Cup the following season, but little did I suspect that our passport into Europe would be franked all the way to the final. Prior to the final I had been honoured by the Scottish Football Writers' Association with their Player of the Year award. I was the second recipient of the award and it meant a great deal to me to be considered worthy of the honour by those who write about the game on a regular basis. The fact that there were so many outstanding candidates was the icing on the cake.

I was also thrilled to be able to take my father, Tom, and my brother, Tam, to the presentation dinner in Glasgow. My father was not a huge football fan, but he was nonetheless proud of my achievements and Tam, of course, played a very big part in my early development as a player. It was on this occasion that my father met Scot Symon for the first time and they got on like a house on fire. So much so, that Mr Symon told my old man that if he ever wanted tickets for a game not to bother asking me, but to contact him directly at Ibrox. My father didn't require any further encouragement and I cringed when Rangers were playing in Edinburgh and he informed me that he was planning to phone my manager for briefs for him and a couple of pals.

Regrettably, neither my father nor Tam was alive to see me presented with the Scottish Football Writers' Association's award again in 1976. Both had by then passed away and I felt a sense of sadness that they couldn't share in my delight at becoming the first person to be named Player of the Year for a second time.

By then I was thirty-three and in the twilight of my career, but clearly the scribes reckoned that I had been partially instrumental in Rangers' success in again completing the treble of League Championship, Scottish Cup and League Cup. My former Rangers team-mate, Sandy Jardine, also went on to win the Player of the Year award twice and others have achieved the feat since, but being the first to do so was special and I make a point of attending the writers' annual dinner. However, with Jock Stein masterminding Celtic's rise to prominence, there wasn't a great deal to cheer about over the next few seasons.

WANT TO KNOW
A SECRET?

I t was murder trying to keep my mouth shut when I learned that I was about to make my Scotland debut in the biggest game of the home international season, against England, at Hampden Park, on 11 April 1964. No one was supposed to know, including yours truly, but I had a friend who was a friend of a bloke who worked at the Scottish Football Association and I was tipped the wink.

In those days the SFA selectors had a powerful say in the composition of the team and it was usually selected weeks in advance and then kept firmly under wraps. But Ian McColl was the Scotland manager and he knew me from our brief time together at Rangers and clearly thought I could do a job for him. Ian, in fact, had been my partner at training on my first day as a full-time player. When the team was announced to the press I had to pretend it was the first I knew, but I had been getting myself psyched up for several days beforehand. Not that I needed any motivation. I was like a kid let loose in a toy shop at the idea of playing for my country.

I had played a few times for the under-twenty-three team and represented the Scottish League on several other occasions. In fact, it appeared that I had been selected for the full squad on the strength of my performance in a 2–2 draw with England at Sunderland's Roker Park the month before. I had been in direct opposition to Jimmy Greaves, with the task of marking a centre-forward who had few equals in the game. I must have acquitted myself quite well, because while I was selected for my international debut, Greaves was dropped to make way for Roger Hunt of Liverpool.

These representative matches were quite a big deal, drawing large crowds wherever they were played. The players also regarded them as important to the extent that tackles went flying in, often with brutal intent. I remember, on the occasion of an under-twenty-three game, overhearing Billy Bremner and Jimmy Gabriel having a half-time discussion concerning the number of players they had 'sorted out' during the first half. However, being picked for your country was a sizeable step up in class and there were no guarantees of a second chance if you flopped first time round. So I naturally felt a degree of apprehension when I met up with the rest of the squad at Kilmacolm in Renfrewshire two days before the game.

There were no elaborate preparations or in-depth discussions about tactics. Those selected had been chosen on the strength of their current club form in the hope that we would replicate that form in an international jersey, but the manager wanted us to play four-two-four, because he felt we were more flexible than England. He was correct in his assessment that the opposition would struggle to counter-act our formation.

I could hardly have wished for a more auspicious start to my international career. Scotland were looking to complete a hat-trick of victories over England for the first time in eighty years and Alan Gilzean supplied the winning touch with a header eighteen minutes from the end when he rose above the Spurs centre-half, Maurice Norman, to head past Gordon Banks. The key to our success was probably the inspirational midfield play of Jim Baxter and the way he linked up with Willie Henderson and Denis Law. England, despite fielding five of the players who would go on to become World Cup winners two years later, simply could not cope with Jim's deft touches and Denis's aggressive challenges.

Our line-up that day was: Campbell Forsyth (Kilmarnock); Alex Hamilton (Dundee) and Jim Kennedy (Celtic); Greig, Billy McNeill (Celtic) and Baxter (Rangers); Henderson (Rangers), John White (Spurs), Gilzean (Spurs), Denis Law (Manchester United) and Davie Wilson (Rangers). The England team was: Banks; Armfield and Wilson; Milne, Norman and Moore; Paine, Hunt, Byrne, Eastham and Charlton.

One of my fondest memories is of the post-match lap of honour. The fans refused to leave until we had taken a bow and we re-emerged from the dressing room by popular demand, some of the lads barefoot, to run round Hampden in the wind and rain.

It was the start of an unbroken run of twenty-one international appearances stretching across thirty-six months, but, having enjoyed a flying start to my Scotland career, I reckoned it was hoping for too much to expect it to continue in a similar vein. The following month we faced West Germany in Hanover in a warm-up for our World Cup qualifying matches and forced a 2–2 draw, with Gilzean again supplying the cutting edge with both goals.

Following a 3–2 defeat by Wales in Cardiff, we faced Finland at Hampden in the first of six World Cup qualifying matches on 21 October. It turned out to be a dream start to the campaign when goals from Denis Law, Stevie Chalmers and Davie Gibson secured a 3–1 victory.

Our second qualifying match was scheduled for May 1965 and, in addition to the Home International Championship matches against

Northern Ireland and England, which resulted in a 3–2 win over the Irish and a 2–2 draw at Wembley, the SFA also fitted in a warm-up game against Spain. It was a measure of the quality of the Scotland squad of that era that the game at Hampden finished goal-less. The strength of the Spanish team was underpinned by the success of that country's club sides in Europe.

A 1–1 draw with the Poles in Chorzow on 23 May, when Denis Law supplied the finishing touch, represented another good result, especially when we followed up with a second win against Finland just four days later. Yours truly and my Ibrox team-mate, Davie Wilson, did the damage in Helsinki. It was the first of three goals I scored for my country and the pick of the crop, small as it was. People still talk about my last-gasp goal against Italy at Hampden in November 1965, which kept Scotland's hopes of qualifying for the World Cup finals in England the following summer alive, but while it was certainly the most significant of my three goals, it wasn't the best. Even though I say so myself, my strike in the Finnish capital was a belter. I hit a cracking thirty-yard drive wide of the keeper and the ball flew into the top corner of the net like a rocket, to ensure that we came away with the victory we craved. Hopes were high that we could qualify to play in the finals in England the next year.

Jock Stein had replaced Ian McColl as manager on a temporary basis while the SFA searched for a replacement and Jock's initial brief was to take charge for these two games only, as he also had his club commitments with Celtic to consider. In actual fact, though, he remained in charge for our remaining qualifying games.

It was clear to us then that Jock paid almost fanatical attention to detail and he was also a strict disciplinarian who wouldn't stand for any nonsense, no matter the status of the personalities he was dealing with. When Jock discovered a group of players playing cards past curfew time in Poland he let rip with a few choice words before ripping up the playing cards and flushing them down a toilet, prior to ordering the 'guilty' to bed.

The fans and the media alike took the view that if we could win our remaining home games against Poland and Italy there was a fair chance that the final fixture in Italy would be of little significance, but our next match, against Poland in Glasgow on 13 October, didn't follow the script. Not to put too fine a point on it, we screwed up big time against the Poles and that game effectively sealed our fate. One day we were rubbing our hands in anticipation of strutting our stuff on the World Cup stage; the next we were in the depths of despair.

The fact that the Poles had managed to lose to a very ordinary Finnish team had actually increased our hopes of qualification. An early goal from our skipper, Billy McNeill, who was also Jock's captain at Celtic, had a six-figure Hampden crowd in a frenzy of delight. But then the roof caved in – and then some. We were just seven minutes away from a third win in four games when we became slack at the back and allowed the Poles to snatch victory from the jaws of defeat. First Liberda equalised and then Sadek plunged the dagger even deeper into our prospects of joining the world's elite the following summer. It was one of my worst moments as a Scotland player and left us facing the mammoth task of beating Italy twice.

The game against the Italians at Hampden one month later, on 9 November, was a clear case of win or bust. Defeat would spell the end of our World Cup dream and even a victory might not be enough unless we somehow dug out a result in the return. However, we were fortunate to have an outstanding manager and Jock Stein showed his tactical awareness that evening to out-do the Italians. Jock was alive to the likelihood that they would man-mark and try to remove the threat posed by our wingers, Willie Henderson of Rangers and Celtic's John Hughes.

In an effort to counteract the Italian game plan I was selected to play right-back for the first time for Scotland. Jock knew that the full-backs would stick like glue to our wingers, so Henderson was instructed to drag his marker inside to enable me to overlap. It was a real ding-dong battle. I also recall that our keeper, Bill Brown, had damaged a thigh muscle and struggled to take goal kicks, but we managed to give a good account of ourselves.

Scotland, in fact, dominated much of the play without creating a great deal in front of goal. The reason for this was the Italians' defensive mind-set. They had perfected the art of defending and playing on the break and for all that they adopted such a negative approach were capable of posing a genuine threat. I'd had to make a couple of goal line clearances, due largely to Bill Brown's physical state, but the game remained goal-less with just moments remaining.

When I glanced up and noticed that the lights in the main stand had been switched on I realised that time was rapidly running out for us. That was done for safety reasons, for the benefit of fans leaving the stadium, so I knew that we had to act quickly if we were to retain any realistic hope of qualifying. With the seconds ticking away, I spotted an opportunity to go inside the winger for once and broke upfield in a last desperate attempt to snatch a winner. I spotted Jim Baxter to my left and squared the ball to him just outside the box. Jim judged his return pass perfectly and I ran on to it and hit the ball first time with my left foot.

The ball flew into the left hand corner of the net and Hampden erupted. Italy, who were to be installed as favourites to win the World Cup, had been beaten and the Scotland fans were euphoric. Consider-ing that my Rangers team-mate, Ronnie McKinnon, was making his debut and Bobby Murdoch, the wonderfully talented Celtic midfield player, was also a complete newcomer, it was a wonderful result.

A fortnight later we played Wales at home and our hopes of upsetting the odds in Italy soared when we thumped our Celtic cousins, 4–1, with a performance that many said was the best they had seen from a Scottish side for years. Murdoch crowned an outstanding display with two goals and Henderson and yours truly got the others. Two goals in two games! I wondered if scoring was becoming habit-forming. But, despite a highly promising debut by Charlie Cooke, the former Aberdeen and Dundee ball-playing inside-forward who was to go on to star for Chelsea, we realised that we would need a great deal of good fortune against Italy to even draw and force a play-off.

The return, sadly, turned into a disaster. See Naples and die? In our final qualifying match, my first as Scotland captain, we quite simply died the death. Jock had somehow persuaded the SFA to part with a £250 bonus per player for a win in Naples. This sort of money was unheard of in British football circles, but there was a grim acceptance that it would take more than a three-figure cash sum to clinch this match. The Scottish League even agreed to cancel any weekend fixture where one of the competing teams had more than one international player involved, but they had no control of the situation involving the Anglos. Consequently, a number of the squad had to return from a planned get-together at Largs on the Ayrshire coast to satisfy the demands of their paymasters.

We were already without our regular goalkeeper, Billy Brown, Billy McNeill and Jim Baxter because of injuries. Denis Law then joined the list of withdrawn players when he was injured on Football League duty. The club versus country conflict also deprived Jock of the services of others, such as Pat Crerand, Billy Stevenson, Dave Mackay, Ian St John and Willie Johnston. Then, shortly before kickoff, there was another hammer blow, when Willie Henderson was forced to cry off because of injury. You couldn't have made it up. The Italians had pulled the stroke of making a late switch in venues from Rome to Naples, but it probably made no difference. Given the many problems he'd had to deal with, it was remarkable that Jock Stein even managed to assemble a team of eleven fit players.

We lined up: Adam Blacklaw (Burnley); Davie Provan (Rangers) and Eddie McCreadie (Chelsea); Bobby Murdoch (Celtic), Ronnie McKinnon (Rangers), and Greig; Jim Forrest (Rangers), Billy Bremner (Leeds), Ron Yeats (Liverpool), Charlie Cooke (Dundee) and John Hughes (Celtic).

Between us we had made a total of thirty-nine international appearances. I was the most experienced of the bunch with thirteen caps to my credit, the only player in double figures. Jock attempted to confuse the opposition by naming Yeats, the Liverpool centre-half, at centre-forward, but we were up against it from the word go. Ronnie McKinnon, never one to take any sort of interest in tactics, was sharing a room with me and I remember him expressing surprise the night before the game that big Ron was to wear the No. 9 jersey. I had to explain to Ronnie that it was simply a ruse designed to confuse the Italians. Once the game kicked off, Ron would revert to his normal role in the centre of defence, but our makeshift side was no match for the Italians and we were soundly beaten, 3–0.

We held the opposition until just before half-time, but once we went a goal down it was curtains. Looking back, it was perhaps just as well that we lost, for heaven knows what fate might have befallen us had we knocked Italy out of the World Cup. The game in Naples was one of the most frightening experiences of my career. The pitch was surrounded by a deep moat to prevent the fans from invading the playing area, but there was nothing and no one to stop them pelting the team coach with stones and bricks as we left the stadium. However, the real damage to our hopes of qualification had been done by Poland when they beat us at Hampden. The draw in Chorzow had looked a positive result up until then.

Jock had handed me the responsibility of captaincy largely, I suspect, on the grounds that I had undertaken the role at Rangers and because circumstances had dictated that I was the most experienced player in the team. Consequently, and as a result of the defeat in Napes, I imagined that my captaincy would be short-lived and I fully expected to be replaced by one of the bigger name players for our next game against England the following May, which resulted in a 4–3 home defeat. However, I retained the skipper's arm band and held the rank for the next four years, missing out on the honour only when Ian McColl was in charge. Even when I was recalled against Denmark in 1975, after an absence of four years, I was appointed captain by Willie Ormond.

After the first game against Italy at Hampden I was a little concerned that people might get it into their heads that I was a full-back. Jock kept me at right-back for our next game against Wales and, later, his successors as manager John Prentice and Malcolm Macdonald also asked me to fill the role. I didn't have a problem playing full-back, but I was used to playing as a double centre-half for my club, sticking in the centre of defence around Ronnie McKinnon, and felt much more comfortable in that position. I didn't feel that I had the experience to play right-back and I occasionally found myself on the wrong side of wingers. Clearly I must have done better than I imagined, though, because I retained my place and was eventually switched back to the position I felt I was best suited to, alongside McKinnon.

My first full year as captain – 1966 – was one to forget in the main. With the exception of a 1–1 draw with Brazil – Pele et al – at Hampden,

Scotland didn't enjoy very much success. In addition to the defeat by England, we also lost to Holland and Portugal and could only draw with Wales at Ninian Park. Our sole success came in the final fixture of that year, a 2–1 victory over Northern Ireland at Hampden. But better times lay ahead.

Nowadays playing for your country is a lucrative business, but forty years ago the players received a small match fee – I think it was £50 – and one cap a season, no matter how many games you featured in. I was on international duty in my second game against West Germany in Hanover when I got my first taste of the benefits of commercialism and was paid the princely sum of £10 to wear a pair of Adidas football boots. Jim Baxter's entrepreneurial skills came to the fore when he did a deal with a sports rep and asked me if I fancied making a couple of bob on the side. The boots were the latest model and I in fact continued to play in adidas boots for the remainder of my career – without any further financial inducement, I might add.

I remember sitting looking at the boots Jim had given to me and thinking back to my early school days when I had played in a pair of borrowed boots. I also recalled, when I signed for Rangers, being given a pair of James Scotland Symon boots, which had resembled miner's boots with heavy toe caps and long studs. When I worked as a milk delivery boy I saved up my Christmas tips and bought myself a pair of boots modelled on the type worn by Puskas. They felt like carpet slippers, but now I was being paid a tenner to wear a certain brand of footwear. Players who earn a hundred times as much in one game for wearing brand-name boots will laugh at what I was paid in 1964, but it was a very different world back then and we enjoyed few of the luxuries of five-star living that the modern stars take for granted.

Our trip to Warsaw to play Poland was an example of what I'm talking about. We ended up staying in a youth hostel full of students and we were none too pleased about the standard of our quarters. So, when the SFA big wigs headed off to attend an official banquet on the eve of the game, some of the more senior players decided to take revenge of sorts for being forced to stay in sub-standard accommodation.

They found the door to SFA President Tam Reid's room unlocked and set about getting up to mischief. Tam, who was also chairman of Partick Thistle, was a heavy smoker and favoured a brand of cigarettes known as Passing Cloud. Without further ado, the raiding party snaffled a couple of cartons containing two hundred cigarettes each and began distributing them among the students. Tam also had an ornamental axe that had been presented to him by the Polish FA as a memento of our visit and that was promptly embedded in a wooden-topped coffee table. When Tam returned several hours later, somewhat the worse for wear, he went potty when he couldn't find his fags and then discovered his axe sticking out of the table top.

The David Beckhams of the football world live in plush homes complete with all mod cons, including saunas, but I had never even seen a sauna prior to Scotland playing Finland in Helsinki. It held huge novelty value for the players and we all crowded in, but Denis being Denis, he couldn't resist throwing a pail of water on the coals before rushing out and jamming the door shut. By the time the Law Man released us we were pouring sweat and in danger of suffering from heat exhaustion, but we weren't prepared for what happened next. Suddenly this old woman began battering us with twigs. We wondered what the hell she was doing. The only thing I could think of was that the old woman was punishing us as a result of Denis's high jinx. None of us realised that was what was supposed to happen when you emerged from a sauna.

CHAPTER 8

THE STEIN FACTOR

There are great managers and there are bad managers, but I believe that there are also lucky managers, and Davie White was not one of those who enjoyed much good fortune during his brief spell in charge. Davie succeeded Scot Symon in November 1967, having been appointed assistant to Symon just five months previously, and he was dismissed after just a little over two years at the helm. He didn't manage to win any trophies with Rangers, but the bald facts don't offer a fair reflection of Davie's reign.

He later proved himself to be a very capable manager, leading Dundee to League Cup final success against Celtic in 1973, and he had made his mark with Clyde, who had finished third behind the Old Firm the season before he came to Ibrox. When they held us to a draw at home with only two games remaining, the result ultimately cost us the championship and gave Celtic the second of their nine consecutive titles. However, he was still only in his mid-thirties and it was a big ask for any young manager to make the huge transition from managing a club of the status of Clyde to one the size of Rangers.

The fact that Jock Stein's Celtic had established something of a stranglehold on the domestic scene didn't help Davie either. When he became boss, we had already failed to progress beyond the qualifying stages of the League Cup after finishing second behind our arch rivals in our section, following a draw at Ibrox and a defeat at Parkhead. That season's Scottish Cup also turned out to be a big disappointment. After beating Hamilton and Dundee we lost to Hearts in a replay.

Our involvement in Europe in the Fairs Cup lasted until April. Wins over Dinamo Dresden and Cologne set us up for a quarter-final meeting with Leeds United, who were at their peak. The first leg at Ibrox finished goal-less and our failure to make more of our chances, especially in the first-half, meant we lost the opportunity to take an invaluable lead to Elland Road, where Leeds won, 2–0, with goals from Johnny Giles and Peter Lorimer.

The League Championship was a close run affair, however. It's hard to believe that we lost only once in thirty-four games – 3–2 to Aberdeen at Ibrox on the final Saturday – but it wouldn't have mattered even if we had beaten the Dons. A disappointing 3–3 draw with Morton at Cappielow ten days earlier, when I scored a brace, had already handed the initiative to Celtic. In the event, Celtic beat Dunfermline, 2–1, at East End Park on 30 April to clinch the title. How unlucky can you be, though? We had been the only team to beat Celtic – 1–0 at Ibrox the previous September – and we had also drawn the New Year game at Parkhead, when Kai Johansen's late equaliser made it 2–2. Yet we had to settle for second best.

Davie's appointment had apparently not been universally approved by the board, but he had an unshakeable belief in his own ability and I personally liked the man. However, as captain I had to take my share of responsibility for the way his managerial tenure worked out. I think the players in general could probably have given more, too. Indeed, in certain instances that was most definitely the case.

Davie's one full season in charge – 1968–69 – was again a tale of near misses. Once more we were unable to stop Celtic being crowned champions and the League Cup campaign began and ended at the qualifying stage. The season kicked-off on 10 August with an Old Firm showdown at Ibrox and Celtic emerged victors. Willie Wallace, who was also to emerge as Celtic's match-winner in the return a fortnight later, when he scored the only goal of the game at Parkhead, struck twice to put the opposition in pole position. The fact that Celtic went on to slaughter Hibs, 6–2, in the final the following April simply served to increase our frustration, more so because that victory ensured that Stein masterminded a second treble in the course of just three seasons.

Celtic completed the cup-double just three weeks after leathering Hibs – and we were the ones who suffered the next time round. In truth, we never got going after Billy McNeill headed Celtic in front after two minutes. On one of the worst days of my career, Celtic scored three more, helped by defensive blunders in front of a crowd of nearly 133,000. It was Rangers' first Scottish Cup final defeat for forty years and one of the most painful in the club's history. For the fourth season on the trot we finished in runners-up spot, this time trailing Celtic by five points, despite having beaten them both home and away.

Davie spent around £400,000 strengthening his squad, including the signings of Colin Stein from Hibs for £100,000 and midfielder Alex MacDonald from St Johnstone for £50,000, and there was clearly growing discontent in the boardroom and on the terraces, but others let Davie down, of that there can be no doubt.

The 1968–69 season was also overshadowed by the events that took place in Newcastle on 21 May. With all hope of domestic success gone, Rangers still harboured the dream of European glory. With the scalps of Vojvodina, Dundalk, DWS Amsterdam and Atletico Bilbao dangling from our belts, we were drawn to face Newcastle in the semi-finals of the Fairs Cup and we fancied our chances of going all the way in the competition.

Given the 'Auld Enemy' aspect, the relatively close proximity of the two clubs and the fact that Newcastle had several Scots in their line-up, there were a lot of 'verbals' in the build-up to the first leg at Ibrox on 14 May. Most of it was directed at us from the Newcastle end. Unfortunately, the luck factor came into play again. We lost two defenders on the eve of the game when injury accounted for Willie Mathieson and Ronnie McKinnon. The absence of Willie Johnston through suspension compounded the manager's selection problems. Fate had conspired against Davie White and there was further clear evidence of that fact when we were awarded a first-half penalty kick, only for Ian McFaul to save Andy Penman's effort.

Penman had been put on the spot, because I had missed a penalty in the previous round against Atletico Bilbao at Ibrox. We had been going through a spell when penalties were being missed left, right and centre, and Davie suggested that as captain I should accept the responsibility of taking the next one. I didn't have a problem with that, but Davie advised me that the Atletico goalkeeper, Iribar, always dived to his right and that was normally where I placed my shots. The fact that Iribar represented the Spanish national side and was highly regarded gave me further food for thought. Consequently, when we won a penalty just after the restart, with the score standing at 2–1, I elected to 'blooter' the ball rather than try to place it. Ibrox in those days had high banked terracing at the Celtic end of the ground and the ball soared skywards. It was so off target that I'm sure it just missed hitting a plane taking off from nearby Glasgow Airport!

However, late goals from Persson and Colin Stein spared my blushes and gave us a 4–1 lead going into the return in Spain, where we lost, 2–0.

Despite Penman's penalty being saved, we felt confident that we could beat Newcastle in the return. After all, we had plenty of other opportunities to score in the first leg against a Newcastle side intent on keeping a clean sheet, but our failure to score even one goal made the trip to St James's Park seven days later a daunting one. However, at least we had Mathieson, McKinnon and Johnston available again to give us some hope that we might still be capable of nicking the one goal we needed to extend our season to a European final.

It was not to be, though. Exiled Scots Jim Scott and Jackie Sinclair did for us in the second-half and the dream died on the end of a 2–0 score line. But while losing was in itself bad enough, the behaviour of a section of the Rangers fans that night made things a whole lot worse. There was a history of crowd trouble when Scottish sides played in England and, regrettably, events at St James's Park did nothing to enhance the reputation of Old Firm fans.

I like the Geordies and there is always a great atmosphere at St James's Park, but drink and passion don't mix. Having said that, I have always held the view that it was a minority who were responsible for sparking the crowd trouble. The referee, whose nationality escapes me, had riled the Rangers fans with a series of dubious decisions and eventually empty Newcastle Brown Ale bottles began to be hurled from the terraces, followed by a pitch invasion.

Partial order was eventually restored, thanks largely to the appearance of police dogs, but at one point the referee said to me in broken English, 'You are the captain – you must stop them.' I responded by informing him that as he was the one who had made all the mistakes he should tell the 'invaders' to behave themselves. Further trouble erupted at the end of the game and the centre of Newcastle became a 'war zone' for a time.

While I would never condone that sort of behaviour, I could also appreciate how frustrated our fans felt. It was almost like a home game for Rangers, because of the close proximity of the clubs, and we took a large following to Tyneside. Strict control of ticket sales and the ban on alcohol has removed the fear of similar scenes to those witnessed at St James's Park being re-enacted in future, but those who administer the affairs of the game can never afford to allow themselves to become complacent.

The reality was that we had created more than enough openings to win the tie, but Newcastle enjoyed the breaks and subsequently went on to score a crushing 6–2 aggregate victory over Ujpest Dozsa of Hungary in the final. Joe Harvey was, in fact, the last Newcastle manager to guide the club to major trophy success and allegedly he later tried to sign me for the Tynesiders, but I never had a decision to make. I was perfectly happy at Rangers.

In retrospect, Davie's decision to bring back Jim Baxter later that same month was a mistake. Jim had become available when Nottingham Forest freed him and it was hoped that the old Baxter magic would be rekindled by a return to his former stomping ground. The truth was somewhat different. Jim failed to recreate his former brilliance. His fondness for the 'good life' had caught up with him and we saw only flashes of the Baxter of four years earlier. Within eleven months Jim's career was effectively over.

By then Davie White had also departed. Even though the 1969–70 season began with an encouraging 2–1 League Cup win over Celtic in our second game, our hopes quickly nosedived when we could only draw with Raith Rovers and once again we failed to advance beyond the qualifying stage. Our indifferent league form, which included defeats by Ayr United and Celtic – their first win in the league at Ibrox for twelve years – meant that after just eleven games we were sitting sixth in the table.

At least we made it through to the second round of the European Cup-Winners' Cup, having knocked out Steaua Bucharest of Romania, and Gornik of Poland were next up. Not to put too fine a point on it, it was a s**t or bust tie for Davie White. Regrettably, it turned out to be the latter for the manager. Celtic had won five of the six trophies available to Davie and Rangers during the previous twenty-one months and the clock was ticking.

Unfortunately, we enjoyed no respite from our troubles in the first leg in Poland. With the great Lubanski, star of the national team, in scintillating form, Gornik won, 3–1. Lubanski scored twice and, although Orjan Persson's goal gave us some hope that we might repair the damage in the return, the odds were stacked against us. But on 26 November 1969 the roof caved in. A crowd of 63,000 watched Lubanski and company score three brilliant goals after Baxter had given us an eighteenth minute lead and an aggregate score of 2–6 sealed Davie White's fate.

Davie was gone just twenty-four hours later, as much the victim of circumstances as anything. In addition to being desperately unfortunate to have to confront a man of the managerial brilliance of Jock Stein, Davie didn't enjoy the complete backing and respect of every one of his players. He perhaps also lacked the guidance necessary for a young manager to avoid the obvious pitfalls of inexperience. Davie was astute tactically and had sound ideas about how the game should be played, but he understandably made mistakes and should perhaps have been more ruthless at times. But, ultimately, the fact that Davie was the only Rangers manager never to have won a domestic trophy can almost certainly be put down to an appalling lack of luck.

Rangers' choice of successor was not terribly surprising. Willie Waddell had been an outstanding player for the club and had gone on to enjoy further success in management when he guided Kilmarnock to the League Championship in 1964–65. 'Deedle', as he was known from his playing days, when the fans had exhorted his team-mates, 'Don't deedle dawdle – give the ball to Waddell,' had then carved out a new career in newspapers as a sports writer with the *Scottish Daily Express* and his judgement was widely respected. So, too, was his knowledge of the game and his passion for Rangers.

The club was at a low ebb and it was clear that Rangers needed someone with the statesmanship qualities of Jock Stein and a manager who could confront the Celtic boss head on. Willie Waddell had these assets and a week after the Gornik defeat it was announced that he was to be the new manager.

He would take over, it was revealed, on Monday 8 December. Willie Thornton, who had previously been manager of Partick Thistle, before being appointed assistant to Davie White sixteen months earlier, took charge of the team for our league match against Hearts on the Saturday and we won, 2–1, at Tynecastle. Prior to that game, Willie Thornton told me he wanted the players to report to the ground at 2 p.m. the following Monday afternoon, but added that the manager had asked to have a meeting with me at 10 a.m.

I had got to know Willie quite well when he accompanied Rangers and Scotland teams on trips abroad in his role as journalist and had formed a reasonably close relationship with him. I was also aware from his demeanour that there was mutual respect between us and I sensed that he thought quite highly of me. But Deedle immediately became boss and didn't waste any time laying his cards on the table. He said, 'This club is not in the position it should be, but you and I are going to take Rangers back to the top. I need your help to achieve that objective.' I replied that that was fine by me and added that I was willing to do whatever was required of me to try to end Celtic's dominance. It was the start of what I like to think was a close and successful working relationship.

Mind you, I wondered on his first day in charge if the manager was also going to take me to task for an incident that had occurred on a European trip with Rangers a short time before. I had been walking along the corridor of the team's hotel when I spotted a key had been left in a bedroom door. When I unlocked the door I was confronted by the sight of a figure lying face down fast asleep. Thinking it was one of my team-mates, I whacked my victim across the backside and ran out of the room. Having made it back to my own room I peered round the door and spotted Deedle prowling the corridor in search of his 'attacker'. I never did find out if he knew it had been me, because the subject wasn't raised, but I suspect he had a fair idea who had administered the slap.

The manager's message to the players was that all would be treated on an equal footing, irrespective of their status. He also stressed that all first-team members would earn the same wage. The importance of discipline was also highlighted by the new manager. He banned long hair and moustaches and warned that everyone had to behave in a manner befitting an employee of Rangers Football Club – both on and off the park. Image was crucially important. Initially, the boss put on a tracksuit and took charge of training, but within a relatively short period of time he discarded the tracksuit and, like Scot Symon before him, wore a dress suit to work instead.

When Jock Wallace was appointed as coach the following April, he did the physical stuff with the players, but the manager never took his eye off the ball. He oversaw training and dictated most of our tactics. He was the boss in every sense and made me feel good, because of the responsibility he gave me as captain. He also put me under pressure to make key decisions on the pitch and I enjoyed that trust. Even when Jock Wallace eventually became team manager, the boss always hovered in the background. He was the driving force and installed a new-found pride in the players. He also made them realise the importance of the club they were representing.

One of Willie Waddell's first tasks was to regroup and rebuild and he made a number of changes over the next couple of seasons. Players of the calibre of goalkeeper Peter McCloy, defender Tom Forsyth and winger Tommy McLean were signed. Others, such as Baxter, Kai Johansen and Willie Henderson departed and a greater emphasis was placed on youth. That opened the door for younger players, like Sandy Jardine, Alfie Conn and Colin Jackson. However, it would have been expecting just a little too much for the manager to perform miracles and, despite us going on a twelve-game unbeaten run in the league immediately following his arrival, Celtic were once again crowned champions. Celtic also beat us in the Scottish Cup, winning, 3–1, at Parkhead in the third round, but at least the signs were encouraging. There was a new vibrancy about the club and the fans, too, seemed to sense better times ahead.

The manager realised that we were not streets behind Celtic. It wasn't as if they ever totally outclassed us at any stage during their nine in a row, but the club was in need of a major overhaul and it required a strong personality to force through the very necessary changes. Inevitably, there were casualties. A clear-out of the backroom staff resulted in Davie Kinnear, Harry Davis and Lawrie Smith parting company, in the case of Kinnear after twenty-six years with the club.

Jock Wallace, who was assistant manager of Hearts, arrived as the new fitness 'guru'. Jock, who had helped mastermind Rangers' downfall in the Scottish Cup at Berwick three years before, was as hard as nails. He revelled in his clichéd nickname 'Jungle Fighter', acquired as a result of his stint of National Service in Malaya with the King's Own Scottish Borderers. He was a fitness fanatic and not a man to be toyed with. Willie Waddell saw Jock as the ideal person to raise the players' fitness levels and work ethic, which he had constantly criticised during his time as a newspaper man, but if Jock was physically tough, the boss was his match in terms of mental toughness. Some might have described him as a bit of a bully in the way he goaded players into a reaction. Perhaps there was some truth in that assertion. Certainly, he created a slight fear factor and wouldn't stand for any nonsense, but Rangers desperately needed a powerful personality at the time.

The boss was a 'hard man' and you could never hope to win any argument with him. He simply kept arguing until the other person gave it up as a bad job. It was also a waste of time asking for a pay rise. He would lower his glasses, peer over the top of the frames and tell you that was your lot before throwing you out of his office. Fortunately, I didn't have too many run-ins with Willie Waddell, but there was one occasion when I stood my ground – and I'm not sure he ever forgave me.

Rangers had been crowned champions in 1975 and our final game of the season, against Airdrie at Ibrox, was meaningless in terms of points, but the boss was determined to attract a full-house crowd of 70,000. He explained to me that he planned to have a large balloon-shaped structure erected on the pitch, from which would emerge a Hollywood starlet who would then proceed to take the kickoff. He added that he planned to advertise the event in the national press to attract the fans. 'That's good, boss,' I replied, 'but where do I come into this?' 'You'll be the starlet,' he informed me. 'You'll wear a long dress and a blond wig over your playing kit and just before the game kicks off you'll remove both ready to play.'

I couldn't believe what I was hearing. 'What?' I exclaimed. 'You seriously expect me to get dressed up as a Hollywood starlet and stand in a balloon for an hour and a quarter and then play a game of football? No way am I doing that.' I went further and added, 'You and your two pals, Willie Thornton and Willie Woodburn, wouldn't do it and I consider myself just as big a name at Rangers as any of you, so you're not on.' By then the manager's glasses had slipped even further down his face and he was spluttering with rage. 'Get out,' he roared and chased me down the marble staircase.

Next day it was the same script. I was ordered to the manager's office and once more I informed him that I wouldn't be part of his scheme. He warned me, 'I won't forget this.' He didn't. Instead of having to dress up like Marilyn Monroe, I was forced to play the part of Ben Hur and ride round Ibrox on a chariot prior to kickoff. After twenty minutes holding on for grim death while this horse careered round the cinder track, I spent the first twenty minutes of the game shaking from head to foot. In the event, 65,000 fans paid to watch me make a fool of myself and Airdrie beat us 1–0!

We had no silverware to show for our efforts in 1969–70, but the changes Willie Waddell was patiently implementing paid off in October 1970 when Rangers won the League Cup. His philosophy that if a player was good enough, he was old enough, was born out when sixteen-year-old Derek Johnstone scored the winner against Celtic.

But the season was completely overshadowed by the tragic events of the Ibrox Disaster. Winning championships and cups was a complete irrelevance compared to the deaths of sixty-six people. History records that Rangers finished fourth in the league, behind Celtic, Aberdeen and St Johnstone, and were beaten in the Scottish Cup final by Celtic, but many of us lost our appetite for football for a time in the aftermath of the tragedy.

Celtic were at the zenith of their power and their title success

On a charge in my 1978 testimonial.

Aged 14 with my team-
mates in the Edinburgh
Schools team in 1956. I'm
second from the left in the
front row.

The 'big match' and a
contract for life. Janette and
me on our wedding day, 27
March 1967.

That's my boy. With my late mum, Agnes, who sadly died in August 1988.

The arrival of my granddaughter, Kaitlin, on 10 March 2004 was like winning the lottery.

ANDY FORMAN

Tea for two. Celtic rival and Scotland team-mate Ronnie Simpson and me having a cuppa on the Edinburgh–Glasgow express.

Rangers manager Scot Symon and me displaying the two-franc piece that was worth a fortune to Rangers when I called 'tails' against Real Zaragoza on 22 March 1967 and we won through to the last four in Europe on the toss of a coin.

Enjoying ourselves at a club dance in Glasgow's Grosvenor Hotel in the 1960s. Willie Henderson, Jim Forrest, yours truly, Davie Provan and Ronnie McKinnon with wives.

The royal seal of approval. Janette, me and Murray at Buck House for my investiture as a member of the British Empire on 15 November 1977.

Another very proud moment. Rangers chairman David Murray presents me with the trophy as 'the greatest Ranger'.

A couple of swingers. With the legendary Gary Player in Orlando.

Rangers strips but no boots. Gary Player's team on his farm in South Africa

The tension of an Old Firm game is etched on our faces. Dick Advocaat and I side-by-side in the dug-out during the pre-match warm-up.

One of the highlights of my career. Scoring against Italy at Hampden to keep alive Scotland's World Cup hopes on 9 November 1965.

Clearing my lines on the day when Scotland 'humbled' the world champions at Wembley on 15 April 1967. Jimmy Greaves looks on.

While on holiday in Majorca, I managed to persuade Bobby Moore to play a game against the hotel waiters, much to the delight of the locals. The black armbands we are wearing were a mark of respect for the hotel gardener who had just died!

represented a sixth consecutive championship. People have asked me how it felt as captain of Rangers to watch our biggest rivals reel off nine in a row and how that impacted on me. To be honest, I can't really say what I felt at the time. Now, I wonder how I could have played for all those years and allowed them to win so often. It was an affront to my pride and to Rangers, but when I think back to the second half of the 1960s and the early years of the 1970s, I think I can say without fear of contradiction that we never at any time felt inferior to Celtic. We went into each new season believing that we were good enough to win the championship and that our turn would eventually come. It was that approach that kept us going. There was always another fresh challenge just around the corner, but I'm sure I must have been boiling inside with frustration and anger. While it is important to give the appearance of being a good loser and to shake hands with the opposition, it's also vital that you never lose the determination to be a winner.

I think Celtic's achievements probably also had the effect of making me even more determined and drove me on to intensify my efforts to beat them. The example of that was a Drybrough Cup match against Celtic when we trailed 4–0. With time running out there was clearly no way back for us, but I refused to throw in the towel. I was urging my team-mates for one final effort when we broke forward and I scored at the Celtic end. The chant went up, 'John Greig, John Greig.' But it wasn't the Rangers fans chanting my name. Most of them had already left. It was Celtic fans who clearly appreciated the effort I was making on behalf of my club and I'll never forget that.

Jock Stein's record of twenty-five major trophy wins is testimony to his standing in the pantheon of the British game. Only Sir Alex Ferguson can lay claim to a similar record of success, so there is no need for me to endorse his remarkable achievements. I played under Stein when he was Scotland manager, so I had first-hand experience of the man and his method and motivational skills. Big Jock was a new breed of manager in that he didn't just pick eleven players to go out and do a job. He picked horses for courses and had the knack of selecting the correct players for a specific task.

If for any reason he miscalculated, Stein had the ability to change things around at half-time. He was willing to tinker with tactics in the heat of the moment and even if we had the upper hand I used to warn my team-mates at half-time to beware a sudden change in the way Celtic would approach the second-half. Of the current crop of managers I would say that Jose Mourinho is the closest I have seen to Stein in the respect that he can suddenly make changes in personnel and drastically alter Chelsea's approach to combat certain situations.

Celtic were also the first team I had seen use their strikers to chase the full-backs across the park to stop them playing the ball. More often than not the strikers remained fairly static, waiting for the ball to be fed to them, but Celtic front players worked their socks off. Stein was also very crafty and thought two moves ahead of most of his rivals. It was alleged that in the days when teams played two games in the space of twenty-four hours during the New Year holiday period, Stein instructed the Parkhead ground staff to water the pitch and force a postponement of the first fixture if Celtic were playing Rangers at Ibrox the next day, so his players would be fresh. Stein used every trick in the book and some that hadn't even been thought of, but he found a worthy adversary in Willie Waddell.

CHAPTER 9

WEMBLEY WIZARDS

The Tartan Army still eulogises about Scotland's defeat of the world champions at Wembley on 15 April 1967. The score line, England 2, Scotland 3, represented one of the biggest upsets of all time. Just six years before Scotland had been humiliated, 9–3, by the Auld Enemy, so how could we expect to beat an England team that contained ten of the side that had triumphed over West Germany ten months earlier?

Jimmy Greaves in place of Roger Hunt hardly constituted a weakening of Sir Alf Ramsey's side. We, meanwhile, had two players making their full international debuts – thirty-six-year-old Celtic goalkeeper, Ronnie Simpson, and Jim McCalliog, the young Sheffield Wednesday striker.

On the surface at least, we had absolutely no reason to feel confident about our chances, but we had a couple of points in our favour. Firstly, we had considered ourselves unfortunate not to qualify for the World Cup finals the previous year and we were desperate to make a point, in the belief that we could have given a good account of ourselves. Secondly, we got a huge lift from playing the world champions, but there was a third highly significant reason for Scotland's victory – the England players were far too bloody cocky.

I have always hated hearing any player say that he wasn't up for a game. As a professional you should always be ready to give one hundred per cent, but I suspect some of the England players at least played the game down a touch, in the belief that it was no big deal. They probably felt that they only had to turn up to beat us and also it's probably true to say that we had more to gain than England.

I had positive vibes before the game. I had a feeling that we were going to cause a real upset. I couldn't explain it. It was just one of those times when there was a real feel-good factor throughout the team. In fact, I had never known a Scotland side quite so confident or fired up. The English football press did us a huge favour by suggesting that we shouldn't even be allowed to share the same pitch as the England lads. There was even a cheeky comparison with Luxembourg.

Those sorts of comments went down like a lead balloon, especially with the English-based players like Denis Law, Billy Bremner and Jim Baxter. Denis was reputedly playing golf on the afternoon of the World Cup final rather than be anywhere near a television set, so he, more than anyone else, was desperate to stick two fingers up to the opposition.

Maybe if the England players had paid more heed to the stats they would have been a little more respectful. We had, after all, won three and drawn one of the previous five fixtures. No other team in the world could match our record against England at that time. Was it any wonder that Sir Alf Ramsey was not more kindly disposed towards Scotland?

Our manager, Bobby Brown, who had kept goal for Rangers and Scotland in the 1940s and 1950s, was in charge of the national team for the first time and was forced to make a late change to his plans. Jimmy

Johnstone had been injured in Celtic's European Cup semi-final against Dukla Prague the previous Wednesday, so Willie Wallace, who had also played against the Czechs, was drafted in as a late replacement for 'Jinky'. 'Wispy' flew south on the Thursday evening to link up with the rest of the squad, but it made no difference; he fitted in without any bother and gave the England defence plenty to think about.

The sides lined up as follows. England: Gordon Banks; George Cohen and Ray Wilson; Nobby Stiles, Jack Charlton and Bobby Moore; Alan Ball, Jimmy Greaves, Bobby Charlton, Geoff Hurst and Martin Peters.

Scotland: Ronnie Simpson (Celtic); Tommy Gemmell (Celtic) and Eddie McCreadie (Chelsea); Greig, Ronnie McKinnon (Rangers) and Jim Baxter (Sunderland); Willie Wallace (Celtic), Billy Bremner (Leeds), Jim McCalliog (Sheffield Wednesday), Denis Law (Manchester United) and Bobby Lennox (Celtic).

History records that Law, Lennox and McCalliog scored our goals, with Jack Charlton and Hurst scoring for the opposition, but the score line flattered England, in my opinion. We should have won by a significantly greater margin and we might have done had Jim Baxter not chosen to start stroking the ball about in an effort to retain possession and humiliate England further. At one point, Jim, Bremner and Gemmell played more than twenty passes without an England player touching the ball and little Alan Ball ran around like a man possessed as he tried to break up their passing game. Jim even indulged in a spot of 'keepie-up', which the Scotland fans loved.

Afterwards, the English press tried to claim that an injury to Jack Charlton had influenced the outcome, but although he was forced to switch from centre-half to centre-forward, Big Jack was probably more of a nuisance as a striker. My suspicion that England had under-rated our capabilities was confirmed by Nobby Stiles, when he came up to me at the end of the game and said, 'Well done, John. Scotland played much better than any of us thought you could play and that's why you beat us.'

Captaining Scotland that day was the highlight of my international career. To have the honour to skipper a team containing players of the skill and craft of Baxter and Law was a big deal in its own right, but to do so on an afternoon when history was made was extra special.

Scotland's success in becoming the first team to beat the reigning world champions had caused such a furore that I was invited to appear on the *Eamon Andrews Show* the following day. Ronnie McKinnon and I had stayed on in London, because Rangers were flying to Bulgaria on the Monday to play Sofia in the European Cup-Winners' Cup semi-final and we had arranged to join up with the rest of the squad at Heathrow. Also appearing on the *Eamon Andrews Show* was the highly successful crime writer, Mickey Spillane, and a young and emerging Welsh singer by the name of Tom Jones, so it was quite an experience to mix in that sort of company and to have my interview shown nationwide.

The show was recorded in the afternoon and broadcast a few hours later and when I returned to the St Ermins Hotel, where we were staying, the manager invited me to watch the recording in his office and treated me to a bottle of champagne on the house. The champagne wasn't my first drink of the day. Shortly after a late breakfast, Denis Law and I had visited a nearby pub, after Denis had expressed a desire for a pint of shandy. Denis had a habit of wearing polo neck sweaters and on this occasion his maroon number made him look like a member of the Salvation Army. One thing was for sure, though: the barman didn't have a clue who we were.

The pub was empty at that time on a Sunday and when the barman heard us speak he immediately recognised our accents and asked if we had been at the game. 'Yes,' I replied, 'but that fellow Law is seriously overrated.' The barman totally agreed with me, but you should have seen his face when I pointed to Denis, who was by now spluttering with indignation, and said, 'I'd like you to meet Denis Law.'

The Wembley game against England was always the big one for Scotland. Prior to 1974 we rarely qualified for the World Cup finals and had never once participated in the European Championship finals. Part of the reason for that unfortunate state of affairs was the fact that we were invariably drawn against quality opposition in the qualifying stages. We never seemed to get a lucky break, being drawn against powerful football nations like Czechoslovakia, the 1962 World Cup finalists who only narrowly beat Scotland in a play-off for the tournament in Chile, Italy and West Germany. The 1967 game was my twenty-first in a Scotland jersey, but I was forced to miss our next match, a friendly a month later against the USSR at Hampden, because Rangers were preparing for the European Cup-Winners' Cup final, and Scotland lost, 2–0.

I did feature in Scotland's next fifteen games, however. My unbroken run stretched from a single-goal defeat by Northern Ireland in Belfast on 21 October 1967 to a 2–0 loss to Austria in Vienna twenty-five months later, but by and large it was a reasonably successful period for Scotland. There were wins over Wales (twice), Denmark, Austria and Cyprus (twice) and draws with England, Holland, West Germany, Northern Ireland and the Republic of Ireland. On the down side we were thumped, 4–1, by England at Wembley and lost, 3–2, to West Germany in Hamburg, when we also had Tommy Gemmell red-carded. The defeat by West Germany immediately followed by the one in Austria was highly significant, because it ended our hopes of qualifying for the 1970 World Cup finals in Mexico and deprived me of my last chance to appear on the biggest stage of all.

However, while my World Cup dream was over, my international career continued for a further eight games. I, in fact, remained a regular choice from April 1970 until May 1971, playing in every match, but I regret to say that we won only one of them, against Denmark, by a single goal. The other seven resulted in three draws and four defeats, but I had to wait a hell of a long time to notch up my forty-fourth and final appearance for my country – more than four years to be exact.

I had long since resigned myself to having played my last game, a 3–1 defeat by England at Wembley in May 1971, when the call came out of the blue. It appeared that Tommy Docherty, who had succeeded Bobby Brown as manager, was not a fan of mine, but Willie Ormond had clearly not forgotten me and I suddenly found myself back in the international fold for the European Championship qualifier against Denmark at Hampden on 29 October 1975.

Not only was I back, I was also handed the role of captain. The month before, Scotland had beaten the Danes, 1–0, in Copenhagen, but the victory had turned sour when five of the squad were handed life bans as a result of an incident that had taken place at the team's hotel. It was alleged that the five players involved – Billy Bremner, Joe Harper, scorer of the goal, Willie Young, Arthur Graham and Pat McCluskey – had been caught in the room of an SFA official in the act of filling his travel holdall full of water following a visit to a nightclub where there had apparently also been an incident over an unpaid bill. I think there had also been a level of police involvement. I suspect it was little more than high jinx on the part of those involved, but they had their international careers ended by the SFA (the original life bans were later lifted). Billy's ban had added significance as he was captain and that left the team without an established skipper, so I was recalled at the age of thirty-three. I was both surprised and delighted, for it indicated that my club form was still good enough to warrant a place on the big stage.

Scotland won, 3–1, through goals from Kenny Dalglish, Bruce Rioch and Ted MacDougall, to complete the double over the Danes, but it turned out to be a one-off for me. The following month the team drew, 1–1, with Romania at Hampden, but by then Martin Buchan was wearing the No. 4 jersey and my international career was over for real this time. My only regret is never having played in the World Cup or European Championship finals, but I played forty-four more times for my country than some players, so I'm not complaining.

CHAPTER 10

THE TRIALS OF NUREMBERG

Rangers achieved the distinction of becoming the first British club to contest a European Cup-Winners' Cup final when they faced Fiorentina in the newly inaugurated competition in May 1961. It was a measure of just how talented that Rangers team was that they disposed of Ferencvaros, Borussia Monchengladbach and Wolves to claim their place in a two-leg final against the Italians. A crowd of 80,000 watched the first leg at Ibrox, when Eric Caldow missed a penalty and Fiorentina scored a last minute goal to take a 2–0 lead into the return. That left Rangers with a mountain to climb and it was no surprise when Fiorentina secured a second win on their own patch, albeit by the slimmest of margins.

Six years after that 4–1 aggregate defeat, Rangers were back in the Cup-Winners' Cup final, this time against Bayern Munich. By a remarkable coincidence our great rivals, Celtic, had also reached the European Cup final to make it a unique double for Glasgow. The first round draw paired us with Glentoran, who were managed by John Colrain, the ex-Celtic and Clyde centre-forward. Given the lower standard of football in Northern Ireland and the fact that the Irish league had been thrashed, 12–0, by the English league the previous week, we travelled to Belfast expecting an easy ride.

Colrain had watched us lose disastrously to Celtic in a Glasgow Cup tie at Ibrox and claimed that he had spotted weaknesses, but his comments weren't taken seriously and were viewed more as an effort to play 'mind games' rather than a genuine belief that Glentoran could possibly win. However, as we were to discover to our cost later in the season, when the underdogs of Berwick Rangers created one of the biggest Scottish Cup upsets of all time, it's dangerous to assume too much.

We were on the offensive for most of the game and led by a George McLean goal scored after a quarter of an hour, but we failed miserably to build on our early lead and paid the price when Glentoran equalised almost with the last kick of the game. I cannot say for sure that we failed to treat the opposition with sufficient respect, but the result tended to suggest that was the case. Mercifully, the return a week later, on October 5, proved somewhat less problematic. We won, 4–0, with goals from Willie Johnston, Dave Smith, Dennis Setterington and McLean, to restore a semblance of self-respect and progress through to the second round where we were drawn against the holders, Borussia Dortmund.

Borussia had beaten Liverpool at Hampden the previous May and had underlined their fitness and staying power by achieving their 2–1 victory in extra time. Borussia's achievement was further enhanced by the fact that Liverpool had accounted for Celtic in the semi-final, so we hardly needed any reminders about the size of the task facing us. Moreover, two of the Borussia team had played in the World Cup finals in England just a few months before. Left-winger, Lothar Emmerich, and centre-forward, Sigi Held, had been in the West German team beaten by England in the final. It was also noted that

Emmerich had scored more goals than the entire Liverpool team in the previous season's tournament.

However, for all that Emmerich was an outstanding player and Held posed a major threat because of his speed of movement, I felt that we were capable of beating them. I suppose my logic was based on the fact that I enjoyed playing against Germans, whose style wasn't dissimilar to our own in that they tackled hard and didn't resort to the underhand antics of some of the Latins. We had home advantage for the first leg, but although we were much the better team, we could so easily have lost the game because of a refereeing blunder by the Spanish official, Daniel Zariquiegui. It turned out to be one of the most appalling refereeing decisions I witnessed during my career.

Having taken the lead when Kai Johansen scored after twelve minutes, we were controlling the play when, in the thirty-first minute, Held set off down the left wing. He proceeded to cross the ball, but then ran over the by-line as he did so. The ball was picked up by the full-back, Peehs, and as he gathered it ready to make a return cross Held stayed off the field, knowing that he would be offside if he came back on. When Peehs crossed I tried to make a clearance, but the ball struck my leg and broke across our goal. It was at that precise moment that Held elected to re-enter the field of play. He reached the ball first and passed to Trimholdt, who scored.

In spite of our furious protests the referee allowed the goal to stand, even though Held had derived a double benefit. Having been allowed to remain off the pitch when the ball was crossed, thus avoiding being offside, the referee then allowed him to return and did not deem him to be offside because the ball had struck a defender. This was arrant nonsense. Held had deliberately stayed off the pitch and as soon as he returned the game should have been stopped. As it was, we travelled to

Dortmund for the second leg with a slender lead, after Alex Smith had scored with a second-half header.

Held and Emmerich stated publicly that Borussia would win the return and, to be honest, it was difficult to feel in any way optimistic about our prospects in the Rote Erde Stadium. Yet it was Emmerich as much as anyone who ensured that we did upset the odds in Germany, when he crocked our inside-right Bobby Watson, five minutes from half-time. Watson had been one of our key players and it was the sort of tackle designed to inflict damage. The sight of Bobby being stretchered off infuriated the rest of the players and stiffened our resolve. In effect, losing Watson inspired the team and we might even have won the match when Jim Forrest had a chance to score, but a 0–0 draw suited our purposes admirably.

The game in Dortmund was our toughest in Europe that season, but the one against Real Zaragoza in the next round ran it close. In fact, I rated them the most talented team we faced. The Spaniards had already accounted for Everton when we met them in the first leg at Ibrox on 1 March. Alex Smith, who had played against Real Zaragoza for Dunfermline the previous season, gave us the low-down.

Canario, who had been on the right wing for Real Madrid when they defeated Eintracht Frankfurt in the never-to-be-forgotten European Cup final at Hampden in 1960, was in the latter stages of his career, but still commanded respect. The principal striker was Marcellino, something of an idol in Spain, and on the left side of attack they had the graceful Lapetra, a regular in the national side. The forward line – known as the Magnificent Five – was completed by Santos and Villa.

We had one factor very much in our favour – the snow and sleet that swept across Ibrox – but even allowing for the fact that the wintry conditions suited us more than the Real players, we put on an impressive display. We played open, attractive football and Dave Smith was outstanding, scoring the opening goal after just ten minutes. Alex Willoughby scored a second midway through the first-half and each of the scorers also had goals disallowed for offside. By comparison, Real had just one clear-cut chance in the entire game and Canario fluffed it four minutes from the end.

Considering that we had travelled to Dortmund with only a single goal advantage and still disposed of the holders, we began to feel that this might be our year, but our optimism very nearly proved unfounded, especially as we had lost the services of our centre-half, Ronnie McKinnon. He had suffered a broken nose in the league game against Ayr United the previous Saturday and the manager, Scot Symon, elected to replace McKinnon with Colin Jackson, a youngster who up to that point had played only one first-team game, a friendly a few weeks before. That was the only change to our line-up. The opposition also made one change, dropping Canario to accommodate a new young star, Bustilo.

In the event, Jackson settled quickly and held Marcellino magnificently. We lost a goal midway through the first-half when Laperta scored from a free kick and Willoughby had one disallowed for offside. But just when it seemed we would manage to hold out under intense pressure, the French referee, Michel Kitabjian, awarded a penalty against us with just four minutes remaining. I was adjudged to have handled, but I hadn't and I stand by that. The referee made a mistake, because I breasted the ball down, but the official's error enabled Santos to level the tie and create the need for extra time. There was further misfortune when Dave Smith missed a penalty in the fourth minute of extra time.

This was in the days before penalty shoot-outs and when, after the additional thirty minutes, the teams were still locked at 2–2 on aggregate we had the farce of a coin being tossed to decide the outcome. What made the situation worse for me as captain was the fact that I had already called it right twice, at the start of the game and again prior to extra time. I couldn't see my luck holding for a third time, so I chose to share the responsibility of trying to decide Rangers' fate in Europe with the manager. Following a brief discussion we decided to call tails, which in the case of a French two-franc piece was the figure '2'.

All these years later I still break out in a cold sweat when I recall the moment the referee spun the coin in the air and it got carried away by the wind. The referee reached the coin first and covered it. Then he showed it to me and my opposite number, Reija. The '2' was staring up at me! At that moment I leapt in the air along with the manager and Willie Henderson did cartwheels round the pitch while our trainer, Davie Kinnear, went to the dressing room to tell those players who could not bear to watch that we were in the semi-finals.

It was a truly joyous moment, but the sight of Reija trudging away with tears streaming down his cheeks said everything that needed to be said about a ludicrous method of deciding the outcome of any football match, let alone one as important as a European tie. I have the coin as a souvenir. Davie Kinnear talked the referee into giving him the coin and the next day on the flight home he presented it to me.

By the time we faced Hibs the following Saturday the fans could talk about little else other than the drama that had unfolded at the Romareda Stadium and when the referee tossed the coin at Ibrox there was almost a hush. Could I be that lucky a fourth time? Amazingly, I was.

In the time between the ties against Dortmund and Zaragoza I suffered my greatest embarrassment as a Rangers player. The date 28 January 1967 will be forever etched in my memory – for all the wrong reasons. It was the day that we faced second division Berwick Rangers in the Scottish Cup and suffered the humiliation of a 1–0 defeat at Shielfield Park in front of 13,283, who witnessed one of the biggest upsets of all time. We had been expected to steamroller little Berwick, but fate had other plans and the anticipated 'massacre' never happened. To this day I still cringe at the memory.

So, what went wrong? It was simple, really. The Berwick lads played out of their skins and we missed a barrow load of chances. Football is often a great leveller and Berwick's part-time players illustrated the point that day. Jock Wallace, who was later to become manager of Rangers, was Berwick's player-manager and he had a fine match in goal, but for all Big Jock's enthusiasm and 'motivational' skills we should have 'murdered' the opposition. Instead, we saw chance after chance go begging until we eventually ran out of time.

Eddie Thomson was the referee and I knew him well. Eddie was also an Edinburgh man and we had appeared together at various charity events over the years. I recall asking Eddie how long there was still to play and he said thirty seconds. I asked him for a bit longer, but eventually I had to admit defeat and I told him, 'Just blow your whistle, Eddie. We'll never score.'

Sammy Reid scored the first-half goal that earned Berwick a place in the history books and often when I am doing an after-dinner speech I refer to the great players I was fortunate to play against, legends like Pele and Eusebio, and then I add, 'Sammy Reid.' The reaction is usually one of blank stares and I am forced to explain, 'He's the little b****** who scored at Berwick.' Part of my repertoire includes a line about Scot Symon telling me that if Berwick are still a goal to the good with twenty minutes to go to make any tactical changes I want. When I ask why, the manager replies, 'Because I'll already be on the train back to Glasgow.'

But it was no laughing matter. The expressions on the faces of our fans said it all. We let a lot of people down that day and they let us know in no uncertain terms. Who could blame them? Willie Johnston had suffered the misfortune to break his leg and we had to make a detour on the team bus to collect him from the local hospital. That meant driving through the town, past the Rangers' supporters coaches, and they gave us pelters.

I was beaten on other occasions, but I never felt as bad as I did that day at Berwick, but it was our strikers, Jim Forrest and George McLean, who suffered more than most. The defeat effectively spelled the end of their Rangers careers. Yet Scot Symon showed remarkable calm and class in the face of a defeat that sowed the first seeds of his eventual demise as Rangers manager. After the game, he approached the Berwick groundsman and complimented him on the excellent condition of the pitch and rewarded him accordingly with a right few quid. It was the act of a true gentleman.

The following week we played Hearts in a league match at Ibrox and the place was like a morgue. Sandy Jardine made his debut at right-half, but you could have heard a pin drop, despite the fact that we won, 5–1, in front of a crowd in excess of 33,000. Forrest and McLean were dropped for that game and a short time later Jim asked for a transfer, but it was a collective cock-up and it was a long time before the Rangers fans forgave us.

For reasons I cannot recall, we had known the semi-final draw before we played Real Zaragoza in Spain and we were paired with the team considered the weakest of the four, Slavia Sofia of Bulgaria. The other semi-final was to feature Bayern Munich against Standard Liege. The Bulgarians were an unknown quantity to us. In fact, no Scottish team had faced a side from that part of Eastern Europe and our knowledge of Bulgarian football amounted to what we had seen of their international team during the World Cup finals in England the year before.

There were all sorts of horror stories about the food being sub-standard and the hotels little better than hostels, but the grub actually turned out to be much better than we had feared and our living conditions, while spartan, were perfectly acceptable. The same could not be said of the national stadium. We had trained at Slavia's own stadium and the condition of the pitch was ideal, but then we were given the news that the game was to take place at the Levski Stadium, which had next to no grass. What little there was grew in small clumps and the centre circle and the goalmouths were completely bare – hardly ideal in terms of ball control.

To make matters worse, repairs were being carried out and right round the edge of the playing area there were iron pipes and metal spikes sticking up, which were decidedly dangerous. As Willie Henderson commented, 'There are better pitches on Glasgow Green.' However, in the days of the Iron Curtain any-thing could happen and more often than not it did. There was little point in complaining, so we accepted our lot, albeit with certain misgivings, because any protest might have been construed as poor sportsmanship.

In the event, our concerns proved unfounded. Slavia were the poorest team we met. They were tough and uncompromising and reasonably skilful, but never really gave us any problems. Davie Wilson scored the only goal of the game after thirty-one minutes to give us a lead we felt confident would prove sufficient to reach the Cup-Winners' Cup final for the second time in the club's history. Rather surprisingly, the manager chose to make changes for the return leg and Roger Hynd was introduced at centre-forward in place of Willoughby, while Willie Johnston replaced Wilson. Hynd's selection was something of a surprise and I think even he was shocked, but it made little difference to the outcome and a Willie Henderson goal in the first-half secured our place in the final.

By then we already knew that we would be facing Bayern Munich, but Glasgow had a second team in a European final, Celtic, and given the enormously rivalry that exists, I think their success possibly acted as a spur to us. It was a remarkable double and the first time that any European city had ever had a team in each of the two major European finals. The principal difference was that we were to play in Germany, the country where our opponents came from, whereas Celtic would face Inter Milan on neutral territory in Lisbon. Bayern would, in effect, be playing at home. Their fans had a short journey of a hundred or so miles to reach Nuremberg, while ours faced a long trek across Europe. Fate was not kind to us.

I think events in Nuremberg might have panned out differently for us had the Cup Winners' Cup final taken place first, but by the time we lined up against Bayern, Celtic were already European champions by dint of their 2–1 success against Inter. Celtic's success intensified the pressure on Rangers to complete a unique double. Celtic's attacking style of play was hailed as the way forward in European football, because it had exposed the Italian's reliance on defence, which had been a feature of that country's football for some years and which had proved highly successful.

I never felt at any time during that season that there was a significant gap between us and Celtic. Indeed, when we drew the final Old Firm game of the season, 2–2, I thought we had made the point, but comparing the two teams' styles of play was a different matter. Our tactics were based on a strong defence. Rather than scoring a lot of goals we were successful by preventing the opposition from scoring. Our strikers had been so unconvincing that we had always worried about conceding the first goal, but in Europe that had never happened, so we hadn't been tested.

We carried the burden of expectancy, because the critics were looking for our game to match the one in Lisbon – fast, open and attractive. However, Bayern's style was similar to our own. They were a cautious team and we got the impression that they were perhaps apprehensive about playing us. In the circumstances, it was difficult to anticipate a classic. Scot Symon had watched the Germans in a league game against Kaiserslautern and pinpointed their danger men. He also revealed that Franz Beckenbauer, who had been the midfield inspiration for West Germany in the 1966 World Cup, now operated in a sweeper role, which shocked us. We had expected that Beckenbauer would pose the greatest threat to our hopes.

We undertook several warm-up games, including one in Toronto against the Czech champions Sparta Prague, and matches against Morton and Motherwell locally, to ensure that, as the domestic season had ended, we stayed match-fit. The game against Motherwell took the form of a testimonial for Charlie Aitken and their team was supplemented by players like Dave Mackay, Ian St John and Billy Stevenson, which tested us.

The game against Sparta was designed to keep our minds on European football, but we hadn't imagined that they would turn it into a European Cup tie and they defended and tackled as roughly as if they were playing in a major final. Some of it was downright vicious and after scoring early, Sparta retreated into defence and set out to frustrate us by any means necessary. It was not the sort of preparation we had sought.

A fortnight later we were on our way to Nuremberg, where everything began to go wrong. It was decided that we would set up camp in the tiny village of Neundettelsau, twenty miles outside the city. The idea was that in such a secluded spot we would be well away from fans looking for autographs and tickets. We would also be able to sleep at night without having to worry about traffic noise and the other distractions of a big city. The thinking was sound. The reality was something else. The training facilities were terrible and on the first day, when we went for a loosening up session, we found the gates to the training ground locked. It was a good half-hour before the situation was resolved.

The coach journeys in and out of the city added to our frustration. Because of the narrow twisting roads, the trip took an hour. The hotel was also lacking in atmosphere and I am convinced that we lost our edge a little. There was no buzz or sense of anticipation. We sat around playing cards and that's a recipe for boredom. So, was it any real surprise that the dream of winning a European trophy turned into a nightmare? Probably not. It seemed to be that one mistake was compounded by another, but it would be grossly unfair to point the finger at any one individual. It was another collective cock-up.

The teams lined up as follows. Rangers: Norrie Martin; Kai Johansen and Davie Provan; Sandy Jardine, Ronnie McKinnon and Greig; Willie Henderson, Alex Smith, Roger Hynd, Dave Smith and Willie Johnston.

Bayern Munich: Maier; Nowak and Kupferschmidt; Roth, Beckenbauer and Olk; Nafziger, Ohlhauser, Muller, Koulmann and Brenniger.

Regrettably, our manager got his tactics wrong and they should have been changed during the game, but the truth is we failed to produce when it mattered most. We were also punished by the player our manager had warned us was the Bayern danger man and Franz Roth was not picked up when he burst through to score the winner in extra time. In fairness to the manager, our tactics had seemed OK. The feeling in the pre-match team talk had been that we could win the game down the flanks. That approach backfired, however, when the Bayern full-backs marked our wingers, Henderson and Johnston, so tightly that neither could move without a shadow. Everywhere Henderson and Johnston went they had a marker breathing down their necks.

When we saw what was happening, we should have had the nous to vary our approach. For example, we should have tried dropping balls behind the full-backs for the wingers to run on to, but we failed to exploit that option. Mind you, had we done so no doubt Beckenbauer would have swept up. He did his job perfectly and never once made a mistake, although in my view it was a waste of his talent for him to play that position. There were few players in the world at that time with Beckenbauer's genius for attacking from midfield, but only once did he venture forward in the entire game. It was a case of Bayern sacrificing Beckenbauer's unique skills in favour of a safety-first approach – but that approach worked.

The galling aspect was that we had created as many scoring chances as Bayern and had generally outplayed them, but Roth's goal in the nineteenth minute of extra time was the defining moment. It meant that not only had we failed to complete a European double for Glasgow, we had also failed to win a single honour. Celtic had completed a clean sweep.

I wept for the first time in my career as I walked off the pitch, beaten and utterly dejected. I couldn't help myself. The tears flowed with the realisation that we had been so close to achieving something no Rangers team had done before. My mood mirrored the sentiments of every one of my team-mates. Roger Hynd reacted by hurling his runners-up medal into the crowd. Moments later I bounced mine off every wall in the dressing room, such was my disappointment, but it was retrieved for me by Joe Craven, the second team coach, who had played a big part in my early career with Rangers. On the coach journey back to our hotel, Joe handed me the battered box containing my medal. 'I know how disappointed you are,' he said, 'but maybe you'll want to have this when you look back forty years from now.' He was correct. After all, European medals of any colour are fairly unique. That journey, following the post-match banquet, could only be desribed as funereal. The manager was so badly affected that he locked himself in his room and wasn't seen again until the following day, when we flew home.

Thinking back on it now, we should have beaten Bayern. Borussia Dortmund and Real Zaragoza were superior sides. I also remain convinced that Bayern ran scared of us. Why else would they have made such a fuss of getting their international striker, Gerd Muller, fit after he had suffered a broken arm just a month or so earlier? In the event, Bayern had to seek dispensation from the Italian referee, Concetto Lo Bello, to allow Muller to play with a special strapping on his damaged arm, but he wasn't match-fit and was carrying excess weight. Consequently, he made no impression on the game whatsoever. That proved to me that Bayern had not been confident of beating us.

But, in the final analysis, we could offer no excuses. We had been more than capable of beating Bayern, but our performance fell well short of our capabilities. It was as simple as that. Sadly, instead of receiving credit for reaching a European final, Scot Symon faced only condemnation for failure. In reality, Celtic's victory over Inter Milan had already undermined that achievement, even before a ball was kicked in Nuremberg.

By the start of the next season, several signings had been completed, leading to the arrival of goalkeeper Eric Sorensen, from Morton, winger Orjan Persson, from Dundee United and striker Alex Ferguson, from Dunfermline. The £65,000 Fergie cost in actual fact established a new Scottish transfer record. But fate was not kind to Scot Symon. In a cruel twist, we were drawn in the same League Cup section as Aberdeen, Celtic and Dundee United. The perceived wisdom was that the two Old Firm games would determine which of the four teams progressed through to the latter stages of the tournament and that proved to be the case.

Celtic got the better of us, however. We drew the first match at Ibrox, 1–1, with Andy Penman scoring a last-gasp equaliser, but lost the return, 3–1. We had led through an early Willie Henderson goal at Parkhead, when Kai Johansen missed a penalty with fourteen minutes remaining. Lo and behold, Celtic proceeded to score three times and we had to settle for the runners-up place in the qualifying section. To make matters worse, Celtic went on to lift the trophy.

Our progress in the league was steady, though. By the end of October we had played eight games, winning six and drawing two. That run included a win over our arch rivals at Ibrox and we led the championship by a single point over Dundee, with Celtic in third place. We were having trouble scoring, however, and when we drew, 0–0, with Dunfermline at Ibrox on 28 October, a section of the support turned on Scot Symon and the board – but there was no hint of the bombshell that was to come.

Just a few days later the manager joined those players who were taking part in the football quiz programme of the time, *Quiz Ball*, at the Singer Factory in Clydebank. Afterwards, he gave me a lift to Queen Street Station to catch the last train to Edinburgh. The following day Scot Symon was gone, to be replaced by Davie White. While he had been driving me to Queen Street, the directors were meeting in a Glasgow hotel to seal his fate.

I always had the utmost respect for Scot Symon. He was the man who signed me for Rangers, after all, and he was a gentleman to the end. He kept his promises to me and I felt close to him. I viewed him as a father figure and I was shocked and saddened by what happened to him. As an example of his kindness, when Janette and I married he arranged for money to be deposited in a bank in Palma, so we could enjoy our honeymoon. You were only allowed to take £50 spending money out of the country at that time, because of currency restrictions, and the manager ensured that we didn't go short. Scot Symon's departure marked the end of an era at Rangers.

CHAPTER 11
COLD SWEAT

When Derek Johnstone rose to head the winning goal in the 1970 League Cup final I was sitting in the Hampden dug-out wondering if I would ever play again. Much worse, I had been given the chilling warning that I might even lose my right leg. I was just twenty-eight years of age and at the peak of my career when a specialist at Glasgow's Victoria Infirmary, a Mr McDougall, dropped the bombshell. I don't mind admitting that I was terrified.

It was one thing having to face up to the realisation that I had possibly played my last game. It was an entirely different matter trying to come to terms with the possibility that I might lose a limb. Mercifully, my worst fears were not realised, but it was one of the most frightening periods of my life. It also made me realise that I had to make the most of what I had and enjoy every moment, because you just never know what lies round the corner.

The previous Saturday we had played Aberdeen in a league match at Ibrox. The Dons had beaten us, 2–0, and we were, frankly, rotten. It was far from the ideal preparation for a major final, especially one against our greatest rivals, Celtic, but by the following Monday morning

I had more to worry about than the result of a football match. I had woken to discover a nasty swelling in my shin. There was also a noticeable red line running the length of my leg. I suspected that my leg was poisoned, but I realised that I had to get an expert opinion as quickly as possible and telephoned the family doctor. It was the same doctor who had delivered me into the world and one look was sufficient to alert him to the fact that there was a problem. 'You won't be playing this week,' he told me, before prescribing a course of antibiotics.

I also took the precaution of contacting the club doctor, Donald Cruickshank, who advised me to travel through to Glasgow so he could carry out a further examination. His prognosis was the same as my own doctor – I could forget all about playing in the League Cup final. When I asked, 'Why not?' the doctor's answer shocked me. 'Because if you get a kick it could be the end of your career.' There wasn't a lot more that I could say. Talk about laying it on the line.

An appointment was made for me to see the specialist, but if I expected words of encouragement I received the exact opposite from Mr McDougall. His prognosis was very much worse. After carrying out a thorough examination, the specialist looked me straight in the eye and asked, 'Have you ever given any thought to what you will do with your life when your career's over, because if your leg doesn't clear up you're finished?' The second opinion was every bit as bad as the first – but I certainly wasn't prepared for what he said next. 'You could even lose your leg, you know.' One doctor had warned me that a kick could end my career. Here was a second one, an expert in his field, telling me that I faced the grim possibility of amputation – no matter what I did.

I didn't wear shin guards and I had received a nasty gash to my shin when I was caught by one of the Aberdeen player's studs. It hadn't seemed a particularly nasty injury at the time, but the specialist concluded that I had picked up an infection. The most likely explanation, he felt, was that whatever treatment had been used on the grass had entered my blood stream through the open wound and poisoned my system. Mr McDougall told me I was suffering from osteitis. Apparently it is a condition that effects the bone marrow. The more chronic form is osteomyelitis and if I had contracted that form of the infection I would have had to stop playing altogether. I later learned that once osteomyelitis sets in it is very difficult to cure and can often lead to amputation, so I was very lucky all things considered.

When Mr McDougall retired he undertook various lecture tours across Europe and part of his talk involved showing his audience an X-ray of my shin. He also explained what treatment I had been given and how I had managed to continue to play football.

Donald Cruickshank, who had only recently taken on the role of club doctor when I suffered my injury, told me recently that I was given very heavy doses of antibiotics and added, 'Thank God they worked. Otherwise you would have had a serious problem.' Donald also revealed that when he informed Willie Waddell that I wasn't fit for the final he went off his head, but apparently when the boss saw the state of my leg for himself he turned white!

I don't suppose I had much colour in my face either as I sat watching a sixteen-year-old making history at Hampden on 24 October 1970, for I genuinely feared that John Greig was about to become history. It was one of the few big games I missed during my career, but I was back playing just a fortnight later when I returned to action in a 1–1 draw at Dunfermline on 7 November. Four days later I was pulling on a Scotland jersey ready to face Denmark at Hampden. I was coming to the end of my international career and I didn't want to miss out on the chance of adding another cap to my collection, but I realised I was taking a risk playing when my leg still wasn't one hundred per cent.

Although the doctors had reluctantly given me the go-ahead to resume playing, I was forced to take precautions and they included wearing a protective dressing on my leg to cushion the blow from any kick, accidental or otherwise. To that end, Tommy Craig, our physiotherapist, moulded a piece of fibreglass to the shape of my leg and I also wore the makeshift body armour at training. It didn't matter if my team-mates saw me taping the makeshift protector to my leg, but I certainly didn't want others to know, for obvious reasons.

When I was with the international team, when were getting stripped for action and again after the game, which, incidentally, we won, 1–0, I went to great lengths to hide the fact that I was a wearing a protective dressing from the Celtic players in particular. I'm not saying that any of them would have passed on the word to their team-mates or that they would have deliberately tried to immobilise me in the next Old Firm game, but I couldn't be certain and I wasn't going to take any chances.

As it happened, the injury eventually healed and I was never troubled by it again, but I have often wondered just how close I came to making the wrong sort of headlines. Instead of the tabloids waxing lyrical about a sixteen-year-old's fairytale final they might have been announcing that the Rangers skipper was finished!

While it was Derek Johnstone who stole the headlines, the most pleasing aspect of the 1970 League Cup final for me was the fact that, as my stand-in, Ronnie McKinnon had the opportunity to collect the trophy. It was conceivable that Ronnie could have been the Rangers captain instead of me, so he deserved his moment. I was a great admirer of Ronnie, whom I regarded as an excellent player and a loyal team-mate. We met up again recently at a supporters function in Stornoway, where Ronnie now lives, after returning from South Africa, and he reminded me of the game and I'm pleased that it obviously meant so much to him being captain that day.

Although I missed the 1970 final, I was fortunate enough to feature in plenty of others. I am the proud possessor of six Scottish Cup medals and four League Cup-winners' medals. I was also involved in five championship wins as well as, of course, the European Cup-Winners' Cup triumph in 1972, so I have no grounds for complaint. Beating Moscow Dynamo in Barcelona was clearly the highlight of my career, but the 1973 Scottish Cup final ran it close for several reasons.

Rangers had not won the Scottish Cup for seven years, due largely to Celtic's dominance during that period, and the game held the added significance of being the centenary final. There was also the Tom Forsyth factor! If Tam's studs had been a fraction of an inch shorter we might not have beaten Celtic, but fate decreed that the man who hardly ever scored a goal grabbed the glory in front of a crowd of 122,714 Old Firm fans on Saturday 5 May.

Celtic went ahead after twenty-four minutes when Kenny Dalglish ran on to a pass from Dixie Deans and produced a cool finish, but we were level again ten minutes later as Alex MacDonald chipped to the far post and Derek Parlane headed past Ally Hunter. The second-half was less than one minute old when we took the lead. Quinton 'Cutty' Young and Parlane combined to make an opening for Alfie Conn and his shot found its intended target. However, such was the nip and tuck nature of the game that Celtic trailed for only a further nine minutes.

I confess to being the guilty man who presented Celtic with the chance to equalise when I dived to save a shot from George Connelly on the goal line. I had no option, because Peter McCloy was out of his goal, and it was an instinctive reaction, although in the modern age I wouldn't have finished the game. The rules nowadays state that if the last man, other than the goalkeeper, deliberately handles the ball and denies the opposition a goal he has to walk, but at that time I was spared the ignominy of seeing red in a cup final – thank goodness! It's also interesting to recall that Derek Parlane was booked for running off the pitch to celebrate his goal. The referee, John Gordon, deemed Parlane's actions to be excessive, but some things never change and more than thirty years on, some players still haven't learned.

In the event, Connelly converted the penalty I had conceded and the game was once again so finely balanced that it was impossible to call – for six minutes at least. Then Tam struck to earn his place in the history books. With exactly an hour on the clock, Tommy McLean floated over a free kick and Derek Johnstone headed against the post. The ball ran agonisingly along the goal line and for a horrible moment it appeared to have eluded Tam Forsyth, but he stuck out his leg and made contact with the ball with the sole of his boot and stabbed it into the net.

It certainly wasn't the most spectacular goal that's ever been scored at Hampden, but it was one of the most important from Rangers' point of view. Tam was a player noted for power rather than accuracy and when he found the net in training we used to applaud him, because it was such a rare occurrence. However, the look of sheer joy –and maybe also of amazement – on his face said it all, because what greater honour is there than scoring the winner in a cup final? Tam was well respected by his team-mates, but you certainly wouldn't have bet on him being the man to achieve such a distinction. I stood with tears rolling down my cheeks at time up. It was a mixture of joy, relief and satisfaction that we had at last got one over on Celtic.

It was one of the very few occasions when a Scottish Cup final has been graced by the presence of royalty and the fact that Princess Alexandra was there to present the Cup added to the sense of importance. As I made my way up the stairs to receive the trophy, though, I suddenly realised that my hands were filthy. Amid the post-match excitement, I had completely forgotten that I would be required to shake hands with Her Highness. I was just feet away when I noticed the Princess was wearing a pair of white gloves. I knew emergency action was called for, so I spat on my hands and wiped them on my shorts in an effort to remove the muck. The Princess is very popular with the Scots because of her connections with the country, and I found her to be a lovely person, but I hope she didn't spot me rubbing saliva on my hands. I can't for the life of me remember what she said when handing over the trophy, although I often joke that she commented, 'Well, you certainly made hard work of that, Greigy.'

The 1973 finalists lined up as follows. Rangers: McCloy; Jardine and Mathieson; Greig, Johnstone and MacDonald; McLean, Forsyth, Parlane, Conn and Young.

Celtic: Hunter; McGrain and Brogan; Murdoch, McNeill and Connelly; Johnstone, Deans, Dalglish, Hay and Callaghan.

I played my final competitive game for Rangers on 6 May 1978 in yet another cup final, but I didn't know at the time that it would turn out to be the last. Aberdeen were the opposition at Hampden in the Scottish Cup final and I had planned to go on playing for one more season at least, but subsequent events dictated that the clash with the Dons would in fact be my farewell appearance.

There were seven survivors from the 1973 team in a Rangers side that was: McCloy; Jardine and Greig; Forsyth, Jackson and MacDonald; McLean, Russell, Johnstone, Smith and Cooper.

Aberdeen lined up: Clark; Kennedy and Ritchie; McMaster, Garner and Miller; Sullivan, Fleming, Harper, Jarvie and Davidson.

Happily, my team-mates managed to give me a winning send-off. To be perfectly honest, though, Aberdeen were never really in the hunt and goals from Alex MacDonald in the first-half and Derek Johnstone early in the second period put Rangers' name on the trophy once again, before Steve Ritchie scored a somewhat freakish consolation goal for them near the end.

While that turned out to be my last competitive game for Rangers, I still had one more duty to fulfil that summer. Sandy Jardine and I had been invited to play in Willie Maddren's testimonial match at Middlesbrough and for the first time since my international career had ended nearly three years earlier, I brought my boots home with me. When I returned from Ayresome Park in the early hours of the following morning and threw my boots into the garage, I didn't realise that I would have no further use for them.

CHAPTER 12
DISASTER

No words can ever adequately describe the horror of the greatest single tragedy to befall Scottish football. More than thirty years on from the Ibrox Disaster I still can't fully get my head round the fact that sixty-six people died as a consequence of attending a football match. It just seems utterly absurd that such a tragedy could occur. Those old enough to recall the scale of the tragedy will not need reminding of the sequence of events that led to such an appalling loss of life on 2 January 1971, but a sizeable percentage of the current generation of Rangers fans weren't even born when the steel barriers on Stairway 13 gave way.

The game had not been a classic and remained goal-less with little more than a minute remaining, but it suddenly exploded into life when Jimmy Johnstone gave Celtic an eighty-ninth minute lead and Colin Stein equalised with a mere fifteen seconds remaining. It was initially thought that Stein's equaliser had caused fans who were leaving the ground to return, with horrific consequences as they were met by hundreds of jubilant supporters coming from the opposite direction down the stairway, but the enquiry that followed found this to be untrue. Whatever the exact cause of the catastrophe, dozens were suffocated and another 145 injured. Yet, it had been a good-natured game with only two arrests for drunkenness, even though it was an 80,000 all-ticket crowd.

In spite of the magnitude of what happened, none of the players was aware of the tragedy that had unfolded just a goal kick away from the dressing rooms. In fact, most had left the ground completely unaware of the horror. It was a typical Scottish winter's day; dull, dreich and prematurely dark. The floodlights had been switched on early and a light mist hung over the ground. I had taken two friends from Birmingham to the game and I was keen to get changed as quickly as possible so I could transport them back to my home in Edinburgh, but I had suffered a knock and required treatment from the physiotherapist. I was the last to be seen by the physio and just as I was leaving the treatment room half an hour later, someone was carried in and laid on the table in an effort to revive them. That was the first inkling I had that all was far from well.

When I returned to the dressing room to get dressed, my teammates had gone and the place was deserted, but the scene suddenly changed as all hell broke loose. Bodies began to be carried in and laid out on the floor. Thankfully, I didn't see the faces, as they were covered, but I remember asking someone what was happening and being told that there had been a terrible accident. I was also asked to get changed straightaway and leave the dressing room as quickly as possible.

I didn't need any further prompting, but I wasn't prepared for the sight that confronted me when I walked down the tunnel and saw a row of bodies laid out along the touchline. It was unreal. There was also a great deal of activity and ambulances were arriving at regular intervals to transport the injured to the Southern General Hospital nearby. The fact that the mist was thickening added to the eerie atmosphere, but I had no real idea of the enormity of what had happened. I knew some people had lost their lives and others had been injured, but I was completely unaware of exactly how many had died.

I suppose I must have left the ground around quarter to six to collect my friends and return home, but when I switched on the TV news later that evening the realisation dawned that there had been a major disaster. Remember this was in the days before new technology and instant news updates. It took time for the authorities to collate the necessary information before releasing details to the media. There was also the grim task of officially identifying those who had died.

Mobile phones hadn't been invented, but I knew that the parents of the two lads I had taken to the game would already have heard that there had been a terrible accident and would be concerned about the safety of their sons. It wasn't until we arrived back in Edinburgh, though, that they were able to telephone home to say they were OK.

Janette and I had become friendly with the pair during the World Cup finals in Mexico the previous summer. *TV Times* magazine had run a competition for readers to select a player of their choice to accompany them to the finals and I was called in as a late replacement for Mike England, the Spurs centre-half, when he had to call off. A couple from Belfast nominated me and it meant being away from home for a month, but there are certainly worse ways to spend the summer than watching the World Cup finals and we were in the company of several other players.

We were part of a group that included Terry Hennessy of Nottingham Forest, Gary Sprake, Johnny Giles and Billy Bremner of Leeds, my Rangers team-mate Colin Stein, the Wolves player, Hugh Curran, and Bobby Hope of West Bromwich Albion. I had first met Bobby Hope when the pair of us were involved in schoolboy trials and we remain friends to this day. I actually 'tapped' Bobby on behalf of Rangers, but the club refused to meet Albion's asking price. His dad,

Bill, also worked for me as a scout during my time as Rangers manager. Bremner and Giles were unaccompanied, but Bobby and his wife took a couple of friends and we struck up an instant rapport with them. It was as a result of that friendship that we had invited the two lads to spend the weekend with us, so they could take in the Old Firm game.

Looking back the whole thing was mind boggling. How could it be that sixty-six people left their homes on a Saturday morning to watch a football match and never returned? The tragedy was not just the deaths of so many, but the effect their loss had on so many others. The suffering continues to this day for many of the families who lost a loved one and I have kept in touch with some of the relatives of those who died. I think one of the reasons I have always felt close to the families of the victims is that their loss was also my loss. They had come to watch me and ten other Rangers players play football and that support cost them their lives.

In the days following the Ibrox Disaster playing football seemed an utter irrelevance. There was no way we could train or even think about playing in the immediate aftermath. Rangers were fortunate to have a manager of the strength and foresight of Willie Waddell. He immediately swung into action and organised it so there were players and other club representatives at the funeral of each of the victims.

I have no idea exactly how many funerals I attended, but it must have been dozens, and I was in a daze for much of the time. I simply couldn't comprehend fully what had happened. The manager also detailed groups of two or three players to visit each of the grief-stricken families. It was a harrowing experience, especially for the younger players like Derek Johnstone and Alfie Conn, and a very sad time for everyone associated with Rangers and football in general.

We were heroes to many of the people whose doors we were knocking on, to offer our condolences, but there's a very fine line between sharing in grief and interfering, so it was also unnerving, wondering what sort of reception we would receive at each of the homes we visited. One family took it very badly and made it clear that they didn't want anybody coming round at such a time. I could understand that reaction and sympathise with their sentiments, but most seemed grateful that we had bothered to make the effort and I am glad that we did.

The club also donated a five-figure sum of money to the Lord Provost's Appeal Fund for the relatives of the victims and the Old Firm came together when a Rangers and Celtic Select XI played Scotland. A crowd of just over 80,000 packed into Hampden Park on 27 January to see Scotland win, 2–1. Archie Gemmill and Peter Lorimer scored for Scotland and George Best, one of three guest players in the Old Firm Select – Chelsea goalkeeper Peter Bonetti and Manchester United legend Bobby Charlton were the others – netted our goal.

The sides lined up as follows. Scotland: Jim Cruickshank (Hearts); Davie Hay (Celtic) and Tommy Gemmell (Celtic); Pat Stanton (Hibs), Ronnie McKinnon (Rangers) and Bobby Moncur (Newcastle); Peter Lorimer (Leeds), Archie Gemmill (Derby), Colin Stein (Rangers), John O'Hare (Derby) and Charlie Cooke (Chelsea).

Old Firm Select: Peter Bonetti (Chelsea); Sandy Jardine (Rangers) and Greig; Bobby Murdoch (Celtic), Billy McNeill (Celtic) and Dave Smith (Rangers); Willie Henderson (Rangers), John Hughes (Celtic), Bobby Charlton (Manchester United), Willie Johnston (Rangers) and George Best (Manchester United).

Although it had been Rangers fans that had died, there was a sense of shared suffering among Celtic supporters and I doubt that there has ever been a time when the two groups of fans were closer. The clubs were united in grief and I can't say that I was surprised, for despite the intense rivalry that will always exist, I believe it is wrong for people to claim that all Rangers and Celtic fans hate one another. Of course, there will always be a small minority on both sides of the divide whose fanaticism outweighs common sense and decency, but in the majority of cases there is mutual respect.

Some people can't understand why I have a close relationship with Billy McNeill, for example, or why I regularly phone wee Jimmy Johnstone. I am friends of both and it's tragic that Jinky has suffered the misfortune to be struck down by motor neurone disease. We go back a long way, to the days when we played in the same Scotland team and formed relationships which have endured for more than forty years. Sure, we wanted to beat each other in Old Firm matches more than we wanted to win any other game and never asked or gave any quarter, but there was never any hatred. We respected each other and still do.

History records that Celtic were crowned champions that season, with Rangers finishing in fourth place behind Aberdeen and St Johnstone. Celtic also beat us in a Scottish Cup final replay after a late goal from Derek Johnstone, providing another fairytale occasion for him against Celtic, had cancelled out Bobby Lennox's strike in the first game. Derek had replaced Andy Penman with twenty minutes remaining before heading the vital equaliser to give us a second bite at the cherry. Derek retained his place for the replay four days later, but was unable to replicate his magic a third time. Celtic hit us with two goals in the space of two minutes in the first-half when Lou Macari and Harry Hood – from the penalty spot – struck and all we had to show for our efforts was a Jim Craig own goal.

Europe turned out to be a one-stop affair. We were drawn against Bayern Munich in the first round of the old Fairs Cities Cup and lost, 2–1 on aggregate, after Franz Beckenbauer scored in the first leg in Germany and we drew the return. But I do recall hitting the crossbar with a header in the first match and Sepp Maier pulling off a succession of fine saves to deny us. However, the remainder of the season was largely overshadowed by the devastating disaster and the club was affected for a very long time afterwards. To this day, the spectre of the Ibrox Disaster hangs over Rangers and will continue to do so for generations to come, because of the enormity of what happened.

Our first game after the tragedy was against Dundee United a fortnight later, on 16 January. The atmosphere was unreal and I don't think the crowd of nearly 28,000 really had much appetite for football. The players, too, found it difficult to focus and the game ended, 1–1. I had put Rangers in front after thirteen minutes and Alex Reid had equalised in the latter stages of the second-half, but the result seemed so unimportant, all things considered.

It is regrettable that, in most walks of life, a tragedy has to occur before steps are taken to improve safety and that was true of the Ibrox Disaster and ground safety. Thankfully, once an appropriate period of mourning had passed, Willie Waddell made it his number one priority to change Ibrox beyond all recognition to try to ensure there could never be a repeat of the events of 2 January 1971. It was a big and bold decision on his part. The ground had a capacity of 80,000 and a record crowd of 118,000 had once watched an Old Firm game. So by cutting the capacity when he kick-started the operation to turn Ibrox into an all-seater stadium, Willie Waddell was effectively reducing Rangers' potential earning power. However, he quite correctly put the safety of Rangers fans before any financial considerations. The new Ibrox is Willie Waddell's legacy and testimony to the changes that took place in the wake of the disaster.

I recall Lord Justice Taylor visiting Ibrox after the Hillsborough Disaster some years later and basing much of his report on the major improvements that had taken place at Ibrox in terms of ground safety. I derived a lot of satisfaction, on behalf of the club, that Rangers was being used as a blueprint to improve safety standards for fans in England

and elsewhere. The Ibrox Disaster was too high a cost to pay for improvements in safety, but if any good did emerge from that tragedy it was that football was forced to react to what was effectively a chilling wake-up call. You should never say never, because that's tempting fate, but I think it's fair to say that the major changes that have been made in football stadia over the past thirty years have enhanced the safety of the fans, although Heysel and Hillsborough were distressing reminders of the dangers of complacency.

THE GLORY ROAD

R angers' European Cup-Winners' Cup team of 1972 (a competition we qualified for after coming second to Celtic in the 1971 Scottish Cup) has never been given the credit that it deserved, in my opinion. The enormity of our achievement has been played down in some quarters because the Cup-Winners' Cup was always regarded as being of secondary importance to the European Cup. That was true in a sense, but it takes a hell of a lot to win any European trophy and the calibre of the teams we faced on the road to Barcelona would not have disgraced any league in the world.

French football was perhaps not of the standard it later reached, but Rennes were a first-class side nevertheless. Portuguese football was recognised as being of a very high standard, however, and Sporting Lisbon, whom we beat in the second round, boasted several international players. Don't forget, either, that Portugal had lost narrowly to England in the 1966 World Cup semi-final.

The third of the teams we beat, Torino, were one of the top sides in Serie A, while Bayern Munich, our semi-final opponents, went on to supply more than half the West German team that won the World Cup just two years later, beating Holland, Johann Cruyff et al., in the final. I'm referring to Sepp Maier, Franz Beckenbauer, Paul Breitner, Uli Hoeness, Gerd Muller and Hans Schwarzenbeck. Need I say more? And if anyone still needs to be convinced about the size of our achievement in drawing in Munich and winning, 2–0, at Ibrox, stop for a moment and consider what I have just said: Maier, Beckenbauer, Breitner, Hoeness, Muller and Schwarzenbeck! Not one, but six World Cup winners. Now, try and tell me that we didn't deserve the highest praise.

Rennes, I have to admit, were something of an unknown quantity to us. Remember, there was nothing like the same level of media coverage of European football thirty-three years ago, but we hadn't heard or read anything that gave us reason to fear the opposition. We were also fortunate to have a manager in Willie Waddell who left no stone unturned. He was meticulous in his preparation. By the time we lined up against Rennes in France, on 15 September 1971, we had a pretty good idea of their strengths and weaknesses.

The boss had been to see Rennes in action and he knew their style of play and which players posed the biggest threat to our hopes of progressing through to the next round. A significant part of our game plan was to prevent the opposition from scoring in the away leg. If we could succeed in doing that, we reckoned we had a very good chance of finishing off the job in the return. It was a case of trying to remain completely focused and staying watertight at the back.

Even at home we adopted a similar philosophy, although I want to stress that we didn't put the emphasis on defence at Ibrox. Obviously, we needed to try to score and we had players capable of troubling any defence. Willie 'Bud' Johnston had pace and could finish to devastating effect. Colin Stein was a centre-forward with an established reputation and a proven track record in front of goal and Alex MacDonald regularly popped up from midfield to grab important goals. It was Bud, in fact, who gave us the lead in Rennes. They equalised a short time later, but we held out for the remaining ten minutes or so and were thoroughly satisfied with a 1–1 result.

We were confident of being able to beat any team at Ibrox, because of the intimidating atmosphere and, with a crowd of 40,000 roaring us on, Rennes were duly dispatched. Alex MacDonald's first-half goal was all that separated the sides in terms of the result, but a 2–1 aggregate scoreline flattered the opposition to an extent.

As I said, the second round draw paired us with Sporting Lisbon and, having played against the likes of Eusebio previously, I was well aware that we faced a significant step up in quality. Thankfully, there was no Eusebio to worry about, but even though Sporting didn't possess an individual of the Black Panther's status, they were an excellent side and the manager warned us that it was imperative that we established a first leg lead, given that the match was at Ibrox.

I had injured my chin in a training accident on the day of the game and played with nine stitches and a handful of painkillers. Jock Wallace had taken the squad to the Marine & Curling Hall at Largs and on the morning of the game disaster struck while we were having a kickabout on the lawn in front of the hotel. I ran for the ball and failed to spot a bench in my path. Next thing, I went crashing into the bench chin first and knocked myself out in the process. When I came to, Colin Stein was standing over me. 'Greigy, you've got two mouths,' Stein casually informed me. He was referring to the fact that a huge gash had opened up across the length of my chin and I was pouring blood.

I was immediately bundled into a car and whisked off to see a local doctor, who did a quick repair job before handing me a bottle of painkillers with the instruction that I was to go straight to bed because I was in shock. After sleeping for three or four hours I woke up at around 4.30 p.m. and declared my myself fit for action, despite having a huge plaster across my chin.

I played at right-back that night and couldn't believe it when we found ourselves three goals in front after just twenty-eight minutes. A double from Stein and another from Willie Henderson seemed to suggest that the manager had over-estimated the quality of the opposition. But it all started to go terribly wrong in the second-half. On reflection, maybe it had something to do with the effects of the painkillers wearing off. Whatever the reason for our late collapse, one minute we were gliding along in cruise control, the next we were in grave danger of tossing away a substantial lead and a place in the last eight. Goals from Chic and Gomes in the final twenty minutes completely transformed the picture. We had produced some sparkling football for seventy minutes, only to see so much of our good work undone as a consequence of slack defending. Sporting's two late goals meant that the return in the Stadium of Light a fortnight later, on 3 November, was much tougher than it had needed to be.

I appeared for the press conference after the game with a two-day growth on my face and the journalists were intrigued as to why I hadn't shaved, given that Willie Waddell insisted on all the players having a clean-cut appearance. He had, in fact, banned moustaches, beards and long hair. I pointed to the plaster on my chin and explained what had happened that morning. Then I made the mistake of adding that perhaps my unshaven look was a good omen and declared that I wouldn't shave again until we had been knocked out of Europe.

The press lads jumped on my statement and that explains why photographs of me with the Cup-Winners' Cup show a bearded John Greig. Initially, I grew a beard to protect the wound, as I had been warned that if I nicked myself shaving it would re-open. The manager was quite happy for me to be sporting a beard in the circumstances, but I hated it. I reckon it made me look like Rasputin and by the time a couple of months had passed I was regretting my promise not to shave for the duration of our European run. I have the scar to this day, but it was worth the pain. Some people used to say that I would have run through a brick wall for Rangers, so a garden bench was easy!

Predictably, the second leg, played in front of 60,000, was full of drama. It was also a game that alternated between heartache and sheer joy in the most remarkable circumstances possible. Sporting took the lead after twenty-six minutes to level the aggregate score, only for Stein to equalise sixty seconds later and put us back in front. But Sporting regained the initiative before half-time. Stein again equalised, however, within a minute of the restart, and the tie was balanced on a knife edge. We were just seven minutes away from the quarter-finals when Sporting's Gomes, who had scored their second goal at Ibrox, struck again to make it 3–2 and 5–5 on aggregate. That meant extra time.

The situation again swung back in our favour when Henderson scored ten minutes into the additional thirty, but the amazing sequence of events continued. Perez equalised the over-all score four minuets later. That made it 6–6 and we imagined that we would go through, by dint of having scored more away goals.

The referee's reading of the situation was somewhat different, however. He ruled that a penalty shoot-out would decide which team went through. As captain, I had been elected to take the last of our five kicks, but I was never called on to face my moment of truth. We missed every one of our penalties, while Sporting converted theirs, and we trooped off believing that the European adventure was over for another season. Worse still, Ronnie McKinnon had been the victim of a horror tackle and suffered a double fracture of his right leg. When we returned to our dressing room, Willie Waddell's efforts to console the players were a waste of time.

The drama was far from over, though. Within minutes, journalist John Fairgrieve of the *Scottish Daily Mail*, a close friend of the manager from their days together as members of the Scottish press corps, came bursting in waving a UEFA rule book. John, who sadly passed away some years ago, insisted that, according to his interpretation of the rules, the referee had got it wrong. John's view was that away goals did count double in extra time. The manager reached into his briefcase and produced his own copy of the rules and, after further consultation, agreed with his former sports writing colleague's reading of the situation. The manager immediately left to seek out the official UEFA observer and after a short delay returned to inform us that we had won the tie. You couldn't have made it up, but I have often wondered how the bulk of the 60,000 spectators, mostly Sporting fans, felt when they heard the news, having left the stadium convinced that their team was through to the last eight.

By now I was starting to wonder if the luck needed to win any trophy was perhaps on our side. I also held the view that the more games a team played in Europe, the stronger they became, once they were in the swing of things. But Torino were one of the giants of Italian football and we travelled to the Communale Stadium, which our rivals shared with city neighbours, Juventus, knowing that we would once again have to produce an outstanding performance on foreign soil to give ourselves a realistic chance in the return leg.

We had beaten Kilmarnock, 2-1, at Rugby Park the previous Saturday, but the manager had expressed dissatisfaction at the poor quality of some of our defending, especially at set pieces. So on our arrival in Turin he took us to a local public park and made us practise defending corners and free kicks for more than an hour. It was the manager's birthday and we had a whip-round to buy him a cigarette lighter. He was a heavy smoker and when I made the presentation I recall he was embarrassed after the way he had made us work on our game in public.

The boss also produced his customary in-depth dossier on the opposition. I had assisted him this time by obtaining copies of Italian newspapers from a hotelier in Edinburgh with whom I was friendly and who translated them for me. He was a Torino fan and the newspapers concerned contained detailed reports on the opposition. I had also asked my Italian friend to teach me a few choice phrases, after explaining to him that I wanted to wind up the Torino players with an insult or two!

During the pre-match team talk the boss held up a photograph of one of the Torino players and said to me, 'John, this is their number one player, Claudio Sala. He is just nineteen and he is the new Italian wonder boy. I want you to put him out of the game.' Being a bit of a Jack the Lad, I asked, 'Just for this one game, boss, or for good?' 'I'm serious, John,' he rapped and I replied, 'So am I, boss, so am I.'

There wasn't a breath of wind in the stadium prior to kickoff and I surprised the referee by electing to take the kickoff after winning the toss of the coin. But there was method in my thinking. Normally, if we kicked off, Colin Stein would pass the ball to Alex MacDonald and he played it back to Dave Smith in turn. But this time I told MacDonald to pass to me when he got the ball from Stein. 'Doddy' asked if we were adopting a new game plan, but I told him to trust me, because I had my tactics worked out.

When I received the ball I deliberately knocked it a yard in front of me, knowing that Sala's inexperience would almost certainly result in him making an immediate challenge. I was correct, but when Sala committed himself to the challenge I hit him with all my force and knocked him six feet in the air. I immediately bent over Sala with my back to the referee, making out as if I was apologising for the tackle, but instead I grabbed the startled youngster by the throat and said, 'Figlio di Puttana', which translated means, 'Son of a whore!' I also drew my forefinger across my throat and growled, 'Glasgow.' I had conceded a free kick after just five seconds, but it was worth it. I had delivered a very clear warning. Sala got the message and was so ineffectual against me that he didn't even play in the return. I suspect that Sala said to himself, 'If he does that to me here, what's he going to be like in Glasgow?'

I realise that some people might question my action and accuse me of being unsporting, but by then I had had plenty of experience of how a lot of foreigners played the game. They thought nothing of spitting on opponents or delivering a sneaky punch when the referee's back was turned, so I was prepared to take them on at their own game in other ways. The experience of Seville all those years earlier, when Canario head-butted me and kicked off a pitch battle, was still fresh in my mind. I had learned to look after myself in a battle and I felt it important to get my retaliation in first, especially playing abroad.

I didn't set out with the express intent of flaunting the rules, but I was always ready to stand up and be counted. There were certain tackles you went into and others it was best to avoid. My first priority was to win the challenges against my direct opponent and once I had done that I looked to assist the team as best I could. My philosophy was simple: to win the war you have to first win the battle. Whether or not people agree with the way I approached my task, Rangers got off to a flying start against Torino when Willie Johnston scored after just twelve minutes. Toschi equalised for Torino in the second-half, after we had frustrated them, and 1–1 was a bloody good result.

However, we had to bear in mind that all Torino required in the second leg was a single goal and we adapted our tactics to counteract their attacking flair. By that I don't mean we simply sat back and soaked up pressure. We were, in fact, pretty much the aggressors and our persistence paid off immediately after the restart when Alex MacDonald finished off a superb move featuring Tommy McLean and Willie Johnston.

Our victory over Torino paired us with old foes, Bayern Munich, for the third time in European competition. In addition to their 1967 Cup-Winners' Cup final win over us, Bayern had also knocked us out of the Fairs Cup the previous season, so there was the added incentive of revenge.

We were drawn to play away from home first and the first leg took place at Bayern's original stadium. Following the 1972 Olympic Games in Munich, the club moved to the brand new Olympic Stadium and I remember Bayern officials telling me years later that they had regretted doing so, because they couldn't recreate the same intense atmosphere that had existed when they'd played at their previous ground.

Our game plan was the same as it had been in the earlier rounds. The intention was to keep the score as tight as possible in the away leg. If we managed to score that would be a bonus. We believed that the key to success was not to concede, but how we managed to survive the opening twenty minutes I don't know. Bayern threw everything at us in one of the most sustained onslaughts I have ever experienced. With the exception of a Paul Breitner goal, we somehow survived until half-time in the knowledge that the tie might already have been over.

As we walked off the pitch at the interval, I recall turning to Sandy Jardine and making the point that every one of the Bayern outfield players had produced a shot on goal. The way the game had gone it was amazing that we hadn't been slaughtered, but we were a resilient bunch and we stuck to our task. We hustled and harried the opposition and Colin Jackson, at centre-half in place of the injured Ronnie McKinnon, did a superb marking job on Gerd Muller. The defence in general was outstanding.

You also need the breaks to go for you in Europe and we enjoyed a stroke of good fortune four minutes into the second half when Colin Stein's shot across the face of the Bayern goal was headed into his own net by Zobel, who was attempting to make a clearance. Another 1–1 result represented a huge achievement and, with the backing of an anticipated 80,000 crowd at Ibrox, I was confident that we could go one better – but fate intervened to deprive me of the chance to be part of a famous victory.

Our Scottish Cup semi-final with Hibs was sandwiched between the games against Bayern and I had the misfortune to be injured in a 1–1 draw at Hampden. That put me out of the return and the replay, which, incidentally, Hibs won, 2–0, five days after we had clinched our place in the Cup-Winners' Cup final. The defeat by Hibs was a sore one, because it effectively meant the end of our bid to win a domestic honour. We had finished runners-up to Celtic in our League Cup qualifying section and our league form had been disappointing. We had begun the season badly and finished poorly, winning just two of our last seven matches. Celtic ran away with the title by a margin of ten points over Aberdeen and we found ourselves back in third spot, a further six points adrift of the runners-up.

Possibly the players' minds had been focused on Europe, but whatever the reasons for our failure to mount a serious title challenge, eleven defeats in the league represented the club's worst tally of losses in the post-war period. It was also very frustrating to miss a second big game nineteen months after being forced out of the League Cup final win over Celtic with a leg injury, but the rest of the lads did magnificently in the absence of yours truly.

My place in the team for the second leg against Bayern on 19 April was taken by Derek Parlane, one of the emerging youngsters Willie Waddell had been grooming for stardom. We couldn't have wished for a better start. Bayern were rocked by the loss of a goal after just one minute when Sandy Jardine scored with a left foot shot that Sepp Maier had assumed was going wide. It was most unusual for Sandy to score with his left peg and we kidded him on afterwards that he had actually intended to cross the ball. The manner of the opening goal resulted in Franz Beckenbauer and Maier having a stand up row in the penalty box. Beckenbauer was clearly furious that his goalkeeper had misread the shot and gave Maier 'pelters'. When, to cap a glorious European debut, Parlane scored a second just twenty-three minutes into the game, Bayern became demoralised. Rangers, meanwhile, oozed confidence and self-belief and the team was able to play within itself to reach a third European final in the course of twelve seasons.

Moscow Dynamo, who had beaten Dynamo Berlin in a penalty shoot-out in the other semi-final, were something of an unknown quantity to us, but we knew that the Russians were superb athletes and very good technically. However, while we had respect for their achievement in reaching the final, we also realised that the best time to play a team from Eastern Europe was following their winter shut-down, when they might be suffering from a lack of sustained match practice. I considered that probably the greatest danger to our hopes of at last being crowned European champions was complacency. We needed to guard against the thought that because we had beaten the favourites, Bayern, the Cup was already ours for the taking.

Mind you, when I reflected on the fact that we had enjoyed a stroke of good fortune in Portugal after appearing to have lost the tie against Sporting Lisbon, and then survived a fierce first-half onslaught in Munich before grabbing a vital away goal through another player's misfortune, I began to think that perhaps we were fated to win the European Cup-Winners' Cup after all.

BARCELONA

I should never have played in the 1972 European Cup-Winners' Cup final against Moscow Dynamo. It was an act of sheer folly. On the morning of the game I could hardly walk, let alone run, as I would have to do for ninety minutes in the Nou Camp that evening. But I pose the question: how could I not have played in the biggest game in Rangers' 132-year history? I make no apology for the fact that I took a massive gamble. Of course, it could so easily have backfired on the team, but even if I had held my hands up and admitted that I was unfit to take part in any game of football, Willie Waddell would have told me to shut up and get on with it. Mind you, at the time neither of us knew I had a broken foot. In fact, it was weeks later before the full extent of my injury became clear – and I thank God for the delay. Otherwise, I might have missed the greatest occasion of my career.

As I've said, my problems began in the Scottish Cup semi-final with Hibs the month before which put me out of the second leg of the Bayern game. John Blackley, a Scotland team-mate no less, had caught me on the instep of my right foot on the turn and I wanted to get my own back, so instead of doing the sensible thing and coming off, I played on for another half-hour, before being replaced by Jim Denny.

Initially, I put strapping round my boot to give my foot additional support, but I hadn't a clue about the damage I was doing to myself.

Rangers didn't bother sending me for an X-ray before or after the Bayern game, perhaps because the manager didn't want to know how bad the injury was. I think he reckoned that if they put my foot in plaster that would effectively rule me out of the final, but Jock Wallace, our coach, felt that a cure might be found in the icy-cold waters of the Firth of Clyde. Even in April the Clyde is no place for the faint-hearted and his suggestion that I bathe my foot in the sea in the belief that the salt water would be highly beneficial didn't meet with my approval. The squad had gone to the Marine Hotel at Troon on the Monday prior to the second leg. It was obvious that I wouldn't be taking part in the game, but how exactly a dip in the sea was meant to help a stress fracture, I don't know. I would probably have ended up with pneumonia had I followed Jock's advice.

There was a twenty-three-day gap between our final league game against Ayr United on 1 May and the final itself and the manager was fully aware that he would need to arrange a series of warm-up games to ensure that the players stayed match-fit. Meantime, I had been consulting a physiotherapist in Edinburgh privately. His view was that I should have had my foot X-rayed at the time I sustained the injury, because it was too painful simply to be swelling and bruising. The physiotherapist told me that I had two choices. I could either continue to train and further aggravate the injury, in which case I would have no chance of being fit to face Moscow Dynamo, or I could cease training and maybe manage to last out the game.

I couldn't just go to the manager and tell him that I was seeing someone privately, because I was going behind the backs of the club's medical staff, in particular our physio, Tom Craig, so I kept my mouth shut and told the boss that it was simply impossible for me to train.

Willie Waddell agreed to my request to be excused training, but I began to put on a bit of weight as a result of my inactivity and he insisted that I play for at least fifteen minutes in one of the warm-up games, at Inverness. Afterwards my foot throbbed, but by the time we flew to Barcelona on the Sunday prior to the final I was even more determined that I was going to play.

I think the reason for us travelling a day earlier than usual for a European match was the fact that the teams had to take turns visiting the Nou Camp Stadium to familiarise themselves with the playing surface and the surroundings. We stayed at the Don Jaime Hotel at Castelldefels, twelve miles outside the city, but there was very little to occupy our time. It wasn't five-star luxury, but the hotel, which is situated on a hillside, was very comfortable and had old world charm. The beach was also some distance from the hotel and that involved a painful walk for yours truly. I have since revisited the hotel and it has been modernised since 1972, with the addition of a leisure complex, but I think most of us found our surroundings quite boring.

On the Monday we trained on a public park and I restricted myself to some light jogging, but by the Tuesday morning it was make-your-mind-up time. The manager told me that he couldn't wait any longer for a decision. The press, who were fully aware of my situation, were at him to name his team and he looked me straight in the face and asked, 'Are you playing?' I gave him the answer he had expected. 'Fine,' said the boss, 'but you'll have to take part in the full training session this afternoon, otherwise the press guys will smell a rat.' So I joined in on a bone hard pitch and soon had plenty of cause to regret putting on a 'show'.

When I got out of bed the following morning, my foot was badly swollen and the pain was excruciating. Every step I took to the shower was agony and when I re-appeared wrapped in a towel I confessed to my room-mate, Davie Smith, that there was no way I could possibly play. If I expected sympathy for my plight, I didn't receive any. 'But you'll have to play,' said Davie. His reasoning was simple; Ronnie McKinnon was still recovering from his leg break and Colin Jackson had been ruled out because of a badly sprained ankle. The squad was down to the bare bones. There was nothing else for it, but would I live to regret my action? There was only one way to find out.

I had never been the nervous type before a game. Apart from a few butterflies prior to my Rangers debut against Airdrie in 1961, I had generally remained calm, but as we made our way from the squad's hotel to the Nou Camp I began to feel emotional and by the time we entered the city I had a lump in my throat. When we looked out the coach windows all we could see were hundreds of Rangers fans making their way to the stadium. The last two or three miles was a sea of blue and white. There wasn't a single Dynamo fan in sight. The Iron Curtain was still firmly in place and travel restrictions meant that next to no Russians were at the game.

It felt like we were en route to Ibrox and I remember thinking to myself that there was no way we could fail these fans this time. We had lost to Bayern Munich in 1967, just a week after Celtic had won the European Cup, and the ramifications for the manager, Scot Symon, had been far reaching. The fans, too, had suffered bitter disappointment. I was also only too well aware that there might not be another chance for me or the other players to win a European medal, for such opportunities are invariably few and far between.

Regrettably, the scenes that followed our triumph in Barcelona detracted from our success to an extent, but the local police should have been much more aware of the situation before the game even started. When we appeared on the pitch an hour or so before kickoff for our customary pre-match walkabout, some fans ran on to greet the players, but there was no malice aforethought. They were in high spirits and simply wanted to express their emotions, but that should have acted as a warning to the police that they needed to employ tighter controls to avoid any repeat.

With tight strapping round my damaged foot and real hope in my heart, I lined up with the other Rangers players as follows: Peter McCloy; Sandy Jardine and Willie Mathieson; Greig, Derek Johnstone and Dave Smith; Tommy McLean, Alfie Conn, Colin Stein, Alex MacDonald and Willie Johnston.

Moscow Dynamo were as follows: Pilgui; Basalev and Dolmatov; Zykov, Dobbonosov and Zhukov; Baidatchini, Jakubik, Sabo, Makovikov and Evryuzhikbin.

Within fifteen seconds of the kickoff I was given the answer I wanted concerning my foot. I clattered into their captain, Sabo, who was an exceptionally good player, and emerged unscathed. I ended up having a running battle with Sabo, but there were no hard feelings. We met up again years later in Kiev and he wanted me to put together a team of ex-Rangers players to play Moscow Dynamo's Old Crocks in Russia, but the plan never materialised.

I have often wondered what it would have been like to have had the opportunity to play against Sabo with two good feet, because I was very limited that night in Barcelona. I think the only thing that kept me going was the constant adrenalin rush. Believe me, the fans weren't the only ones praying for the full-time whistle. I was also desperate for time up, because by then, after more than a month without proper training, I was completely knackered.

Long before we experienced the joy of victory, though, there was a football match to be won and lost and Moscow Dynamo, as we had anticipated, were a fit and technically gifted side, but we won the game in the first fifty minutes. Davie Smith orchestrated much of our build-up play from deep in defence and was instrumental in the creation of our first two goals. It was from Davie's precise pass from the middle of our half that Colin Stein was able to run on to the ball and score the opener after twenty-four minutes. For the second, five minutes from the interval, Davie ventured further downfield, before chipping the ball for Willie Johnston to produce a head flick.

Bud also scored our third goal four minutes into the second half, after running onto a long clearance from Peter McCloy. I remember turning to Bud when we were 3–0 up and saying, 'Surely to God we can't lose this time,' but a wee while later I was wishing I had kept my big mouth shut. Just when it appeared that we had the game won, the Russians made a tactical substitution, replacing Jakubik with Eschtrekov. It transformed their play and Eschtrekov scored a goal almost straightaway, sparking a Dynamo revival.

It was a long last ten minutes and by the time Makovikov scored Dynamo's second three minutes from the end I was screaming at the Spanish referee, Ortiz de Mendibil, to blow his whistle. Earlier, the referee had kept running past me saying, 'No problemo, capitano. Three-zero, three-zero!' Now I was telling him, 'For Christ's sake, blow your whistle.'

When the fans kept coming on to the pitch while the match was still in progress perhaps the referee should have signalled time up rather than risk the situation deteriorating. But he was in a difficult position and when he did eventually blow his whistle, the Rangers supporters appeared in their thousands.

There is a photograph of me grimacing as I am grabbed from behind by a fan, but the pained expression on my face had nothing to do with being given a bear hug. I was in agony because another fan had leapt in the air and come down on my sore foot. In actual fact, I suffered a second stress fracture, this time on the opposite side of my foot, because of the force with which he landed.

Meanwhile, it was mayhem all around us, with spectators swarming all over the pitch and the Spanish police wading into them with batons in an effort to restore order. Not surprisingly, the players were encouraged to return to the dressings rooms as quickly as possible. This involved us going through a maze of corridors and when we eventually arrived at our dressing room, Willie Waddell and Jock Wallace did their best to try to calm the players down. My team-mates were in a state of euphoria. Personally, I felt buggered and sat with my head in my hands as the emotion washed over me!

The next thing I knew, Willie Waddell and I were being led back along a corridor by a Barcelona club official to a long narrow room with a table at one end and several UEFA officials surrounding the Cup. I was still dressed in my strip and boots and the situation felt a bit unreal. One of the officials said something to the effect of, 'Glasgow Rangers, winners of the European Cup-Winners' Cup 1972', handed over the trophy and then more or less added, 'Right, you can go now.' The manager and I didn't realise at the time quite how bad the situation was, with supporters and police involved in a full-scale pitch battle, but clearly the UEFA delegates were keen to observe what was taking place and wanted us out of their hair as quickly as possible.

By the time we had returned to the dressing room with the Cup, most of the players were dressed. It was their first sight of the trophy and, like Celtic five years before, we were denied the honour as a team of going up to collect it. There was no lap of honour in Lisbon and there was none in Barcelona and that was a great pity. It seemed an injustice, irrespective of whose fault it was, that fans swarmed on to the pitch on both occasions.

As I lay in the bath with the trophy for company, I considered the events of the past few hours and the realisation hit me. I don't mind admitting that I shed a tear at that point. It was the realisation of a dream and the proudest moment of my career. Any professional sportsman who achieves something of note will tell you that he or she derives a great deal of satisfaction when it's over and you have time to reflect on the size of that achievement. It certainly isn't easy to win a European trophy at that level, but nothing that is worthwhile is ever easy.

We returned with our wives and girlfriends, who had been staying at Sitges, to the team's hotel and partied on into the wee small hours. After about the third bottle of champagne I sought out Willie Waddell and in a private moment I admitted, 'I wasn't fit to play, boss.' He looked at me and smiled. 'I know,' he said, 'but I wanted you to play anyway and the rest of the players felt the same way.' I suppose I had done my share in the earlier rounds, but there is little doubt that the others helped me through these ninety minutes in Barcelona. They all mucked in, as they always did.

There were no stars in the 1972 team. We worked hard for each other and there was a good balance about the side. We were strong and resolute in defence and skilful and energetic in midfield. We also had wingers with pace and the ability to cross the ball accurately, and strikers who could finish to great effect. In other words, that Rangers team had no glaring weaknesses and plenty of strengths.

We were a team in every sense of the word and after just a couple of hours' sleep we were still as high as kites. So much so that when I came down for breakfast I found the rest of the players in the hotel's swimming pool and promptly dived in. Nothing unusual in that, I hear you say. True, but of course I don't swim and it's the only time in my life that I'd been in a swimming pool since I very nearly met my maker at Dalguise when I was a kid. I guess my mind must have been elsewhere at that moment!

When we arrived at the airport a few hours later the team coach was directed straight on to the tarmac to avoid the pitfalls of having to go through customs with thousands of fans milling about the airport waiting for their flights back to Glasgow. As soon as we stepped off the coach we were confronted by the sight of dozens of planes lined up ready for take off. Most of these charter aircraft were already full and awaiting clearance when I began walking towards our plane with the Cup in my hands. Next thing I knew the other planes were emptying and hundreds of fans began swarming across the tarmac. Within seconds I was bundled on to the plane to avoid a second invasion!

There is no shortage of stories of the exploits of some of those who travelled to Barcelona. My personal favourite concerns the fellow who was awakened by a policeman at Manchester Airport after being discovered stretched across several seats in the arrivals lounge. 'You can't sleep here,' advised the policeman. 'Where am I,' asked the Rangers supporter?' 'Manchester Airport,' came the reply. 'What am I doing here,' asked the by now bemused fan. 'Why?' enquired the police-man. 'Did you get on the wrong plane?' 'No, I drove to Barcelona!' I have no idea whether he bothered to return to Spain to collect his car, but that story sums up the fanaticism of some Rangers fans.

Rangers winning the Cup-Winners' Cup remains a vivid memory for most who were there and an example of that was an experience I had in a local restaurant some years ago. I had gone there with a friend and my dinner companion couldn't help noticing that a couple at an adjoining table kept looking across at me. He pointed this out to me and I told him not to take any notice, as they would eventually approach me. Sure enough, after paying the bill this guy approached me and said, 'You don't recognise me, do you, Mr Greig?' 'No,' I said, 'I don't. You'll need to give me a clue.'

'Well, I was waiting for you to recognise me, because I was on the pitch in Barcelona.' 'So were thousands of others,' I pointed out. 'Aye,' he said, 'but I was wearing a kilt.' 'How old were you at the time?' I asked. 'Seven,' he said. 'And what age are you now?' 'Twenty-four. Is that why you don't recognise me?' 'No,' I replied. 'It's because you're no wearing your kilt!'

The journey home from Barcelona was uneventful as far as the Rangers party was concerned and I think the only person who took a drink from the Cup was the pilot. The rest of us had had more than our fill of champagne. When we landed at Prestwick I made my way through the green zone at customs, but I had only gone a few paces when a voice asked, 'Where do you think you're going?' I told my inquisitor that I had nothing to declare, because I hadn't even seen a shop for the past five days let alone bought anything from one. 'What's that in your hands then?' asked the customs official. 'What does it look like,' I replied and kept walking. It appears that he was a Celtic fan trying to be smart!

As we made our way to Ibrox, cheering fans began lining the surrounding streets about a mile or so from the ground. There was at least another 20,000 inside the stadium as we made our way round the track on the back of a specially converted lorry. I was still sporting my beard and the supporters began chanting for me to 'get it off,' but I wasn't daft. I had already arranged for a hairdresser in Edinburgh to do the needful and the *Daily Record* newspaper paid me £100 for exclusive pictures of me being shaved. The cash helped pay for a fresh supply of razor blades.

Following the celebrations at Ibrox, Janette and I eventually arrived back at our home in Edinburgh late on the Thursday evening. We were due to collect our son, Murray, who was only three years old, from Janette's sister, Jessie, in Falkirk the following day, but I was informed that the arrangement had changed. Janette explained that close friends of ours, Bill and Jean Mailer, wanted to take us for a celebration meal on the Friday evening. However, I should have tippled that something was up when Janette spotted that I was dressed casually and advised me to change into a suit, explaining that as captain of the newly crowned European Cup-Winners' Cup champions I would be recognised and should, therefore, be suitably attired.

Our friends duly collected us by car, but instead of heading straight for the restaurant I was told that we were first going for a quick drink at a hotel owned by a mutual acquaintance, Hughie McRoberts, who was a Celtic fan. It was a small establishment in Newington and, unbeknown to me, Janette had arranged a surprise party for a group of thirty or so friends and family.

When I walked in I was greeted by the sight of my former Rangers team-mate, Davie Provan, and Neil Martin, who had played for Hibs and whom I had known since we were kids. I was also presented with a *This Is Your Life*-style book signed by all the guests. Part of the way through the evening Hughie approached me to say that Janette had given him a cash advance for a 'free' bar, but that money had run out. Of course, I told Hughie to keep the drinks flowing and we were still there at 2 a.m. I'm sure I must have spent a sizeable chunk of the £2,000 bonus we players received for winning the Cup, but I didn't mind a bit.

It was the largest bonus the club had ever paid and, taking inflation into account, the four-figure sum represented £15,000 to £20,000 in today's money. It was also three to four times what we usually received for winning the league or a domestic cup. I remember saying at one stage that as Hughie and his wife were up early in the morning to prepare breakfast, we should all leave together. I then asked everyone to charge their glass for one final toast, but when I looked around me I was standing in an empty room – they had all left me and were heading back to the bar! The evening was a complete surprise, but I wouldn't have changed it for anything. It was wonderful to celebrate Rangers' achievement with close friends and Janette did brilliantly.

That summer Janette and I decided to holiday in Jersey, as we felt that Murray was still a bit young for exotic foreign travel. What I didn't know was that Willie Johnston and another of my Ibrox team-mates, Alex Miller, had also had the same idea. The three of us met up on the beach with our wives and kids and, inevitably, when we spotted a group of youngsters having a kickabout, we felt a need to join in. Moments later I had cause to regret my decision. I found it well nigh impossible to walk on the rutted sand in my bare feet and I hobbled back to where Janette was sitting with the others and informed her that I still had a problem.

It was nearing the end of June and I hadn't tested my injured foot since the game in Barcelona. As soon as we returned home I made an appointment to see a specialist and it was only then that my injury was diagnosed as a stress fracture. Or two in fact, thanks to that over zealous fan. The only cure was rest, according to the specialist. I somehow made it back for the start of the following season in August and, thankfully, was not troubled again by the injuries.

However, while I was given a clean bill of health, Rangers were sick at being denied the chance to defend the Cup-Winners' Cup, after being banned from playing in Europe for two seasons as a consequence of the Barcelona 'riot'. The club also received a hefty fine. The suspension was later cut to twelve months on appeal, but, to this day, I am adamant that the thousands of Rangers fans who swarmed onto the pitch to celebrate were not out to cause trouble. There was no malicious intent, in my view.

Our fans were carefree and happy. It was the actions of the Spanish police which led to things turning ugly. They completely misread the situation and over-reacted. When they waded into the fans wielding batons, in some instances our supporters responded by fighting back. Who could blame them? After all, if someone comes at you with the intention of causing you harm it's human nature to respond in kind.

I would have sympathised with the police had they been confronted with a situation where two sets of rival fans were at each others' throats, but they knew beforehand that there would be very few Dynamo supporters at the game. Travel restrictions meant that the bulk of the 35,000 crowd were Scots (estimated at between 25,000 and 30,000) and the remainder neutrals, so there was never any real likelihood of trouble. I can never condone any pitch invasion, but what began as a celebration quickly spiralled out of all proportion and the Spanish police should have been held accountable. I was later told that Willie Waddell had threatened to resign unless the club appealed against the ban, such was his sense of injustice. Apparently, some of the directors were reluctant to do so for fear of repercussions if any appeal failed, but eventually they agreed.

It was frustrating not to have the opportunity to defend our trophy and by the time the suspension was up, several of the players had left the club and the momentum that had built up during the European run was gone. When we were readmitted sixteen months later, in September 1973, we lasted just two rounds in the Cup-Winners' Cup. After thrashing Ankaragucu of Turkey, 6–0 on aggregate, Borussia Monchengladbach presented us with a near impossible task. We were beaten, 3–0, in Germany and might have lost even more heavily had Peter McCloy not saved a penalty from Jupp Heynckes, who had already scored twice. Borussia were beaten, 3–2, in the return, but the three-goal deficit was always too much of a handicap. However, I have often wondered what the 1972 team could have achieved had fate – and UEFA – been a little more kind to us.

CHAPTER 15
TREBLE, TREBLE

J ust a fortnight after Barcelona, Willie Waddell dropped a bombshell by announcing that he was resigning as manager. I believe he chose to hand over the reins to Jock Wallace at the height of his success because he felt there were other areas of the club that would benefit in the longer term from his expertise and administrative skills. I remember him saying at the time that team management was a young man's game – he was by then in his early fifties – and adding that it was impossible for one person to run the entire show. He also felt that the club had to be streamlined. So, Willie Waddell became general manager and Jock Wallace succeeded him as team manager, but it remained a partnership, with Deedle very much the senior partner.

Big Jock, whose playing career as a goalkeeper had involved spells with Workington, Airdrie, West Bromwich Albion, Brentford, Hereford and Berwick Rangers, based everything on mental toughness and physical fitness. He was not the sort to suffer fools gladly.

The word most associated with Jock Wallace's reign as manager is 'character'. Invariably when he was asked to assess the greatest strength of his team the reply was, 'Character, kid, character!' I don't think I'm being unkind to suggest that tactics were not Jock's strong point. For him it was more about putting eleven players on the park who played for the jersey from the first minute to the last. He trained the players to a level of fitness that meant we could outlast any team, but Rangers also had some very talented players. In many ways the team picked itself most weeks.

Peter McCloy and later Stewart Kennedy shared the goal-keeping duties at various times and the defence, which at its strongest was Sandy Jardine, Tom Forsyth, Colin Jackson and myself, was solid and dependable. Alex MacDonald and Bobby Russell offered craft, inventiveness and energy in midfield. We also had talented wingers in Davie Cooper and Tommy McLean, and Derek Johnstone posed a powerful goal threat in attack. The other important ingredient the treble-winning sides of 1976 and 1978 had was continuity. There was the minimum of change in the squad and that allowed us to form a close understanding.

From a personal point of view, Jock probably gave me a level of fitness that allowed me to play until the age I did. He gave me a platform and I built on it. The trips to Gullane to train on the sand dunes became a huge talking point. Jock even had his own 'Murder Hill' and forced the players up the slope until some actually threw up, because of the physical exertion.

Pre-season training was not something to look forward to, but those critics who questioned Big Jock's methods were made to eat their words when they saw the results on the pitch. Some considered it absurd that he should take the players across country from Glasgow to East Lothian, just to train on a beach, but Jock's methods were vindicated when we won two trebles in the space of three seasons. We went to Gullane purely to run and train. The manager didn't take any footballs. Neither did he bother with the niceties of showers and changing facilities at the end of the shift. We were made to bathe in the sea, dry ourselves as best we could and then change on the coach.

I recall one occasion when I was the only one running up the sand dunes. I had been sidelined by an ankle injury and Jock told me to report to Gullane for a one-on-one fitness session. It was sheer torture and one of the toughest days of my entire career. The rest of the players were given the day off and I drove down from my home in Edinburgh to be given the 'Wallace treatment'. Afterwards it felt like I had been run over by a steamroller!

Later, when I was manager, I also took the players to Gullane to train, because I felt that they would benefit from a change of environment, but I always made sure we had a plentiful supply of footballs. As a kid I had played on the sands at Gullane and had good memories of the place.

Big Jock was a hard man and it took a brave one to speak back to him, but he also had a heart of gold and the players liked him because he was a player's man. He also allowed us an element of leeway, in particular on European trips. Jock placed trust in the senior members of the squad – guys like me, Alex MacDonald, Sandy Jardine, Colin Jackson, Tommy McLean, Tam Forsyth – to show common sense. Usually, when we arrived at our destination, one of us would head for the local supermarket to buy a quantity of beer and lager, so we could enjoy a drink after the game. Jock didn't have a problem with that as long as the younger players weren't involved. In fact, more often than not he would join us for a beer and discuss the game that had just taken place.

For all that Jock was a strict disciplinarian, he also allowed us to have a bit of fun. There was a good spirit about that squad and that was one of our strengths and a key ingredient in our success. We got on well as a group and played for each other. We tended to do things together, too, and I remember after we had clinched the title in 1976, all the players and their wives and partners spent the evening following our final match at Tannadice celebrating our success at Dunblane Hydro.

On another occasion I took my life in my hands by trying to wind up Big Jock on the eve of a European tie in Berne in what turned out to be my final season as a player. We had gone to the Young Boys of Berne ground to train and as we made our way out on to the pitch I spotted that the door to the groundsman's hut was open. When I took a peek inside I saw a large plastic coat hanging up and decided to have a bit of fun.

A pal of mine had given me a latex mask of a grotesque old man with wrinkled skin and long flowing grey hair and I quickly pulled on the mask, followed by the coat, and proceeded to run on to the pitch. Big Jock was standing on the other side and when he spotted me he bellowed, 'Here, you get off the effing pitch.' But I kept coming and he began to move towards me. I honestly thought for a moment that he was going to hit me, but when he realised I was the one wearing the mask he told me to keep it on. I always led the players in training and there were quite a few locals gathered in the stand on the far side of the ground to watch us work out. They must have wondered what the hell was happening when the 'old man' went jogging past them, but that was the sort of thing Jock encouraged.

He was a motivator and he browbeat his players into believing that they couldn't lose. As a result, we regularly ran over the top of teams in the final fifteen minutes of games. Jock knew his strengths and weaknesses and didn't spend a lot of time on tactics, but he did learn a great deal from Willie Waddell and the pair of them formed a formidable partnership.

Willie Waddell liked to practise psychology in the hope of unnerving the opposition and before a European tie against Bayern in Munich he used me to demonstrate that Rangers weren't in the least intimidated by the prospect of facing Franz Beckenbauer and company. I had suffered a nasty injury the previous Saturday, when one of the Motherwell players raked his studs down both my shins. By the following Tuesday my legs looked even worse, because of the severe bruising, and I was ordered to remove my trousers and climb on the treatment table. Willie Waddell then threw open the door and ushered in several German journalists and photographers and invited them to take pictures of my legs. 'You can see how bad they are,' he said, 'but he's playing.' That sort of bravado was easy for Deedle, but when the game got under way the Bayern players had been alerted as to the state of my legs and proceeded to kick lumps out of me!

When Jock was coach we referred to him by his Christian name, but it was 'Boss' as soon as he became manager. I didn't have a problem with that and I like to think that we enjoyed a good relationship. I was given free rein to make whatever changes I saw fit during a game and I took full advantage of my position as captain.

When Jock assumed the duties of team manager, Rangers hadn't won the league championship since 1964 and that became his top priority. However, from the outset of the 1972–73 season we made things difficult for ourselves by losing three of our first five league games, including a 3–1 defeat by Celtic. Our poor start was compounded by Alfie Conn tabling a transfer request, Colin Stein also expressing a desire to move on, and Willie Johnston being landed with a whacking nine-game SFA suspension. Stein was sold to Coventry and Johnston moved to West Bromwich Albion before the year was out. Former Ayr United winger, Quinton 'Cutty' Young, came to Rangers as part of the Stein deal and Jock also added Tom Forsyth and midfielder-cum-forward, Joe Mason, to the squad.

Despite an embarrassing home defeat by Stenhousemuir in the League Cup, we qualified for the knock-out stages and made it to the semi-final, where we lost to Hibs. In the absence of European football caused by the club's twelve-month ban, Willie Waddell worked hard behind the scenes to gain some compensation and was partly instrumental in the creation of the Super Cup. We faced Ajax of Amsterdam over two legs in January and lost to the World Club champions home and away, but the team was in no way disgraced. Playing against players of the calibre of Johann Cruyff, Johnny Rep and Ruud Krol, we matched the Dutch side in most departments and the 6–3 aggregate score was not a particularly accurate reflection of our general play.

Although we led the title race by the end of February, Celtic maintained their remarkable run when they edged us out by a single point. We did, however, enjoy the satisfaction of beating our arch rivals in the Centenary Scottish Cup final.

The following season was preceded by the departure of Ronnie McKinnon. Ronnie had been a key player for Rangers for almost a decade, but, in truth, he never recovered fully from the horror double leg break he suffered against Sporting Lisbon.

Season 1973–74 is not one I recall with any affection. I prefer to skip over the detail of a campaign that failed to yield any silverware and will confine my comments to the bald facts. We finished third in the league, reached the semi-finals of the League Cup, the fourth round in the Scottish, and fell at the second hurdle on our return to Europe.

On a personal level, one of the rare highlights was scoring Rangers' 10,000th goal in all competitions. It was the second goal in a 4–0 win over Clyde at Ibrox on 30 March. In the same game, Derek Johnstone scored the club's 6,000th league goal. I'll let you into a secret, my shot actually deflected off the Clyde player, Eddie Aherne.

I suppose, technically, it was an own goal, but Eddie was persuaded to say nothing!

Persistent problems with my hamstring limited me to just twenty-three appearances the following season and the timing of the injury could hardly have been worse. After a wait of eleven long years, Rangers were crowned champions at long last. In retrospect, it hardly mattered a great deal that we 'bombed' in the cup competitions after finishing second to Hibs in our League Cup qualifying section and losing to Aberdeen in the third round of the Scottish Cup. All of us associated with the club craved the title.

For the record, we finished seven points in front of a very fine Hibs side and the nucleus of the two treble-winning teams was firmly in place. In fact, the team changed very little over the next three seasons as a hard core of twenty players took the club to new heights. In stark contrast to the previous season, I played in every game; fifty-five in total as we produced a clean sweep of the domestic honours. The 1975–76 championship was won from Celtic by six points and we also beat our deadly rivals in the League Cup final when Alex MacDonald headed the only goal of the game.

The final piece in the jigsaw, the Scottish Cup, was fitted into place on 1 May, when we accounted for Hearts, 3–1. That final is also remembered for the opening goal being scored before the official kickoff time. Derek Johnstone's header after forty-two seconds hit the net before 3 p.m. after referee, Bobby Davidson, began the game early. I suppose the only disappointment we suffered came in the European Cup. Having beaten Bohemians of Dublin we met the eventual finalists, St Etienne of France, in the next round and lost home and away, by a 4–1 aggregate margin.

But if we imagined that the pendulum had swung back completely in Rangers' direction, we were in for a rude awakening. The 1976–77 season was a bit of a nightmare. It soon became evident that certain changes in personnel were necessary and Jock Wallace acted accordingly, when we relinquished our grip on the title.

Having been thrashed, 5–1, by Aberdeen in the League Cup semi-final the previous October, a month after going out of the European Cup to FC Zurich, there was further bitter disappointment in store the following May when Celtic won the Scottish Cup at our expense. It was our last chance of success, but fate conspired against us. Celtic's match-winner was controversial, to say the least. Derek Johnstone was judged to have handled a shot from Johannes Edvaldsson and the award of a penalty stood, in spite of furious protests. In the event, Andy Lynch took the kick and scored the only goal of the game, but nothing will ever convince me that big Derek actually made contact with the ball. Mind you, the referee's judgement was all that counted and Bob Valentine did not hesitate in pointing to the spot. Although I have to admit I was furious at the time.

Almost inevitably, Jock Wallace went into the transfer market, and winger Davie Cooper and striker Gordon Smith were signed from Clydebank and Kilmarnock respectively, in deals totalling £165,000. Midfielder Bobby Russell, who turned out to be a highly significant signing from Shettleston Juniors, was also added to the squad.

Interestingly, it was Aberdeen who emerged as our closest challengers that season, but the cornerstone of our success results-wise was the 3–2 victory over Celtic at Ibrox in early September. After losing our first two league matches – to Aberdeen and Hibs – we hardly looked back following the Old Firm win. The influence of the new signings, Cooper, Smith and Russell, was evident, but we never managed to shake Aberdeen off our tails and eventually we won the title by a mere two points over the Dons. We then proceeded to complete a league and cup double over our north-east rivals in the Scottish Cup final.

We had completed the first part of the treble in March, beating Celtic, 2–1, after extra time in the League Cup final, but that success was very much overshadowed by the death of Bobby McKean, just two days earlier. Bobby was found dead in his car in the garage at his home and the tragedy cast a dark cloud over the club for a time. Bobby had drifted out of the first-team picture and his death was a shattering blow for everyone at Ibrox.

Although I didn't know it at the time, I scored the last of my 120 competitive goals for Rangers at Somerset Park on 8 April. We beat Ayr United, 5–2, and I hit the second in what was a crucial win, given that Aberdeen were still breathing down our necks. That same month I also became the first Rangers player to be granted a testimonial match. The Scotland team, which was preparing for the World Cup finals in Argentina, provided the opposition and 70,000 packed into Ibrox for what turned out to be an emotionally charged occasion for me. Rangers won, 5–2, and I scored twice, taking my goals tally to 140 in all games. I'm proud of that record which puts me in the top ten Rangers goal-scorers of all time – not bad for an inside-forward turned defender.

When we lined-up against Motherwell at Ibrox on 29 April, for the game that clinched the title, there were eight survivors from the previous treble team – Peter McCloy, Sandy Jardine, Tom Forsyth, Colin Jackson, Alex MacDonald, Tommy McLean, Derek Johnstone and me.

But just a month after we had clinched the title with a two-goal victory, Jock Wallace stunned the players and the fans by announcing his resignation. It appeared that he no longer felt that the board valued his services. Although it was never publicly stated, I suspect that Jock's decision to quit was taken in a fit of pique over his personal terms. By then Jock had also soured a wee bit towards me. He gave me a right rollicking one day at training for suggesting a tactical change and our relationship cooled after that.

It had been his custom to invite me to join him in the boot room on a Friday after training to discuss tactics for the next day's game, but that stopped. Jock began consulting my deputy, Sandy Jardine, instead, but as Sandy and I travelled together I quickly found out what was happening anyway. Sometimes, I thought that Jock was unsettled by the fact that I was nearing the end of my career. Whatever the case, at the end of the 1974–75 season, when I was thirty-two, he issued an ultimatum to me with regard to my fitness. This was the season when my hamstring injury forced me out of around fifty per cent of the games. It was to be my worst season for injuries and I was forced to shorten my stride to compensate. The club had organised a month-long tour of Canada, New Zealand and Australia and Jock told me around March time that I wouldn't be going unless my fitness improved. Then he added that he might even consider 'freeing' me.

However, I later discovered that it was an empty threat, for Willie Waddell continued to make the decisions regarding signing and transfers and when he called me into his office at the end of the season he explained that he would be offering me year-on-year deals from now on, because of my age. I said that a year's contract was certainly better than a free transfer and I was asked what I was talking about. When I told Willie Waddell what Jock has said, he replied, 'That'll be right!'

I think it was at that moment that I first realised that when Big Jock left I would become manager, but I won't have a bad word said about Jock Wallace. I had only respect for the success he achieved. Two trebles is some going in anyone's language and there was not a fitter team in British football at the time. I also doubt that there was a happier bunch of players and I have a lot of good memories of the 1975 tour.

I also remember one particular incident I would rather forget. We had just finished training at a sports ground in Melbourne when I heard this voice say, 'Hi, John. Do you not remember me?' As it happened I didn't and my latest 'new best friend' – an exiled Scot and a Rangers fan – refused to give me a clue. I am always concerned in those sorts of situations in case the person addressing me is someone I should remember from my past, because I would never want to appear dismissive of anyone.

It was a long walk back to the changing rooms and eventually I exhausted every avenue – school, boys club, former workmate, one-time opponent? The answer was always, 'No,' but still he wouldn't say where our paths had crossed. I was becoming increasingly irritated and eventually I told him, 'Look, you'll need to tell me, because this is giving me a sore head.' In actual fact I felt like hitting him for refusing to end my suffering. Then he told me. 'I bought your first car, a Ford Prefect registration, TSF 21. But I traded it in for a new model.' I replied. 'You must have bought the car directly from the garage.' As it turned out that's exactly what had happened. The only reason he knew I had once owned the vehicle was because my name was listed in the log book. In actual fact this guy had never met me in his life, so how the hell he expected me to recognise him I have no idea, but for almost quarter of an hour he had kept at me. Not much wonder I wanted to hit him.

The positions were reversed on another occasion as the team flew to Canada for another close season tour the following summer. Only this time it was my team-mate, Tam Forsyth, who felt like committing an act of violence against me and Derek Johnstone. Tam had played for Scotland against England at Hampden the day before and had made a great tackle on Mick Channon to prevent the loss of a goal. Scotland won, 2–1, and Tam had been able to stick two fingers up at Tommy Docherty for making several unkind comments about him prior to the game. Tam had taken Martin Buchan place in the team and

Docherty said it was like comparing a Clydesdale horse to a thorough-bred. The remark had obviously annoyed Tam and he didn't take too kindly to being reminded of what had been said, but that didn't stop Derek and I from playing a trick on Tam.

We persuaded one of the cabin crew to link us to the plane's intercom system before he then told Tam that there was a telephone call for him. The rest of us positioned ourselves at the rear of the plane as Tam, by now somewhat bemused, made his way to the phone. It was agreed that I would be the one to speak to Tam and that Big Derek would relay the conversation to the rest of the lads. When Tam answered I disguised my voice and put on an English accent, informing him that I was a sports writer from the *Daily Mirror* and I wanted to interview him about the previous day's game. Tam thought this was tremendous, but he was also intrigued to know exactly how I had managed to get the aircraft's telephone number! Thinking on my feet, I replied that all the leading national newspapers had contacts at the various airlines and because of this I had been patched through. Meanwhile, Derek was providing a running commentary for the rest.

After praising Tam for the brilliance of his display at Hampden and asking him a couple of questions, I then informed him that he would receive a fee of £200 for the interview, but when I asked him for his home address, he requested that the cheque be sent to the team's hotel in Vancouver and duly proceeded to reach in his pocket and read off the address from the itinerary that he had been given by the club. Tam also commented that the call must be costing me a fortune, but I explained that the *Mirror* was sharing the cost with the *Sun* and that my colleague would also like a word with him.

I handed the phone to Derek, who proceeded to engage Tam in a conversation about yours truly along the lines of, 'How's that old guy Greig playing these days?' Tam considered the question for a moment before replying rather diplomatically that there were no stars at Rangers. Derek then informed Tam that he was passing him back to the journalist from the *Mirror*. 'Your cheque is in the post,' I said. 'Have a great time in Canada, but can you do me one more favour?' 'Sure,' said Tam. 'Can you please turn round and look up the plane, because there are a couple of the guys at the back who are desperately trying to catch your attention?' The look on his face was a picture. There we all were rolling about the aisle in hysterics, but for the next month Derek and I had to watch our backs everywhere we went, because Tam would have committed 'murder' had he managed to catch either of us alone.

But Tam had the last laugh when Derek and I copped a £200 fine for having the nerve to drink Bertolla Cream Sherry while airborne. Jock Wallace had banned the players from drinking alcohol, but Derek reckoned that we would be safe enough, because the sherry could be mixed with Coca-Cola and the boss would think we were having a soft drink. But Jock wasn't daft. When he spotted us drinking our 'Coke' he picked up one of the glasses and took a sip, before immediately spitting out the contents. A short time later Tom Craig, the physiotherapist, was dispatched to inform the pair of us that we had just been fined £200 each. I turned to Derek and said, 'Well, big man that's the most expensive sherry you and I will ever drink,' but Derek was undaunted. 'It could have been worse,' he said. 'At least he didn't spot the empty bottle!' As it happened, no fine was ever docked off our wages.

When Jock quit as manager he got out at the right time, in my opinion, because we were an ageing team. The upshot was that I was the one left with the onerous task of getting rid of the older players and bringing in younger ones. Jock eventually returned as manager, when I resigned five and a half years later, but he was not first choice. Rangers couldn't persuade the likes of Alex Ferguson, Jim McLean or John Lyall to succeed me. I recall Fergie phoning me and, following a twenty-minute conversation, he told me he had decided against taking the job. So Jock ended up back at Rangers – and Fergie eventually found his way to Old Trafford. The rest, as they say, is history!

CHAPTER 16

A ROYAL SEAL
OF APPROVAL

I t appears that even the Queen is a football fan. Her Majesty was certainly clued up on my career when I stood before her to be invested as a Member of the British Empire. I have no difficulty recalling the exact date of my one and only visit to Buckingham Palace. It was 15 November 1977. I am pretty sure that her Majesty also remembers the occasion, although not for the same reasons as myself. The name 'John Greig' may not mean anything to her, but she's bound to recall the birth of her first grandchild.

The Queen became a granny with the arrival of Master Peter Phillips, son of Princess Anne, at around the same time as several hundred recipients of various 'gongs' shuffled nervously in anticipation of coming face to face with the monarch. Janette told me later that the Queen had apologised to the family members gathered in another room for keeping everyone waiting, explaining that she had just become a grandmother for the first time. Years later I met Mark Phillips on a visit to Gleneagles and told him I would never forget the day that his son was born. Mark smiled when I explained the circumstances and then informed me that Peter is, in fact, a big Spurs fan.

My meeting with The Queen was without doubt the proudest day of my life. I am a self-confessed royalist and Janette and I are very fond of the royal family, so it was both a huge honour and a real privilege to be given the award of an MBE for my services to football.

I was one of the last to be presented to the Queen and I had imagined that she would simply hand me my medal and it would be all over within a few seconds. How wrong I was. Her Majesty floored me by saying, 'You have played a long time for Glasgow Rangers and you have had a great career. Your team has been doing very well.' Considering how many others had been presented to her beforehand, I was amazed by Her Majesty's powers of recall. She had clearly been fed all the relevant information by her private secretary in advance of the investiture ceremony, but it struck me as very impressive indeed that she was able to remember such detail.

Mind you, I feared that I would be late for my appointment with the Queen when the taxi driver I hailed to take me, Janette, and my son, Murray, to the Palace at first refused the hire. When I told him to take us to Buckingham Palace he declined the fare on the basis that it was just around the corner, but when I explained to him that I wished to be dropped inside the grounds of the Palace he soon changed his tune.

'That's different,' he said. 'I've never been inside the place. Jump in.' A couple of minutes later we were deposited at the appointed dropping off point. 'That'll be three quid, mate,' said the driver. However, I only had a twenty pound note and, surprise, surprise, the cabbie didn't have any change. Given the circumstances and where we were standing, I wasn't going to wait for him to start asking others who were arriving if they had change of twenty quid, so I told him to keep the change – albeit more than a tad reluctantly!

When we emerged from the investiture ceremony and appeared on the Palace quadrangle, where several journalists and photographers were assembled, we had our picture taken by Eric Craig, the *Daily Record*'s sports photographer. I was prepared for that to happen, given that I was captain of Rangers and the award of an MBE constitutes a story of sorts on the sports pages, but I hadn't anticipated that I would also have my own little fan club.

I couldn't believe my eyes and ears when I heard the chant, 'Follow, follow,' and looked up to see four Rangers fans decked out in the club's colours standing on the other side of the Palace railings. Believe it or not, they had made the trip specially to see me emerge with my MBE.

I was even more pleased that Janette and Murray had been able to accompany me to the Palace than I was for myself. The wives and children of football players have to put up with a lot and it's not often that they are given the opportunity to share in such special moments, but there wasn't time for any elaborate celebrations. I had to head straight back to Glasgow as Rangers were playing just twenty-four hours later.

By then the Ibrox kit-man had embroidered 'John Greig MBE' on the back of my training gear. The fans also joined in with the chant when I scored the opening goal in a 3–1 League Cup quarter-final second leg win over Dunfermline at East End Park. The Supporters' Club is also named after me – John Greig MBE Loyal.

I think largely because of my loyalty to the club I have always enjoyed a close affinity with the fans. They appreciate that I chose to spend my entire playing career with Rangers when it would have been easy to have sought bigger earnings elsewhere. But while money is important in terms of allowing you to enjoy a certain standard of living, cash has never been my God. I was also well paid by Rangers. The fact that my dad spent forty-nine years working as a warehouseman with the same company in Edinburgh must have rubbed off on me, I guess. There was certainly never a moment during my eighteen years as a player when it seemed likely that I would be transferred to another club.

I suppose the closest that came to happening was in the mid-1960s when Harry Catterick, then manager of Everton, made a move to sign me. Catterick was a pal of Scot Symon's and he wanted to buy me to further strengthen what was a very fine Everton side, which went on to win championships and cups. But Scot Symon wouldn't hear of it. Not that I was told of Everton's interest at the time. I found out by pure chance years later during a conversation with Howard Kendall, who was by then manager at Goodison Park.

In 1964, when he was still a teenager, Howard had become the youngest player ever to appear in an FA Cup final. He was a member of the Preston side beaten by West Ham and, despite that defeat, quickly made a name for himself. According to Howard, when Harry Catterick failed in his bid to sign me, he turned his attention to Howard, who went on to enjoy a successful career with Everton and England.

Newcastle also tried to sign me in the latter stages of my career. I was thirty-three when Joe Harvey made his move, but I had no wish to uproot my family and no real desire to play in England. As things turned out, I am very glad I chose to remain at Rangers, because I would have missed out on the 1976 and 1978 trebles had I chosen to go to St James's Park. Mind you, I doubt very much that Willie Waddell would have allowed that to happen in the first place.

If there were any other moves to try to prise me away from Ibrox I was never made aware of them and I'm glad I was never forced to make such a decision, because it would have meant that Rangers no longer felt a pressing need to retain my services and that would have hurt. I can truly say, hand on heart, that I have absolutely no regrets that I was a one-club man and that that club was Rangers.

CHAPTER 17

IBROX GREATS

I was given the accolade of 'Greatest Ever Ranger', but Jim Baxter would have been my personal choice. Jim was one of the true greats of the game; a player who would have left his mark on any generation, because he would have been able to adapt to suit the demands of the modern game. He was blessed with magnificent talent and the ability to win a game almost single-handed – and he knew it.

That was what made Jim the player he was. He had the utmost confidence in himself. Jim gave the appearance of being the coolest man around and he probably was. He refused to show nerves and the bigger the stage the better he played. Jim loved beating the English, especially at Wembley, because he was playing against some of the biggest names in British football and it was his chance to upstage them by showing just how good he was.

The facts bear out my assertion that Jim revelled in the big occasion. He played against England five times and was on the losing side only once, in 1966, when we went down, 4–3, at Hampden. Scotland won the other four, including beating England on their own patch in 1963, when Jim scored twice, and again in 1967, when he was outstanding in our 3–2 victory over the world champions.

It was a measure of Jim's standing in the game that he was selected to play for the Rest of the World against England at Wembley in 1963, in the FA's centenary match. Rubbing shoulders with the likes of Lev Yashin and Ferenc Puskas did not faze Jim in the slightest. In fact, he became a pal of Puskas and when he learned what sort of money the Hungarian was earning at Real Madrid, that friendship probably helped influence his decision to seek a move from Rangers.

Despite his antics off the field and the way he lived, Jim was also very competitive and played from the first whistle until the last kick of a game. He was able to do so because he was naturally fit and could run around all day long. Those who questioned his fitness didn't know what they were talking about.

The tragedy was that Jim left the game so early. He made a mistake, in my opinion, in electing to sign for Sunderland for the money. Rangers had his best years from 1960 until 1965, but he was capable of remaining at his peak for much longer. I think breaking his leg in the European Cup tie against Rapid Vienna in Austria in December 1964 probably influenced Jim's decision to move, in that it brought home to him the precarious nature of a footballer's career and the need to cash in while the going was good.

Jim loved a laugh and a joke, but he didn't suffer fools gladly and you had to pull your weight. Otherwise, Jim would give you both barrels, as happened in the case of George McLean. 'Dandy' had been signed from St Mirren in January 1963 at a cost of £27,000, largely on the strength of his performance against us in the previous season's Scottish Cup final. Much was expected of him, but Dandy had a stinker on his debut and Jim turned to him at half-time and rapped, 'That's the worst exhibition I have seen by an inside-forward in my entire life.' Quick as a flash, Dandy snapped back, 'Well, you'd better get used to it, because there's plenty more where that came from.'

Jim was speechless, but he was rarely lost for words – or cheek. Like the time he was lying in the slipper bath at Ibrox one Monday morning and the doorman arrived with a message that there was a phone call for him. 'Tell him I'll see him on Wednesday,' announced Jim. 'But he says you have to come back today,' argued the doorman. He was wasting his time. Later I asked Jim who had wanted to speak to him. 'Oh, it was just my sergeant at Stirling Castle,' he blithely declared. Jim was doing his National Service and simply couldn't be bothered reporting for duty, but that was typical of Jim and he very probably got away with it.

After spells with Sunderland and Nottingham Forest, Jim returned to Ibrox in 1969, but he wasn't half the player he had once been. Sadly, Jim died in April 2001 at the age of just sixty-one, but he had few regrets, publicly at least. He used to say that he had lived three lifetimes in one and I suppose there was a lot of truth in that statement. He certainly knew how to enjoy himself.

I saw quite a lot of Jim in later years, because his two sons, Alan and Stephen, attended the same school as my boy, Murray, and he never lost his talent for raising a smile, often in a manner that made others cringe. But no matter what anyone says about Jim Baxter, he stands alongside any of the greats of the game. He was blessed with a remarkable football brain, great vision and an abundance of skill. I could never praise Jim highly enough as a football player and you rarely see his likes in the modern game – more is the pity.

Bobby Shearer and Eric Caldow were not great players in the sense of being hugely gifted, but they formed an outstanding defensive partnership for Rangers in the 1950s and early 1960s, because they blended so well. They were experienced players and captains at different times, who helped me understand what was involved in being skipper of Rangers and what the role represented. Shearer was known as

'Captain Cutlass', a nickname that suited his build and style of play, while Caldow was a more refined player, but whereas they differed a great deal as individuals, both were hugely influential.

Shearer had calf muscles as broad as some other players' thighs and he tackled with the force of a tank. The story goes that during a European tie Shearer actually tackled one of the opposition's substitutes, who was warming up on the touchline. Substitutes had only just been introduced into the game and Shearer was clearly oblivious of the fact. So, spotting the unfortunate sub running along the touchline, he launched himself in a powerful challenge and whacked the fellow's legs. One of Shearer's team-mates asked what the hell he was doing and he explained that his victim had looked 'too macho'. I recall on another occasion Shearer put in a challenge on Gerry Baker, brother of the late England striker, Joe, and sent him flying ten yards into the Ibrox enclosure.

Caldow, who played forty times for Scotland, was very different. He was never booked, because he relied on speed of thought and blistering pace rather than brute force. The leg break he suffered at Wembley in 1963, when Bobby Smith launched a horrific late challenge, effectively cut short Caldow's career.

Willie Henderson couldn't see the length of himself. Wee Willie was as blind as a bat and was one of the first players to wear contact lenses. I remember on one occasion we all ended up searching the pitch after one of them popped out. Getting in a car with Willie behind the wheel was the equivalent of a white-knuckle ride. I got the fright of my life when I was in a rush to catch my train and he offered to drive me to the station. Willie had bought himself a second-hand Mercedes that had seen better days and was still in the process of taking driving lessons. Suffice to say, he still doesn't drive to this day!

But, boy, could Willie play – despite being plagued by bunions! He was blessed with blinding pace and ball control and could be relied on to get to the by-line and deliver crosses with pin-point accuracy. Hence the reason Rangers scored so many goals. I had played against Willie at under-seventeen level. He was with Edinburgh Athletic and I was with Edina Hearts and the local papers were full of the fact that the pair of us were heading for Rangers. That Rangers were prepared to sell a player of the calibre of Alex Scott to Everton to accommodate Willie on the right wing tells you just how good he was.

Ian McMillan was twenty-seven when Rangers signed him from Airdrie. Known as the 'Wee Prime Minister' after Conservative leader, Harold McMillan, Ian remained part-time to enable him to work at his day job as a surveyor. Ian was a highly intelligent, graceful midfield player, whose ability to pass the ball to his strikers with tremendous accuracy meant he set up goals galore. He was also a gentleman and great with me when we trained together on Tuesday and Thursday evenings, so I have always had a soft spot for him. I made my Rangers debut in place of Ian, after he was injured, but he nevertheless always tried to encourage me. Ian is now in his seventies, but hardly looks a day older than when he played for Rangers and he is still a low handicap golfer.

It's the best man's duty to toast the bride, but my best man somehow managed to toast the minister. That, though, is typical of Jimmy Millar, who formed a deadly spearhead with Ralph Brand in a partnership daubed M&B. Between them Jimmy and Ralph scored an incredible amount of goals. Jimmy would drop slightly deeper while Ralph was as sharp as a tack. Our friendship began when I travelled with Jimmy and Ralph on a daily basis from Edinburgh. They always ensured that I was included in the conversations about football and I learned a great deal from the pair of them. I was also a regular visitor to Jimmy's home on a Saturday evening for a sing-song.

Jimmy was called-up for National Service, but didn't fancy the idea of serving Queen and Country and did a runner after just a couple of days at his barracks at Glencoarse, near Edinburgh, where the late Ally MacLeod, who became Scotland manager, was his sergeant. Having enlisted on the Monday morning, Jimmy returned home forty-eight hours later. He explained to his father that he had been granted leave, but his old man was having none of it. He knew damn fine that Jimmy had gone AWOL and when the MPs arrived on the doorstep asking if Millar senior knew the whereabouts of his son, Jimmy's dad pointed to a cupboard and said, 'Aye, you'll find him in there!'

Like Willie Henderson, Jimmy was a nightmare behind the wheel of a car. One day we were driving along the old A8 between Glasgow and Edinburgh when steam began pouring out from under the bonnet. I suggested we pull into a garage to find out what the problem was and straightaway the mechanic asked Jimmy if he ever bothered to top up the radiator with water. 'No,' he replied. 'I just put petrol in the car.' Jimmy's driving wasn't much better. On another occasion he pulled out into the middle lane in a three-lane road to overtake another vehicle when I saw a lorry heading straight for us. 'Pull in,' I yelled. 'Why?' asked Jimmy. 'I moved out first!'

I'll never forget the day I met Jimmy walking out of Ibrox clutching a brown paper bag containing his boots. I asked him where he was going and he told me he had just been transferred to Dundee United. Jimmy later tried his hand at management, when he became boss of Raith Rovers, but he was never cut out for that role, because he was too laid back. He phoned me prior to meeting the players and asked what he should say to them. I advised that he should just say what was in his mind. Later that evening Jimmy called me back. 'I walked into the dressing room and said, "Right you lot, my name is Jimmy Millar and I'm the manager and you'll do what I tell you because I'm a better player than any of you."' Not surprisingly, Jimmy didn't last too long.

Management wasn't for him and he chucked it in after the club refused to buy a new washing machine. 'My wife's fed-up having to wash the strips,' he explained.

Ralph Brand's partnership with Jimmy owed a great deal to their daily train trips from Edinburgh. They talked football constantly and even roomed together, so they could continue the conversation. But the talking stopped on the park, where Ralph's blistering acceleration and lethal finishing enabled him to cash in on Jimmy's clever knock-downs and intelligent link-up play. Between them, M&B scored a total of 368 goals for Rangers in 634 games for the club. By a remarkable coincidence, each played 317 times.

Only Willie Johnston could match Davie Wilson's tally of goals. There were few wingers with his ability to put the ball in the net. Davie was skilful, with good close control, and was able to cut in from the left side and shoot with either foot. He was good at winning penalties, too, because of his skills as a diver. He was also deadly from the spot.

Johnston was probably quicker and more direct than Davie. He was also naturally two-footed and one of the best young players I have seen. He was just fifteen when he arrived at Rangers from his native Fife and made his Scotland debut against Poland in 1965, while still a teenager. We christened him 'Bud' because he wore a long fur coat like the one favoured by the comedian, Bud Flanagan, but defenders never had any reason to smile, because of Bud's lightning pace. He would regularly pull on a pair of heavy miner's boots at training and still beat any of us in a sprint.

Bud could play on the left wing or through the middle and score goals, as he proved in the 1972 European Cup-Winners' Cup final, when he got two against Moscow Dynamo. Apart from his electrifying speed, Bud had great ball control and was good in the air for a wee fellow, but he started to worry unnecessarily about certain aspects of his game and became increasingly frustrated, instead of just getting on with what he was good at. Consequently, he would lose his rag and end up being sent off. Eventually he was collecting red cards at a frightening rate. Bud was eventually tempted to join West Bromwich Albion for the money and I think that was a mistake. Don Howe was coach and Bud phoned me a short time after his move to the Midlands. 'Don Howe thinks I'm uncoachable,' he said. I wasn't all that surprised, because Bud was a law unto himself, the way he played the game.

Sandy Jardine lived close to me in Edinburgh and when he joined Rangers we travelled together by train. I tried to do for Sandy what Jimmy Millar and Ralph Brand had done for me and gave him as much encouragement as possible. I had spotted that Sandy was an intelligent player, who thought about the game, and if you get five or six players prepared to think about tactics, there's a fair chance you'll end up with a successful team.

Like me, Sandy started out as a midfield player, but eventually found his natural position at right-back. He worked to develop his game and became one of the best full-backs in the country, to the extent that Scotland switched Danny McGrain of Celtic to left-back to accommodate Sandy in the national team. One of Sandy's great strengths was his pace. He and Willie Johnston used to compete in the Border sprints during the close season and regularly dominated these races.

I will never forget Sandy's wonderful gesture when Rangers clinched their first championship for eleven years, when we drew 1–1 with Hibs at Easter Road in March 1975. I was suffering from an injury and was left on the bench, but what I didn't know was that the manager, Jock Wallace, and Sandy had agreed that Sandy would come off a couple of minutes from the end to make way for me. That said a lot about the person Sandy is and I will always be grateful to him for allowing me to be part of what was a momentous day for the club. Sandy and I remain very close and I am glad that he is back at Rangers, working behind the scenes.

When I was working for the BBC, after I quit as Rangers manager, I interviewed Franz Beckenbauer and was taken aback when he enquired after my former team-mate, Ronnie McKinnon. It transpired that Beckenbauer thought that Ronnie had been an outstanding centre-half – and compliments don't come much bigger than that. Ronnie kept things simple and gave people the impression that he was as cool as a cucumber. In fact, he was a nervous wreck. When we played together he liked me to stay a yard behind him, to leave him to win the headers. He hated the responsibility of being last man.

Ronnie read situations quickly and was great in the air. He also liked to man-mark and I remember a game against Ayr United when he was assigned the task of marking their striker, Alex 'Dixie' Ingram. Scot Symon had warned Ronnie that he would have to stay tight on Ingram, but we found ourselves two goals down at half-time and Dixie had scored both of them.

The manager asked Ronnie to explain why Ingram had managed to evade him twice and my team-mate replied, 'Because he keeps doing stupid things.' By that Ronnie meant that Ingram hadn't kept it simple and stuck to conventional tactics. Ronnie just didn't want to know if it wasn't straightforward. Tactics were alien to him. He played the game as he saw it.

If Ronnie suffered the slightest nick he would lie in the bath after the game and make a huge fuss over it. That led some players to imagine he was soft, but the March 1972 evening when he suffered a double fracture of his right leg in the Cup-Winners' Cup quarter-final against Sporting Lisbon showed there was another side to Ronnie. He had been subjected to a horrific tackle and you would have heard the crack a mile away, but Ronnie lay on the pitch as cool as you like and said to our trainer, Davie Kinnear, 'Davie, my leg's broken.'

Alex MacDonald wasn't big, but my goodness he could jump the height of himself and he was invariably first to reach the ball. You also had to admire 'Doddy's' work rate. He always gave one hundred per cent and scored important goals in big games. Doddy was a grafter, who was underrated, in my view, but not by those who played alongside him.

Tommy McLean was a different type of winger from Willie Henderson, but he made a heck of a lot of Derek Johnstone's goals. Wee Tam could land the ball on a sixpence and his knowledge of the game was excellent, as were his deliveries from dead ball situations.

I suppose Davie Cooper was reminiscent of Jim Baxter in some ways. He possessed a great left foot, like Jim, but was unable to use his right to the same effect as Baxter. 'Coop' also had his best years at the beginning and end of his career, while the middle part wasn't quite what it might have been. I played with and managed Coop, so I knew his strengths and weaknesses. I became aware early on not to do overlapping forty- or fifty-yard runs, because Coop would use you as a decoy, but he didn't like checking back.

Coop was happiest when he had a free role. However, give him the ball when he was in the mood and Coop was terrific. He was so talented and it was testimony to his all-round sporting prowess that nobody could ever beat him at head tennis. Davie had as good a left foot as I have seen and if he had been blessed with the same sort of pace as Henderson or Johnston he could have played for any team in the world, but sometimes he just wasn't switched on.

When Coop joined Motherwell in the latter stages of his career and was given a free role he revelled in it. He was a big fish in a small pond and the way he passed the ball he brought the best out in others. It's just so sad that he is no longer with us after dying at such a ridiculously young age from a brain haemorrhage.

Colin Stein was Scotland's first £100,000 footballer and an old-fashioned centre-forward who rumbled up the opposition. He was also fortunate to get off to a flier when he grabbed a hat-trick against Arbroath on his debut, just days after joining us from Hibs. Colin had a great attitude and couldn't have cared less who he was playing against. He just went out and gave it his best shot, without fear or intimidation – he was a great, brave competitor. But, like Jim Baxter and Willie Johnston, I always felt that Colin made a mistake in deciding to move south – in his case to Coventry City. When he eventually returned to Rangers he wasn't the same player he had been previously. Colin was also one of those lucky sods who excelled at most sports. He played off a handicap of just one at golf and later became an outstanding bowls player.

At an age when most teenagers are still giving thought to their future, Derek Johnstone was thrust into the limelight in the most dramatic fashion possible when he scored that winning goal against Celtic in the 1970 League Cup final at just sixteen years old. But even at that tender age I spotted something in Derek that suggested to me that he possessed the qualities necessary to one day become captain of Rangers. Sandy Jardine was the obvious candidate to eventually succeed me as captain at that point, but I felt that Derek would be a more beneficial choice in the long term and I began sharing a room with him on trips, so I could pass on the benefit of my experience. Derek suffered to an extent from his versatility. He was capable of scoring thirty goals a season, but he liked playing centre-half, in much the same way as John Charles had alternated between the two positions. However, he was an outstanding player who was big, strong and brave and excellent in the air.

Jock Stein didn't do Rangers any favours during Celtic's nine-in-a-row years, but he certainly did me one when he recommended that I sign Jim Bett from Belgian side, Lokeren. Jim was a natural. He was imbued with the competitive Scottish spirit, but played the game in a continental fashion from his time in Belgium and the period he had spent in Iceland. Jim had a great idea of how the game should be played and wanted to make short passes, which he was excellent at doing, and diagonal runs. He should have made a lot more of his career, but he was maybe too quiet for his own good, although I admired him nonetheless.

Brian Laudrup was one of the truly great Rangers players and one I was very close to, after I was detailed to look after him when he signed for the club. He was also a player I would go out of my way to pay big money to watch – and there are not many I can say that about. Laudrup was a true entertainer and you could hear the buzz of expectation from the fans every time he got the ball. I was amazed at the way he could accelerate from a standing start, be up to full speed within five yards and then stop dead in his tracks.

Apart from supplying the ammunition, Laudrup was also capable of scoring his share of goals, but I genuinely believe that he was embarrassed about scoring. He seemed to derive much more pleasure from making goals. When Gordon Durie scored a hat-trick in the 5–1 Scottish Cup final win over Hearts in 1996, I was convinced that Laudrup could have achieved the same, but instead he elected to set them up for his team-mate.

Laudrup is a genuinely nice man, who was graceful in the way he played the game and glided past opponents. I would have hated to have played against him. In 1998, after Rangers, Laudrup joined Chelsea and starred in that summer's World Cup for Denmark, but just three months into his Stamford Bridge deal he sensationally quit and returned home to FC Copenhagen, before eventually announcing his retirement.

*

I just wish he had stayed around for a while longer, but when I asked Brian why he had called it a day, when it was patently obvious that he had a couple more seasons in him, he told me he had grown tired of the demands of training and preparing for matches. But no matter that I disagreed with his decision, Brian Laudrup was a truly Great Dane.

What can I say about Paul Gascoigne that hasn't been said before? Gazza was the nearest I have seen to Jim Baxter, in as much that he has the same confidence in his own ability, with every bit as much self-belief as Jim. What a talent! Gazza's hat-trick against Aberdeen in 1996, when Rangers clinched an eighth successive league title encapsulated a wonderful performance. I don't think I have seen many better individual performances, but I wonder whether Gazza made the most of his sublime skills. When Gazza was discarded by Glenn Hoddle on the eve of the 1998 World Cup finals, I felt heart-sorry for him. The fact was, though, that his fitness was clearly not what it should have been and he had denied himself the chance to make a final appearance on the biggest stage of all.

For all his faults and problems, it was impossible not to warm to Gazza. He was a loveable rascal with an astonishing ability to land himself in hot water – and others along with him. I well remember the day he asked to swap cars with me. I was driving a club-sponsored Honda Accord and he had a top-of-the-range two-seater BMW, but he explained that he required a roomier motor, because he had his close pal, Jimmy 'Five Bellies' and a cousin visiting, so I handed him the keys to my car.

I warned him to look after my motor, but moments later I was standing at the front door at Ibrox when Gazza flashed past me doing 70 mph and honking the horn in an attempt to wind me up. To be honest, I had half-expected that sort of reaction, but I was totally unprepared for what happened next. I went off to the gym for a work-out and switched on the radio, only to hear on the local news that police were investigating a death threat against Gazza. Here I was about to drive home in a car you couldn't fail to notice, complete with tinted windows, and someone was threatening to shoot the owner. Needless to say, I insisted on having my car back first thing the following morning.

You could never remain angry with Gazza for long, though, even when you were detailed to act as his chauffeur, as I was when he was ordered home from a trip to New York by the manager, Walter Smith. Gazza had been given permission to take time off to recover from an injury, but he was supposed to spend the time relaxing away from the spotlight. Instead he elected to fly to the States for the weekend to watch the St Patrick's Day Parade. That was bad enough, but much worse was to follow when the Monday morning tabloids carried front page pictures of Gazza sitting with a bunch of Celtic fans and clearly enjoying a few drinks. Walter went ballistic and word was sent to Gazza to catch the first available flight home.

I was dispatched to pick up him and his agent, Mel Stein, at Glasgow Airport and I was fortunate enough to be given clearance to drive on to the tarmac, so we could avoid the waiting horde of journalists who had gathered to report the latest instalment in the story. But when Gazza and Stein emerged from the aircraft they couldn't understand what all the fuss was about. 'What's he done wrong?' asked Stein. 'Gazza,' I replied, 'the only way you could have beaten that was to have led the parade sitting astride a white elephant.' Stein responded by declaring, 'That's a great line for your next book, Gazza.'

For all that I admired Gazza, the lad obviously had problems. But would he have been the same player without the troubles that dogged his career? Possibly not. He might have started worrying about the game in the same way that Willie Johnston did and never have become the player he was at his peak. Perhaps Gazza didn't get as much from his career as he should have, but for a few years at least he was a supreme entertainer and he was loved by the fans.

Ally McCoist wasn't always loved and there was a period in his Rangers career when he became a victim of the boo-boys, but by the time Coisty left Rangers to join Kilmarnock, in the twilight of his career, he had become an idol of the Rangers fans.

I had first tried to sign Coisty for Rangers as a fifteen-year-old, but he decided to join St Johnstone instead. He quickly made a big impression at Perth and I again made a move for him when I learned that St Johnstone were prepared to sell him, only to be told that Coisty had set his heart on playing in England. Why Coisty chose Sunderland I have no idea, but it turned out to be the wrong move for him.

He never managed to make much of an impression at Roker Park and when I received a call from Iain Munro, who was at Sunderland at the same time, informing me that Coisty was available, I reactivated my interest. Munro, who had been a Rangers player, warned me that both Aberdeen and Celtic were also interested, but I had a slight advantage in that I knew the Sunderland manager, Welshman Alan Durban, from playing against him in international games and I quickly organised a meeting.

We eventually agreed a transfer fee, which was less than half what I had originally offered to St Johnstone. I think we had been prepared to pay Saints £375,000, but in actual fact I got Coisty for around £160,000. Once the deal had been agreed I met Coisty at a hotel in Carlisle and we quickly agreed personal terms, but I was about to discover to my cost that nothing is ever straightforward where Coisty is concerned.

I had arranged for a press conference to be held at Ibrox to announce the signing. I impressed upon Coisty the need for us to make quick time to Glasgow, but we had only gone a few miles when Coisty flashed his lights, signalling me to pull over into a petrol station. Coisty was almost out of petrol, but he informed me rather sheepishly that I would have to pay, because he had no money. Come to think of it, I am not sure that he ever reimbursed me! But he repaid me and Rangers many times over with the goals he scored. Coisty did go through a rough patch, when the goals dried up temporarily and some fans got on his back, but I was amazed when I learned that my successor as manager, Jock Wallace, had been prepared to sell him.

Graeme Souness also dropped Coisty and stuck him on the substitutes' bench for so long that he earned the nickname of 'The Judge', but there have been few more prolific goal-scorers. I never saw Coisty play as a schoolboy, but I was impressed by the way he scored goals of the sort that were way above his age group when he was a teenager. He could score seemingly from nothing, because of his great movement. Coisty was a natural, but he was almost too good-looking to be a footballer. He was the sort you would take home to meet your mother – but not your daughter! Coisty was not only an outstanding player for Rangers, he was also a marvellous ambassador for the club, because of his infectious personality. I have always found him to be a very respectful individual, too.

I recall being close to tears when the squad broke up after the 1998 Scottish Cup final against Hearts, because it was the end of an era. Walter was also leaving to take charge of Everton, but I felt it most when I looked at Coisty and Ian Durrant, because I had signed them both and I felt sad when I was leaving the post-match reception.

The term 'True Blue' might have been coined with Ian Durrant in mind, because he is the epitome of a real Rangers man. Born just along the road from Ibrox, Durranty was a fan and still is. The story goes that he climbed over the wall to watch my testimonial match and I joke with him that I only gave him a fiver when he signed, because I didn't have a single pound note in my pocket.

Durranty was a bag of bones when I first clapped eyes on him, but it was clear from the outset that he could play all right. I could see early on that he had the makings of a great player. There are some players that you have to keep coaching in the hope that they will develop. Others you can coach, but they invariably do things off the cuff and Durranty was one of the latter. He had natural ability, wonderful vision and awareness that enabled him to read situations before they fully developed. He was also one of the few players capable of getting in front of the ball from midfield and making runs into the box. He was always prepared to take a chance and that mentality paid off in the form of the great goals he scored.

For such a slightly built lad, Durranty was solid and had unbelievable reserves of energy. It was a tragedy when he suffered an horrific injury playing against Aberdeen at Pittodrie in October 1988, when Neil Simpson's challenge ripped his right knee apart. He was never quite the same player after that, but it was amazing that he even made it back, because his knee is one hell of a mess.

However, even though Durranty lost something as a consequence of that reckless challenge by Simpson, he remained a cut above the majority of his rivals. In fact, he told me recently that Marseille were keen to sign him after he scored the equaliser with a classic swerving half-volley against the French side in a Champions League match in 1993. I am delighted that Durranty was invited to return to the club recently in a coaching capacity, because he is a Rangers man at heart and as a player he was a one-off.

CHAPTER 18
SEEING RED

Given the reputation I had with some people of being a 'hard man', it will come as a major surprise to many that I saw red only three times in my career – a record of which I am fairly proud. Sure, I was booked more times than I care to remember, but I think the facts bear out my contention that I was not a 'dirty' player who set out with the express intention of injuring opponents. I played the game hard, but I also tried to play fair within the rules. I was capable of 'sorting out' opponents who tried to do the 'dirty' on me and I never shirked a tackle, but while I always played to win, I refused to do so at all costs.

Although the record shows that I was sent off three times in eighteen years, as far as I'm concerned I deserved my punishment only once – when I hooked Joe Smith of Aberdeen for deliberately trying to injure me. The first time I walked I did so on the grounds of intent, rather than as the result of a premeditated act of violence. The second time was a joke, but I am prepared to hold my hands up and admit that my third and final sending off was fully justified.

Don't laugh. The first time I saw red I was the victim of a Russian referee who couldn't tell the difference between the aggressor and the aggrieved. In October 1968 Rangers were playing the second leg of a Fairs Cities Cup tie against Vojvodina in Yugoslavia when one of their players swung a punch at me and the pair of us ended up being ordered off. Exactly what I did wrong I don't know. The Vojvodina player in question was a fellow by the name of Trivic. Bobby Moore had warned me about him when we had met on holiday a few months earlier, because he was the same player who had been involved when Alan Mullery had become the first England player to receive a red card.

Trivic was captain of Vojvodina and when he put in what I considered to be an over-the-top challenge on one of our players, I immediately ran across to try to defuse the situation. The next thing I knew Trivic had tried to stiffen me. In actual fact, his punch missed, but I fell back anyway and when I was getting back on my feet the referee was pointing in the direction of the dressing rooms. I couldn't believe it. He was sending the pair of us off and it was a long walk back. The stadium reminded me of Wembley, with the dressing rooms at the back of one of the goals and a wide track running round the pitch, which had resembled a lake the previous evening. The heavens had opened to the extent that it was impossible to train on the surface, which was covered by thousands of tiny frogs, hopping about.

However, I had more to worry about as I made my way down the touchline. The vastness of the stadium meant it was exposed to the fans and the locals began to pelt me with fir tree cones, but, amazingly, instead of leaving me to my fate, Trivic put his arm round my shoulder and they stopped. The pair of us actually stood together at the side of the pitch and watched the remainder of the game, which resulted in a 1–0 defeat for us, but as we had established a two-goal advantage in the first leg that was enough to take us through to the second round.

In those days there was no such thing as charter flights and we travelled by scheduled aircraft. As a consequence, we were unable to fly back straight after the game and had to spend an extra night in Vojvodina. Davie White was manager at the time and it was decided that we should attend the post-match banquet, in spite of what had happened. Imagine my surprise, though, when Trivic approached me and asked me to accompany him to where the referee and the two linesmen were sitting. The next thing I heard was Trivic telling the referee that I was innocent and, to my amazement, the Russian agreed not to make any mention of my sending off in his report.

That effectively meant I was free to play in the next round against Dundalk, who we beat, 9–1 on aggregate. We scored six in the first leg at Ibrox and Davie White thought it best to leave me out of the return just in case, but Rangers never heard any more about the sending off and there was never any mention of a suspension.

It would never do to put the boot into a Knight of the Realm, but Sir Alex Ferguson was just plain 'Fergie' the second time I saw red, on 5 September 1970, after aiming a kick at my former Rangers team-mate. Fergie had moved on to Falkirk when we faced them in a first division match at Ibrox and he was obviously keen to put one over on Rangers. But I drew the line at being elbowed and when Fergie did that to me I reacted in anger and swung my boot at him. I missed completely, but when the referee ran up to me I admitted I had been out of order. 'I'm sorry, ref,' I said. 'I deserve to be yellow carded.' He responded by saying, 'You deserve more than that – you're being sent off.'

The referee was Bert Padden from Saltcoats in Ayrshire and I didn't take too kindly to being red-carded. Before leaving the pitch I had a few words for the official, which included advising him he would be in trouble with the SFA, because Rangers were a big club with friends in high places. I also declared that I would get him back somehow. In actual fact Padden did me a favour of sorts, because my pal's daughter was being married in Edinburgh and it meant I got back to the capital in time for the meal in the evening.

But, all joking apart, I was not at all happy. Neither was Fergie. I was lying in the slipper bath raging at my misfortune when I was suddenly pushed under the water. When I resurfaced and looked up, Fergie was standing over me. 'What are you doing here?' I asked. 'I've been sent off as well,' he replied. In the event I was given a two-week suspension and Fergie received a one-match ban. We were also fined for what I considered to be an overreaction on the part of the referee.

The next time I encountered Bert Padden was when he was appointed to take charge of a league match at Ibrox. I cannot recall who we were playing, but I do remember that when Padden came to the dressing room to check the players' boots I was deliberately unhelpful. 'Can I see your boots?' he requested. 'They're sitting there,' I said, pointing to my footwear. 'Help yourself, because I don't want to speak to you. You were out of order sending me off.'

I even refused to toss the coin to decide ends. I had vowed to get Padden back and there was no way I was going to assist him and make his life any easier. However, I hadn't figured on the referee keeling over as a result of suffering a heart attack in the middle of the game. I was just about to play the ball out of the penalty box when I heard Alex MacDonald shout to me to boot it out of play. That was never usually a problem, but this time I did so through choice. It was a freezing cold evening and when I turned round and saw Padden lying in the penalty area, I imagined he had pulled a muscle. When he was put on a stretcher and carried past me to the dressing room I took pleasure in reminding him that it was pay-back time, but you can imagine how I felt when I learned Bert had suffered a heart attack. I met his daughter at an Open golf championship at Turnberry a few years back and she reminded me of the occasion. Thankfully, she was also able to tell me that her dad was doing fine.

I took my third and last 'walk of shame' at Pittodrie on 30 April 1977. Bob Valentine was the referee and, to make matters worse, Aberdeen beat us, 2–1. I'd had a running feud of sorts with Joe Smith, brother of Jimmy, who had featured in a £100,000 transfer from Aberdeen to Newcastle some years earlier. We just didn't see eye to eye and the mutual dislike had led to one or two hefty challenges. But what Smith did that day was inexcusable. He challenged me with his studs showing and a less experienced player than me could easily have ended up with a broken leg.

I was playing left-back and was about to play a long ball out of defence when the incident happened. I was on the point of swinging at the ball when Smith came across me with the sole of his boot raised and I was wise enough to realise that if I followed through he would catch me and the force of the contact could leave me crocked. I pulled back and Smith missed my leg, but as he went past me he elbowed me in the face. Now, I can't stand anyone touching my face and I reacted in fury. I grabbed Smith and twisted him round to face me – and landed a right hook flush on his chin.

Smith collapsed in a heap and was out cold before he hit the deck. I had never hit anyone like that in my life and the Aberdeen trainer had to use smelling salts to bring Smith round. When he did and realised what had happened he made to have another go at me and I made to hit him again. The trouble was all of this had taken place in full view of the linesman, who was standing just a couple of yards away.

The referee quite correctly pointed out that I had lifted my hands and added that he had no option but to send me off. I argued that Smith had deliberately tried to injure me and followed up by elbowing me in the face, but I couldn't really complain. The fact that I had chinned an opponent meant I was guilty, but so was Smith and he escaped, which was infuriating.

My sending off came just a week before the Scottish Cup final, where we were to meet Celtic at Hampden. By a remarkable coincidence, Bob Valentine had also been appointed to take charge of the showpiece game of the season and I was only too well aware of the fact. As it happened, Sandy Jardine and I always made a point of catching the Aberdeen-Glasgow express before changing trains at Dundee and joining the Edinburgh connection. We did so because there was a full restaurant car service on the Aberdeen-Glasgow train, so we were able to have a meal.

Bob, who was from Dundee, and his linesmen caught the same train and we were tucking into our grub when one of the linesmen appeared in the restaurant car. When I asked where Bob was, the linesman explained that he was a little embarrassed about what had happened and had decided to maintain a low profile. I told him there was no need for Bob to feel bad and sent a message inviting him to join us for a drink. Sandy thought I had lost my marbles until I explained that, with the Cup final coming up, there was method in my madness.

Bob joined us and I bought him a few beers, also making the point that I hoped there would be no hangover from the Pittodrie game. I was assured that the slate had been wiped clean, but, lo and behold, seven days later, Bob gave Celtic the penalty that won them the Cup, adjudging that Derek Johnstone had handled a shot from Johannes Edvaldsson on the line.

As I said previously, it was a questionable decision to say the least and I went off my head. I gave Bob dog's abuse and reminded him that he had been happy to accept my hospitality the week before. I was wasting my breath, of course, but I suppose I should consider myself fortunate that I was free to play in the final. Under the present rules I would have missed out, because a red card for violent conduct results in an automatic suspension from the next game. I have never considered that ruling to be fair or just. My view is that any ban should be incurred for the competition in which the player was ordered off.

Tom 'Tiny' Wharton was, without doubt, one of the best referees Scotland has ever produced. He stood 6ft 5ins and weighed around 18 stone – hence his nickname – and automatically commanded respect because of his size, although he also earned that respect through his style of refereeing and knowledge of the game. Tiny always treated me well and we used to have a natter on the pitch, because at that time, in the 1960s, you were able to talk to referees. Tiny didn't so much run as perambulate round the pitch and many a time he would say to me, as he glided past, 'Mr Greig, I have twice given you the benefit of the doubt. Don't let there be a third time.'

Tiny would give you a couple of chances. He always also used the prefix 'Mr' and you felt obliged to address him in a similar manner. This led to several amusing exchanges. For example, if I disagreed with his decision I would say, 'Mr Wharton that was a terrible decision.' Tiny would then ask, 'Why is that, Mr Greig?' to which I would reply, 'It wasn't a goal. The scorer was offside.' Tiny was always adamant. 'It was a goal, Mr Greig.' 'No, sorry you're wrong, Mr Wharton' I would persist, but Tiny always had the last word. Eventually he would bring the exchange to an abrupt ending by declaring, 'Mr Greig, when you read the Sunday newspapers tomorrow you will find that a goal was scored. So who is right and who is wrong?' There was no answer to that.

Tiny was in charge of a game at Tynecastle when the Hearts player, Johnny Hamilton, with whom I was friendly, had a difference of opinion with him. Now, as it happened, Johnny wore dentures and was forced to play minus his teeth. This meant he spoke in a strange and amusing manner, but he was still able to make himself understood and when I whacked him with a heavy tackle at the Gorgie end of the ground and the challenge went unpunished, Johnny reacted in fury. 'That was an effing foul, ref,' shouted Johnny. 'Are you in the Masons the same as this lot? The only colour you can see is blue.' Eventually, the ball ran out of play and Tiny called Johnny over, but Johnny was incredulous. 'Don't tell me you're effing going to book me,' spluttered Johnny. 'No, I am not, Mr Hamilton,' replied Tiny. 'Please go and join your teeth in the dressing room!'

One of the things I liked about Tiny was the way he treated players as adults. He didn't wag his finger and make you walk twenty yards to be reprimanded. He appreciated that football is a tough game, full of hard tackles, and he reacted with common sense. Tiny revealed to me that if he was having a problem making players see sense, he would send someone off, and if that didn't have an instant effect he would quickly balance up the sides again with a second ordering off, and so on until the message got through. Tiny also told me that when he was a young man he had been given a trial, but at the end of the game the two fellows running the team advised him that he would never make it as a footballer – because his brains were too far from his feet!

There was no shortage of characters among the referees of my generation. Bobby Davidson was another excellent referee, although a touch officious. Then there was JRP Gordon of Dundee. John had a habit of telling the press photographers that he would appreciate a print if they happened to take a particularly good shot of him in action.

I made several visits to SFA headquarters in Glasgow's Park Gardens, more often than not to appeal against a caution, because Jock Wallace had a terrible habit of making the players lodge an official protest, irrespective of the circumstances. On one occasion, having requested a personal hearing from the association's disciplinary committee, I drafted an appeal running to six pages, because I was in danger of missing a big game – I can't remember exactly which one – as a consequence of being booked. However, by the time I appeared before the 'beaks' I had picked up another caution and the timing of the second booking meant I would serve my suspension before the game in question.

When I appeared at my appeal hearing the chairman of the committee commented that I had written an extensive report, before asking if I had anything to add. When I said, 'Yes,' he nearly fell off his chair, but he told me to proceed and I duly informed the assembled company that I wished to withdraw my appeal on the grounds that, having reflected on events, I considered that I was very probably guilty as charged. The committee knew I was 'using' the system to suit my own ends, but they went along with my request anyway and that was the end of the matter.

Things didn't always work out quite so well though. I had thought I was on to a good thing the first time I was sent off along with Fergie, but on that occasion things backfired on me. Shortly before I appeared before the disciplinary committee, I bumped into Jimmy Aitken, who was SFA President and whom I had got to know on Scotland duty, and he assured me he would look after me when my case came up. When I sat down to face my accusers, though, no sooner had the chairman read out the charge than Jimmy announced that he would have to leave as he had another urgent appointment. He then stood up and walked out. Without Jimmy's support I ended up being handed a two-match suspension.

I was somewhat more fortunate on another occasion. Brian McGinley, another referee who was a cut above the majority of his colleagues, had booked me for a tackle and I was appealing as usual. Brian's report contained the comment that I had 'arrived an hour late' when making my challenge. I replied that I had got there as quickly as possible and added that, while I was not the quickest thing on two legs, an hour seemed a slight exaggeration, as Allan Wells had done the Olympic sprint in a time of around ten seconds. So it would hardly have taken me sixty minutes to complete a distance of fifteen yards – even at my age. Not surprisingly, I won my argument, the case was dismissed and my caution expunged from the records.

Even when I stopped playing my visits to Park Gardens did not cease entirely. When Dick Advocaat was Rangers manager he once sent me with Jorg Alberts to help in the German's defence of a charge that he had criticised referees in the Scottish press. That sort of thing is frowned upon by the SFA, but it's perfectly permissible for a player to pass comment on a match official in the German media and Jorg had assumed he was free to do so in Scotland. Consequently, he got away with it.

I suppose the only time I actually enjoyed receiving a summons to Park Gardens was when I got a telephone call from Ernie Walker, the former SFA secretary, asking to see me. I was working in the travel industry at the time and Ernie was keen for me to make arrangements for the Scotland team for a match in Spain. Ernie ended our discussion by informing me that if I ever required a couple of match tickets all I had to do was pick up the phone. I immediately burst out laughing at the kind offer and Ernie was somewhat bemused by my reaction. He asked what I found so funny and I replied, 'Ernie, most times I have come here in the past it was to be fined or suspended. It makes a welcome change for it not to actually be costing me money to visit this place.'

CHAPTER 19

SUCH EXALTED COMPANY

Pele, Eusebio, Di Stefano, Puskas, Beckenbauer, Cruyff, Best, Charlton and Moore. What would that lot be worth in today's crazy world of multi-million pound deals? I can't even offer a guess, but I can offer an assessment of them as football players, because I had the good fortune to play against them. Sharing the same pitch was an honour and a privilege, and they were great players in an age of outstanding ones.

My one regret is that I never had the opportunity to take part in the World Cup or European Championship finals, but I did at least rub shoulders with many who did – and Pele was the best of them all. I encountered the player generally regarded as the greatest of all time at Hampden in June 1966, just prior to the World Cup finals in England, when the Brazilians played Scotland in a friendly. We had missed out, after finishing behind Italy in our qualifying section, but we at least had the consolation of meeting the holders of the Jules Rimet trophy.

So much has been written about Pele that I don't have to list his achievements, but suffice to say that he had everything. If there is such a thing as the complete football player, Pele was that person, but it may surprise some to learn that Pele was not only a wonderful player, he was a hard bugger as well and capable of looking after himself. I was taken aback by his remarkable upper body strength and powerful thighs.

Eusebio was exactly the same. The legendary Benfica and Portugal star was built like a tank and when you tackled him your whole body shuddered. I was at right-back against Brazil and Billy Bremner played directly in front of me. I suppose we must have done OK, because we drew, 1–1, with Stevie Chalmers of Celtic getting our goal.

Pele was special, but Alfredo Di Stefano and Ferenc Puskas weren't bad either. Real Madrid's legendary strike force were in the twilight of their careers when, in September 1963, Rangers were drawn to play the Spanish giants in the preliminary round of the European Cup, but they were far from past it. One flash of genius from Gento – one of the quickest players I have ever seen – three minutes from time in the first leg at Ibrox sealed our fate, as the winger raced half the length of the field before crossing for Puskas who slammed the ball into the net. But Puskas was far from finished with us and his hat-trick in the return a fortnight later left us on the receiving end of a six-goal thrashing.

My first memory of Puskas was watching him help destroy England at Wembley in 1953, when the Hungarians shattered the myth of England's invincibility on their own patch. Seven years later I saw him for the first time in the flesh, when the magnificent Real Madrid team beat Eintracht Frankfurt, 7–3, to claim a fifth consecutive European Cup triumph. Little did I think that one day I would eyeball the 'Galloping Major' on the same pitch. Perhaps I should have been more careful about what I wished for. By the time our paths crossed, Puskas was thirty-six, but the 'old man' was still some operator. He was deceptive, because he was all left foot, but what a left peg it was. It was like a magic wand and he was still weaving spells, because of his remarkable speed of thought and sharpness.

Di Stefano was no less prolific. He, too, was technically past his sell-by date, but age had not diminished his talents. Di Stefano was what I would describe as the first of the deep-lying centre-forwards, with marvellous all-round vision and control allied to superb dribbling skills and a lethal finish. Not so long ago I had the honour of meeting Di Stefano again, in Monaco, when he presented me with an award on behalf of UEFA in recognition of Rangers' achievement of winning a hundred trophies. It was the nearest I got to Di Stefano in forty years, but I was glad to see that he was no longer limping!

Franz Beckenbauer was a genius. The 'Kaiser' could play sweeper, but he was at his best when he was dictating tactics from midfield. Beckenbauer rarely made a mistake and his coolness and awareness of how the game was unfolding around him, allied to his distribution skills, made him a world-class player.

Johann Cruyff had balance, skill, speed and was naturally two-footed, but I would rather have faced the Dutchman than George Best. Best was a nightmare to play against. At his peak he ran at defenders and was prepared to take on the whole defence in one movement. In some ways Best reminded me of Jimmy Johnstone, only quicker and more direct. Besides being blessed with a god-given talent, Best, like so many of the truly outstanding players, was also supremely self-confident.

Scotsmen aren't supposed to have anything good to say about the English, but there are exceptions and Jimmy Greaves, Sir Bobby Charlton and the late Bobby Moore were three of my favourites. Greaves was the sort of player you couldn't take your eyes off even for a split second, otherwise the ball was in the back of the net. He had remarkable speed of thought and movement and could score goals out of almost nothing. He was one of the best finishers ever. The only two strikers who ran him close in the art of 'poaching' goals were Gerd Muller of Bayern Munich and Uwe Seeler of Hamburg.

Both these Germans were stocky and powerful and incredible in the air.

Bobby Charlton was what I would class as a model professional. He didn't kick opponents and he steered clear of confrontation with referees. The way he opened up play with his graceful movement and pace was also exciting to watch. Charlton could suddenly switch the play to the other side of the pitch and hit shots with tremendous power and accuracy. I would have chosen Charlton for any world eleven, because he was a graceful thoroughbred and the genius in Sir Alf Ramsey's team. He was also the complete gentleman and I never heard a player criticise or complain about him.

Bobby Moore was not the quickest off the mark, but he had a unique football brain and the ability to read situations before they developed. In fact, he didn't need to be fast, because of the immaculate timing of his interceptions and challenges, and his ability to emerge with the ball and make telling passes. I played against Bobby several times, including the never-to-be-forgotten 3–2 win at Wembley in 1967, and he was a man I warmed to. I remember after that game we joined the England players for a reception at the Café Royal and Bobby came across to speak to Ronnie Simpson and I after the meal was over.

It could not have been easy for him, given the result, and I appreciated the gesture, but I was slightly taken aback when he said, 'It's OK for you two. Your season is over and you can go and enjoy yourselves. I'm off to Houston first thing in the morning with West Ham to try out this new Astro Turf they're all talking about.' I looked at Bobby and smiled. 'Just a minute,' I said. 'Ronnie's got a European Cup semi-final next week and I'm playing in the Cup-Winners' Cup semi-finals.' Bobby blushed at his faux pas and then burst out laughing.

We met up again the following year, on holiday in Majorca, when we found ourselves staying at the same hotel in Palma. It was my second visit there and the previous year I had organised a game against the hotel waiters. With the captain of the World Cup holders in residence they were desperate to organise another match and begged me to ask Bobby to play. However, when I approached Bobby he told me he didn't feel like playing, because he had a badly blocked ear caused by swimming in the hotel pool, but I eventually persuaded him to play for five minutes to keep the locals happy. Billy McNeill had just left after a family holiday, but his Celtic team-mate, Willie Wallace, was staying at the hotel and he also took part. I remember we had to wear black armbands as a mark of respect for the hotel gardener who had just died. Despite his initial reluctance, Bobby played the whole game, much to the delight of the opposition and the locals – and myself, because I was captain and that meant the England skipper played under me.

My boss at Rangers at the time, Davie White, was also staying at the same hotel with his wife, Jean, and the hotel manager invited all of us to his home that evening for dinner. The drink flowed with each course, but Willie Wallace wasn't much of a drinker and he soon succumbed to the effects of alcohol, to the extent that he ended up steaming drunk. Eventually, Willie's wife, Olive, asked me if I would escort her husband back to the hotel and I agreed. On the way back, Willie was desperate to relieve himself and I led him behind a tree where he was instantly sick all over my suit. Despite this inconvenience, I led Willie back to his room and put him to bed, because he was in no fit state to undress himself.

The holiday over, the next time I saw Willie was just an hour or so before the first Old Firm game of the following season, a League Cup tie at Ibrox. Normally, I never spoke to a soul before these games, but who should I meet when I walked through the front door at Ibrox but Willie, who insisted on showing me his holiday snaps. No mention was made of me having looked after him when he was throwing up or tucking him up in his bed because he had been incapable of looking after himself. No, sir. Willie repaid me with an elbow in the face and then added insult to injury by scoring both Celtic's goals in a 2–0 win.

When it came to strikers there was none braver or more aggressive than Denis Law. My Scotland team-mate may have looked puny, but he had the heart of a lion and would have fought with his shadow. Denis was a tiger who loved playing against England – and hated losing to them because of the stick he took from his English team-mates at Old Trafford. He was also deceptively strong and fought for every ball, but it was in the air that Denis really excelled. He seemed to have the capacity to actually hang in the air when he jumped for the ball. When you met him for the first time, Denis made an instant impression and he had an almost magical aura, because of his personality. I remember early in my international career, when the squad was based at Largs on the Ayrshire coast, going to Denis's room just to chat to him. He sat with a pot of tea and a packet of fags and regaled me with fascinating tales. Denis is quite a private person, but he was a truly great player.

John White never had a great deal to say, preferring to do his talking on the pitch, where he displayed sublime skills. John tragically died at the peak of his career after the tree he was sheltering under on a London golf course was struck by lightning, but he had already left his mark on the game. John was a key member of the great Spurs team of the early 1960s. I didn't play in either of the games when Rangers faced Spurs in the Cup-Winners' Cup in the 1962–63 season, when they went on to lift the trophy, but to appreciate the value of a player like John White I didn't have to.

John was ahead of his time. He had great vision and was an integral part of Spurs' pass-and-run style of play. Yet, a lot of the bigger clubs rejected him when he started out at Falkirk, largely on the grounds of his slight build. However, Bill Nicholson, the Spurs manager, was more astute. Nicholson went to see John while he was doing his National Service and had the foresight to quiz the PE instructor, who informed him that John won every cross-country race hands down. That was enough for Nicholson, who immediately signed him.

John was undoubtedly a great guy, but that wasn't quite how I felt about him on the eve of my Scotland debut in April 1964. The team was staying at Kilmacolm in Renfrewshire and I was chosen to room with John. We had gone to bed, but I suddenly woke with a start at 3 a.m. It seemed that all hell had broken loose. There was all sorts of shouting and bawling coming from the adjoining bed. John was having a dream of some sort and I was part of his nightmare – like it or not. John went straight back to sleep, but I lay awake for hours afterwards – not exactly the ideal preparation for someone about to face a baptism of fire against England. John was originally from Musselburgh and for a number of years they held an annual five-a-side tournament in his memory, which Rangers participated in.

Billy Bremner is another who is sadly no longer with us, but the wee man won't ever be forgotten by those who played with and against him. Billy was an out-and-out competitor and the bigger the reputations of those he was playing against, the more he responded to the challenge. Billy was as hard as nails and would have tried to run through walls if you had asked him to. He could tackle and pass the ball and had a great awareness of the game, which I think he got from Don Revie.

I could go on to name a whole host of other outstanding players who helped enhance my career, but just to have walked on to the same pitch as the ones I have mentioned was mind-boggling.

Great managers help make great players, of course, and there can be little doubt that Sir Alf Ramsey's achievement in masterminding

England's World Cup triumph was a momentous feat. Sir Alf was not short of critics. Considering he achieved so much and took England to the pinnacle of world football, the number of Englishmen who subsequently sniped at him and questioned his management skills never ceased to amaze me.

If Sir Alf had been a Scot and guided Scotland to the World Cup, the Tartan Army would have built a statue to him, but, naturally, he was not the most popular man north of the Tweed. The Auld Enemy winning the World Cup did not go down well with at least five million inhabitants of the British Isles.

My one and only direct encounter with Sir Alf happened in 1969, when I was selected for the Great Britain squad to play Wales in Cardiff as part of the celebrations to mark Prince Charles' investiture as Prince of Wales. However, my father was regrettably rushed into hospital just before I was due to report for international duty. Dad had been admitted to hospital to have his appendix removed. That's not normally a life-threatening operation, but my old man hadn't enjoyed the best of health and he was also getting on in years, so in the circumstances I wasn't keen on the idea of travelling to Wales. However, he insisted that I go, telling me that he would watch the match on TV, so I travelled down on the Sunday by train. However, it turned into a hell of a journey and it took me hours to reach my destination. Nowadays, you just hop on a plane from any one of a number of Scottish airports and a couple of hours later you reach your destination, but back then travelling from Edinburgh to Cardiff was a little more complicated.

Sir Alf was in charge of the Great Britain squad and it was a huge honour to be chosen, but I had a bad feeling about making the trip from the outset and my worst fears were realised late on the Sunday evening, when I received a telephone call from my eldest brother, Alfie, informing me that my father had taken a turn for the worse.

I was sitting with Billy Bremner and Jack Charlton when the call came and Alfie warned me that my father was not expected to survive beyond the following day.

I immediately went to see Sir Alf and explained the situation to him. He was sitting with his trainer, Harold Shepherdson, having a cup of tea when I broke the news that I would have to return home as quickly as possible. Even though it was nearly midnight, I remember Sir Alf was dressed in a collar and tie and wearing a suit. Sir Alf told me to leave everything to him.

He arranged for me to receive an alarm call at 5.45 a.m. and I was also given tea and toast before setting out on my journey. Even at that ridiculously early hour Sir Alf was fully dressed when I came downstairs and was again wearing a collar and tie and a suit – a different outfit from the previous evening, I might add. He explained my travel arrangements, which involved taking a taxi to the railway station, where I was to catch the Paddington Express. Once I arrived in London I would be met by an FA official and driven to Heathrow, where I would catch a flight to Edinburgh. When I arrived back in Scotland I was met at the airport by my brother and was told the sad news that my dad had passed away, but I will never forget the kindness shown to me by Sir Alf. He was perceived by many to be aloof and distant, but I found him to be a gentleman of the old school.

My son, Murray, was just six weeks old when my dad died and I regret the fact that he didn't live longer, to see his grandson growing up. My father didn't have any airs and graces. He was a man of few words and I must have been about fifteen before I realised that my name wasn't, 'Hey, you.' I was small for my age and very picky with my food. In fact, I used to dread a Sunday when all the family sat down to dinner. The sight of me pushing my food round the plate drove my old man nuts and it wasn't long before there was a shout of, 'Hey, you,' quickly followed by a slap across the back of the head. However, meal times apart, we had a lot of laughs. We didn't have a TV, so we had to make our own entertainment and had not one but two pianos in the living room. With one of my brothers playing the piano, another the accordion and my dad using the door to improvise as a drum every party went with a swing. My own party piece involved me blackening my face with coal dust and doing an impersonation of Al Jolson singing 'Mammie'!

And talking of sing-songs, whenever Wales were in town for the bi-annual rugby international against Scotland at Murrayfield, our home was invaded by an army of Welsh fans. My sister, Margaret, had married a Welshman, Clive Jones. Clive was in the army and he, along with members of his family and assorted pals, formed a chorus after the match, no matter the score. It was wonderful and the neighbours would throw open their windows to listen to a medley of famous Welsh songs belted out at the tops of their voices.

Margaret's son, Mervyn, later went on to play for Hibs and I recall one occasion when she gave me a right earful, because she thought I'd been too rough with him when the pair of us were in direct opposition. I wonder what Pele's mum would have said to me?

CHAPTER 20
BOSS MAN

I knew when I broke out in a rash and the skin on my hands started flaking that, for the sake of my health, it was time to quit as Rangers manager. I had also been suffering from migraines for the first time in my life and some days I had to ask one of the ground staff to drive me home. No job is worth that. However, I have never ever regretted becoming manager of the club where I spent my entire playing career. On 24 May 1978, when I was asked to succeed Jock Wallace as boss, I couldn't say 'No,' so I said 'Yes'. I would have hated to have gone through the rest of my life wondering what might have been had I turned down the offer of what I consider to be the biggest job in Scottish football.

Willie Waddell had once made a statement that I would always remain part of the club, for as long as he was at Rangers, but I had never imagined that it would be as manager. I had thought that I might well return in a coaching capacity, but I had not considered the possibility that Jock would walk away to become manager of Leicester City. However, when Jock quit I instinctively knew that I would be in the frame to replace him. People have often asked me whether I feel I was too young for such a role, but I couldn't have refused the job. Had

I done so I might not have been asked again and I could never have taken that chance. Anyway, I have always believed that when I make a decision it is the correct one.

I had dreaded the thought of my playing career ending. I loved playing and had already signed for one more season when Jock took the decision to leave. The day Jock left I arrived home from watching my nephew, Davie Jones, play in a junior game for Arniston Rangers and I told Janette I was off to bed, because I had a big day ahead of me. When she asked what I meant by that statement, I told her that I would get the call from Ibrox the next day asking me to become the new Rangers manager. Janette told me not to be daft. She pointed out that Rangers has just won the treble and I had signed for one more season, but I knew differently.

Under the terms of my new deal I had a gentleman's agreement that if I wasn't playing for the first team I wouldn't be asked to turn out for the reserves, because I didn't want to deprive a young player of his chance. I had pointed out to Jock that I would be thirty-six the following September, but I felt that my experience might be a help to the team in Europe. I had also made it clear, though, that I wanted to go and watch the first team if I wasn't selected and that if I received an offer from another club that genuinely interested me I would be allowed to leave.

To be honest, I hadn't a clue what that actually meant, but the idea of playing and coaching in a place like Florida appealed to me, and I did fancy going to the States for a year to unwind and enjoy myself. However, the decision about my future was taken out of my hands. Rangers made it for me and in many ways I was glad, because that spared me from having to make what would have been a heart-breaking decision about when the time was right for me to hang up my boots. I played in the Scottish Cup final against Aberdeen on 6 May and less than three weeks later I was the manager of Rangers.

By a strange coincidence, Celtic also appointed a new manager that same month. Billy McNeill, who had been a Scotland team-mate and who was my counterpart as captain at Parkhead for many years, succeeded Jock Stein just a few days after I moved into the hot seat at Ibrox. Billy had served an apprenticeship with Aberdeen, so had not had to make the sudden transition from player to manager overnight. Perhaps if the circumstances had been different, it would have suited me to have done the same, but fate decreed otherwise.

I have been asked many times why I didn't opt to become player-manager, but that couldn't have happened, because the necessary back-up simply wasn't in place, as it was when Graeme Souness took on the dual role in 1986. Fitness wasn't a problem. I had lived like a monk for the previous five years, after attending a coaching school in Germany and realising that if I wanted to extend my career by several seasons I had to look after my body. I made sure I was in bed by 8 p.m. on the eve of a game and often I would go back to bed after training, to ensure that I had plenty of rest. To this day I am still an early bedder. I was also careful with my diet.

But the best laid plans and all that. The morning after Jock's resignation had been announced, Sandy Jardine and I went to the Commonwealth pool in Edinburgh for a sauna. Afterwards we met up with Janette and Sandy's wife, Shona, for lunch. But this time the press were on my trail and I recall Eric McCowat, a photographer I have known for years, following us about. After lunch I went to collect my son, Murray, from school and when we returned home, Janette informed me that Willie Waddell had phoned. When I returned his call I was told to get myself through to Glasgow straightaway. Janette was a bit uptight and I felt much the same, because I hadn't had time to prepare myself mentally for what was about to happen.

I can't say I was surprised when I met with Willie Waddell and the chairman, Rae Simpson, at Ibrox and they offered me the job. Up to that point, Rangers had had only six managers and the honour of becoming the seventh in 105 years was enormous. Strange as it may sound in the money-mad world of the modern game, I had no idea what sort of salary I should ask for. To be honest, the thought never even entered my mind. Not that it would have made any difference. I was told what my wage would be and that was it. I didn't ask for a contract either and wasn't offered one. That changed a year or so later, after we had beaten Juventus and PSV Eindhoven, but my view was that I didn't need a contract. Surely, if I respected the club they should respect me in turn? I don't know if I was offered the contract because the directors feared that I would walk away, there had been whispers linking me with PSV, but they had nothing to worry about.

Just after my appointment, knowing that I would have very little free time over the course of the next twelve months, Janette and I took ourselves off to Majorca for a fortnight's holiday. It was while I was there that I received a phone call from Willie Thornton, the Rangers assistant manager, with news of the European Cup draw. Rangers had been drawn against Juventus and they formed more than half the Italian national side. It represented a glamour tie, but a far from easy one. However, I was determined to leave no stone unturned and I reported for duty a week before the players, with the idea that I would test the training schedule I had drawn up on myself first, in the knowledge that I was fit and if I could get through it, so could the players.

Back then the club used the Albion training ground, which had one grass pitch and one ash surface, but each day before training could begin we had to clear broken glass off the pitch as a result of passers-by throwing bottles on to it. When I look at the standard of the training facilities the players enjoy at Murray Park now, I have to pinch myself to make sure I'm not dreaming.

Heads above the parapet. An anxious Rangers dug-out during the 1972
European Cup-Winners' Cup final.

Johnston ... .

Stein ...

Johnston again ... . And European glory was ours.

The joy and the pain. A fan lands on my injured foot at full-time in Barcelona.

We are the champions! Back row, standing from left to right: Alex Miller, Gerry Neef, Andy Penman, Sandy Jardine, Derek Parlane, Derek Johnstone, Peter McCloy, Dave Smith (bending down), Bobby Watson. Front row, crouching from left to right: Jim Denny, Tommy McLean, me, Willie Mathieson and Colin Stein.

My cup runneth over. Proudly showing the Cup-Winners' Cup to the world at Barcelona airport.

It's mine and you're not getting it. Keeping the fans at bay.

Oh, alright lads, let's have a song.

And still leading the sing-song, now with coach Jock Wallace on the flight home.

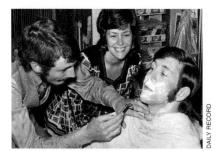

Janette supervises the removal of my beard and I pocket £100 from the *Daily Record* newspaper.

DAILY RECORD

Shake, pal. The great Johan Cruyff and I exchange pleasantries before the very first European Super Cup, at Ibrox in January 1973.

Bowing to HRH Princess Alexandra prior to the 1973 centenary Scottish Cup final against Celtic.

And ninety minutes after that royal greeting we were Scottish Cup winners for the first time in seven years. What a feeling!

'Murder Hill'. Still leader of the pack during pre-season training in the sand dunes of Gullane at the age of 33.

And it paid off.

A. WILSON

Champions!

After 11 long years. Receiving a bear hug from Big Jock at Easter Road after clinching the title in March 1975. I'll never forget Sandy Jardine's wonderful gesture that day.

Move over Ben Hur. The final game of the 1974–75 season, against Airdrie, and we were already champions. Willie Waddell reckoned that my chariot ride would be a crowd pleaser.

Party time at Dunblane Hydro to celebrate the league title and the completion of the second part of the Treble in 1976.

Clearing off the line from Hearts' John Gallacher in the 1976 Scottish Cup final. 3–1, and the Treble, to us.

SNSPIX.COM

'This is no time for your exercises Peter – it's the Scottish Cup Final.' But this was only a consolation goal for the 'Dons.

Our 2–1 victory gave us our second Treble in two years.

Below: Third time lucky. It took two replays but captain Derek Johnstone proudly displays the 1978 Scottish Cup after our 3–2 win over Hearts. My second trophy in my first year as Rangers manager.

SNSPIX.COM

SNSPIX.COM

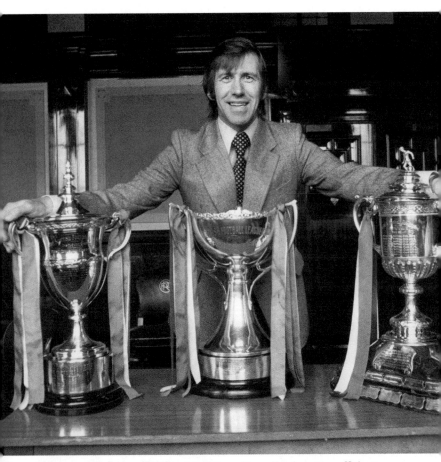

The complete set – for the third time. Proudly showing off the League Championship, League Cup and Scottish Cup trophies at Ibrox in 1978.

Making the instant transition from player to manager was never going to be easy. One minute I was one of the lads, the next I was the boss, but the other players had always shown great respect towards me as captain and that didn't change. Mind you, I didn't feel that they could continue to refer to me as 'John' or 'Greigy' and I pointed out to them that someone had to be the boss and that someone was me. To be fair to the players, they didn't have a problem with that, at least not that I was aware of, but perhaps if I hadn't been captain for thirteen years it might have posed greater difficulties.

My appointment coincided with the rebuilding of the stadium, so for three years only three sides of the ground could be used on match days, while the remaining side resembled a building site, which was very off-putting. I don't want that to sound like an excuse, though, and the first season certainly wasn't a problem, because we had a great squad and a very experienced set of players who had completed two trebles in the space of three seasons. So, talking tactics with the players was easy, because they understood the game and had achieved success. The infuriating thing was that most of them were fast approaching the veteran stage at more or less the same time.

Prior to the game in Turin, we had played with a flat back four, but I decided for the first leg against Juventus that I would operate with a back four and Sandy Jardine as a sweeper behind the defence. That was an easy system to implement, because the players were very adaptable, but the night we went out of the competition in the third round, to Cologne, I could see by the expressions on their faces that a lot of the players knew that their last chance of another European trophy win had gone.

I also realised that as much as it would hurt me, I was going to have to make the decision to bring in younger players. The average age of the second team was twenty-six and, while we had been winning leagues and cups, the problem should have been addressed much sooner and steps taken to build a very much younger squad. I was determined to implement a proper youth policy. The club regularly sent a team to compete in a youth tournament in Croix in northern France and I saw that as an opportunity to develop that side of the club. I recall going to John MacDonald's house in Clydebank in an effort to sign him for Rangers and his dad saying that the problem was that the club didn't have a youth policy. 'You're right,' I said, 'but I'm going to start one and your boy is going to be the first.'

It seemed ridiculous to me that Jock Wallace had borrowed youngsters from other boys' clubs to make up a team to represent Rangers against the likes of Barcelona and Inter Milan. I became the first Rangers manager to accompany our youth team to France for the Croix tournament and we won it two years out of three.

I also took it upon myself to train the youth players on a Monday evening, after they had finished school, to try to build up a relationship with them and over the next four and a half years a whole stack of youngsters became good enough to play for the first team. From memory, the list included Hugh Burns, Scott Nisbet, Dave McPherson, Kenny Black, Gordon Dalziel, Billy Davies, who in 2004–05 achieved the remarkable distinction of guiding Preston to the play-offs, only to fall at the final hurdle to West Ham, Derek Ferguson, Ian Durrant, John Spencer, Gary McSwegan and, of course, John MacDonald. It gave me a lot of pleasure being able to give theses lads a chance and I took a great deal of satisfaction from seeing them develop into first-team players. It is an achievement of which I am very proud.

Six weeks before I resigned, I gave Derek Ferguson his first taste of European football, when I sent him on as a substitute in our Cup-Winners' Cup tie against Valetta in Malta. Rangers won 8–0, but I gave young Derek a rollicking for refusing to take a penalty kick. I warned him that in future if I told him to do something he would have to follow my orders or suffer the consequences of not obeying an instruction. However, for all that I was forced to reprimand Derek, I believed that he would become a key player for Rangers. I envisaged that Ferguson, Ian Durrant and Sigi Jonsson, a young Icelander, would form the midfield, because they played the sort of football I encouraged. Regrettably, for all that he was a very talented player, Derek became unsettled, lost his way a little in the middle of his career and never quite fulfilled his potential.

I recall telling our goalkeepers, Peter McCloy and Stewart Kennedy, in the first practice match I supervised that I didn't want them just kicking the ball downfield. I instructed them to throw the ball to a team-mate so we could build constructively from the back. After all, with a talent such as Davie Cooper in the team there was no point in the keeper lumping the ball into the air and hoping it would land at someone's feet.

On the down side, I eventually had the thankless task of telling some of my former team-mates that the time had come for them to move on. One of those I was forced to let go was Alex MacDonald. Initially, Doddy, was set to sign for Partick Thistle, but Thistle were part-time and when I received a call from Hearts enquiring about Doddy's availability, I informed the club that he was free to choose whichever club he felt suited him best. After the service he had given Rangers, Doddy was entitled to that much. In the event, Doddy landed on his feet, when he became manager at Tynecastle.

I also let Sandy Jardine go, but, in hindsight, I probably allowed him to leave the club too soon. Sandy could have done as good a job for Rangers in the role of sweeper as he subsequently did for Hearts. I also made a mistake in not appointing Sandy captain, but I felt that his best years were behind him and that Derek Johnstone's were ahead, so it would be better if a younger player took over from me. As I have said, there was something about Derek that I always felt would make him captain of Rangers but even still, on reflection, I should have stuck with Sandy.

Willie Johnston was another who eventually joined Hearts and it was no coincidence that Doddy and Sandy became a formidable management team at Tynecastle, narrowly missing out on a league and Cup double in 1986. However, the pair were still key players in my first season in charge and both played a big part in the team's achievement in winning both the League Cup and the Scottish Cup.

When I accepted the manager's job I also had to accept the fact that there wasn't a lot of money available to strengthen the squad. Consequently, I had to display prudence and I acquired left-back Alex Forsyth from Manchester United on a free transfer. Derek Johnstone, with whom I had roomed on trips, had been having problems with the club prior to Jock resigning and I had to talk him out of seeking a move away from Rangers. I'm glad I succeeded in doing that.

What was a successful season, in as much that we won two trophies and finished runners-up to Celtic in the championship, was very nearly a momentous one. In the event, we finished three points adrift of our arch rivals, but at least I had the satisfaction of enjoying a victory over my old mate, Billy McNeill, the Celtic manager – without a ball even being kicked.

We were scheduled to play Celtic on 24 March, just three days after we faced Cologne. Ibrox was under renovation and the Old Firm game was set to take place at Hampden, but heavy snow led to the postponement of our European tie by twenty-four hours and I knew that Billy would be rubbing his hands, because it turned out to be a very physical match. The following day, Billy and I visited Hampden, along with the match referee, Brian McGinlay, to inspect the state of the pitch. It was clear that there had been a thaw of sorts, because we could see blades of grass sticking up through the snow, and Brian felt it best to delay any decision until the morning of the game. Billy agreed. Not surprisingly, I wanted the game to be called off.

I made the point that while the pitch might just be playable, the safety of the fans also had to be taken into account and, in my view, the state of the terracing posed a danger, because it was covered in snow. It was as if Billy had pressed a button! Next moment a squad of workman appeared at the top of the terracing all round the ground. They were members of the Hampden and Celtic ground staff called in to clear the terraces, but, to me at least, they looked more like a bunch of Indian braves massing for an attack. I was having none of it, though. 'It's Rangers' home game and I am the one who will decide what happens,' I pointed out somewhat forcibly. Brian McGinlay had little option, but to call the whole thing off. It wasn't that I was scared by the prospect of facing Celtic. I was simply trying to protect my players. They had been involved in a strength-sapping European tie less than twenty-four hours earlier and needed time to recover. Billy, meanwhile, was trying to gain an advantage at our expense and I could fully understand that. I would have done the same in the circumstances.

The game eventually went ahead on 5 May and we beat Celtic, 1–0, with wee Alex MacDonald scoring the all-important goal. That meant we had the title in our grasp when we travelled to Parkhead on 21 May 1979, needing a single point to become champions. Celtic had to win to snatch the prize from us and when we led by a Bobby Russell goal after nine minutes, the situation favoured Rangers. However, when the late Johnny Doyle was red-carded ten minutes after half-time, as so often happens, Celtic, instead of being hampered by playing with only ten men, raised their game to compensate. The upshot was that Roy Aitken equalised midway through the second half and then George McCluskey gave them the lead. Doddy squared the game two minutes later, but Colin Jackson suffered the misfortune to head into his own net and Murdo MacLeod scored a fourth goal almost with the last kick of the game.

I hated losing to anybody, let alone Celtic, and it was a bitter pill to swallow, but I refused to wear my emotions on my sleeve. It's easy to be a good winner, but much more difficult to be a good loser. However, Eric Gardner, my boys' club leader, had installed in me the need to behave with dignity and with so many eyes on me I was determined to conduct myself in a manner befitting the manager of Rangers football club. I was boiling inside, but I thrust out my hand to Billy McNeill and offered my congratulations. I would like to think that Billy would have reacted in a similar fashion had our positions been reversed and, significantly, he still talks about that moment, so it must have meant something special to him.

Mind you, it was the most disappointing moment of my managerial career, at least in terms of missing out on silverware. To have been within touching distance of achieving another treble in my first season as manager, and then missing out so close to the winning post, was hard to take. Beating Aberdeen in the League Cup final and Hibs – at the third attempt, after two replays – to win the Scottish Cup was compensation of sorts, but the league is the big one and I regret not managing to win at least one championship.

Europe, too, had held a great deal of promise that first season. Having been drawn against Juventus in the first round of the European Cup, the critics didn't give much for our chances ahead of the first leg in Turin on 13 September. Juventus had nine players who were in the Italian World Cup squad, including household names such as Zoff,

Tardelli, Cabrini, Gentile and Bettega. It was hardly surprising that we were considered underdogs, but I didn't share that pessimism.

Willie Waddell and I travelled to Italy to watch Juventus play AC Milan in a local tournament a few weeks before the tie and by half-time I had made up my mind with regard to the composition of our team. When we went for a cup of coffee during the interval, Willie Waddell espoused the view that Juventus were a very decent side. I was forced to agree with that assessment, but I informed him that I had already decided on a formation I felt could achieve a result that would give us a realistic chance in the return. As I have said, adopting specific tactics with the team we had then wasn't a problem as they were all experienced professionals. 'I'm going to play with a sweeper and four at the back, with one striker and another playing off the target man,' I told Deedle.

Juventus were managed by Giovani Trapattoni, who had been an outstanding player for Italy, and he came to Easter Road to watch us play Hibs. The game ended goal-less and I offered him a lift to the airport. As I was still living in Edinburgh I had taken my car – a brand new BMW– to the game. On our way to the airport I made a detour along Princes Street, to let Trapattoni see the sights, and a woman ran into the back of my car. Exchanging details with the other motorist meant we fell behind time and I ended up having to drive at high speed to reach the airport, so Trapattoni could catch his flight. We made it by the skin of our teeth, but when I went to open the boot to retrieve my passenger's holdall I discovered, to my dismay, that the impact of the collision had jammed it tight shut. There was no other course of action but to ask a local workman for a crowbar to force the boot open. So much for my good deed – and the state of my car!

Trapattoni clearly appreciated the gesture, though, for when he discovered that I was celebrating my thirty-sixth birthday on our arrival in Turin, he sent a cake to the team's hotel. However, the team gave me the best present of all. A 1–0 defeat represented an outstanding result against a side of Juventus' quality and gave us a right good chance of overturning the deficit in the return and progressing through to the second round.

Tommy McLean hadn't played in the first leg, as I brought in Alex Miller and Kenny Watson to play deep. We were heavily geared to defend and the players ran until they dropped. Juventus elected to play a man-marking system in the return, but I confused them by switching Tommy McLean from his customary outside-right position to play on the left, with the result that their full-backs were all at sea to start with and kept shouting across to the coach asking which player they should be marking.

Even though Juventus boasted so many players from that summer's World Cup squad, we out-thought and out-fought them at Ibrox to score in each half and those goals from Alex MacDonald and Gordon Smith earned us a showdown with PSV Eindhoven, who hadn't lost at home in a European tie in twenty-five years.

I like to think that, because of the influence people like Willie Waddell and Jock Stein had on me as a player, I went into great depth about the opposition. I felt it was important to equip my players with as much information as possible and I made sure I was clued-up on the strengths and weaknesses of the Eindhoven squad, but our prospects looked bleak when PSV kept a clean sheet at Ibrox. Try as we might we simply couldn't break them down and without a goal to show for our efforts the smart money was on the Dutch.

When PSV scored inside the first minute, heaven knows what sort of odds the bookies were offering on our chances. I had just lit up a cigar when the ball hit the back of our net and I snapped it in two. Alex Miller, who was standing next to me in the dug-out, turned and asked,

'What are you going to do now?' 'Light another one,' I replied without any humour. Plan A had been binned inside sixty seconds and I wasn't sure exactly what Plan B comprised of. But the team went on to produce one of the finest performances by a Rangers side in Europe, smash PSV's remarkable home record and achieve a result that had seemed well nigh impossible so early in the game.

No other side had beaten PSV on their own patch, certainly not one that had to come from behind to achieve the feat. In fact we had to draw level twice, after Alex MacDonald's equaliser had been cancelled out. With just three minutes remaining, Derek Johnstone and Bobby Russell scored the goals that highlighted a performance that was full of character and flair, and which has seldom been bettered by a Scottish team playing abroad. Those Rangers fans who had travelled to Holland in large numbers refused to leave the stadium at full-time and I did something which I never did again as a manager and walked across the pitch to accept their accolade of a standing ovation.

The run ended in the next round when we lost, 2–1 on aggregate, to Cologne following a single-goal defeat in Germany, but I always enjoyed pitting my wits against European opposition, for while there was a familiarity about the domestic game, Europe gave me an opportunity to try to keep the opposition guessing.

While I think I was entitled to consider that my first season in management had been a success, the next twelve months turned into something of a nightmare. We finished fifth in the league, eleven points adrift of the champions, Aberdeen, and got no further than the third round of the League Cup. A Scottish Cup final defeat by Celtic added to my sense of failure. There had been the promise of an extended European Cup-Winners' Cup run after wins over Lillestrom and Fortuna Düsseldorf, but Valencia ended our aspirations in the second round. It was galling that the team produced a wonderfully disciplined performance in the first leg in Spain, only for us to lose, 3–1, at Ibrox in the return.

I had signed defender Gregor Stevens from Leicester and striker Ian Redford from Dundee, with Derek Parlane moving south to Leeds by the time we lost, 1–0, to Celtic in the Cup final, but I realised that further rebuilding was required. So I acquired the services of another striker, Colin McAdam from Partick Thistle, and Jim Bett, who cost the club £180,000 when he arrived from the Belgian side, Lokeren – as I said earlier, a price well worth paying. I also generated cash by selling Gordon Smith to Brighton for a record fee of £400,000.

The 1980–81 season began brightly and we remained unbeaten in our first fifteen games, including home and away wins over Celtic, but our exit from the League Cup at the hands of Aberdeen, and defeat by Chesterfield in the Anglo-Scottish Cup, culminated in a general slump in form. Again the Scottish Cup offered us our only hope of silverware. We met Dundee United in the final and had the misfortune to see Hamish McAlpine make a last-minute penalty save from Redford to force a replay.

I had gambled on leaving Davie Cooper on the subs bench. People will read this now and wonder how the hell I could have done that, but Coop wasn't always the player he became later in his career. He wasn't known as 'Moody Blue' without good reason. There were times when he simply didn't perform as he was capable of doing, considering his magnificent talent. But Coop responded to being left out of our starting line-up by turning in a vintage display in the replay, so my controversial decision was vindicated. Coop opened the scoring, Bobby Russell added a second and John MacDonald, whom I had also left out of the team for the first game, responded to his recall by grabbing a double. Our 4–1 victory was emphatic, but I was even more pleased by the manner of our display, which was one of the best during my time as manager.

During the summer I tried to sign Ally McCoist from St Johnstone to further strengthen the squad, but Coisty chose to become a Sunderland player instead and I had to bide my time for two years, before finally getting my man. It was one of the best decisions I ever made, and I consider that he was one of the biggest legacies I left the club, for Coisty became an outstanding player for Rangers. There was a spell when his form slumped, but I could never understand why my successor, Jock Wallace, was prepared to even consider selling such a prolific goal-scorer.

Dundee United also formed the opposition when I won my fourth and final trophy as Rangers manager, on 28 November 1981. United were bidding for a hat-trick of wins and, predictably, they made it hard for us. Rangers, in fact, had to come from behind, after Ralph Milne had given the Tannadice side a forty-eighth-minute lead. Davie Cooper equalised and Ian Redford, who had replaced Gordon Dalziel, scored a dramatic last-gasp winner with just two minutes remaining. Regrettably, having also reached the final of the Scottish Cup, we were trounced, 4–1, by Aberdeen in extra time. Europe was a one-stop affair. Dukla Prague beat us by three goals in the Czech capital and despite us winning the return, the deficit was too great and we went out, 4–2 on aggregate.

Luck plays a substantial part in the success or failure of any team and without wishing to sound hard done by, Rangers didn't enjoy a great deal of that in season 1981–82. Defender, Gregor Stevens, received a six-month ban from the SFA after being ordered off for a fifth time and we were without him from March until the following August. A month after that body blow, Tom Forsyth was forced to quit the game on medical grounds. On a more positive note, John McClelland, who had cost £90,000 when we signed him from Mansfield the previous year, eventually became a solid performer in defence and went on to play for Northern Ireland in the 1982 World Cup finals.

Robert Prytz, a £100,000 signing from Malmo, also served the club well in midfield.

The following season – 1982–83 – we suffered the double disappointment of losing to Celtic and Aberdeen respectively in the League Cup and Scottish Cup finals. Dundee United, meanwhile, were crowned champions, with Celtic in second place and Rangers finishing fourth. Our UEFA Cup adventure was comparatively short-lived. Having been drawn against Borussia Dortmund, a 2–0 home win following a goalless draw at the Westfalen Stadium brought the reward of a tie against another German side and this time we fell at the second hurdle, to Cologne. The loss of Jim Bett, who was sold back to Lokeren for personal reasons, was a savage blow. Players of Bett's quality were hardly ten a penny and his departure left us short in midfield. The youth policy I had instigated was continuing to produce promising youngsters, but at a club like Rangers the one commodity the manager doesn't have is time.

But no matter how results went, I was always keen to ensure that the players didn't become bored at training by having to follow the same routine day-in, day-out. I knew from my own playing days how tedious training could become and I tried to vary our programme as much as possible, so the players looked forward to coming to work. I never saw the point in trying to 'punish' players on the training ground and thought that it was a counter-productive measure.

When I was a player and we lost I never wanted to go out socially after the game, but I suffered even more when I became manager. I would sit in isolation and wonder whether I was doing the job properly and question the tactics I had employed. The stress eventually began to take its toll and for the first time in my life I began suffering from migraines. Around the same time I woke during the night with a pain in my eye and by the following morning it was badly bloodshot. I consulted a specialist and he administered a course of injections straight into my eye. The next thing that happened was that the skin on my hands began flaking and I was diagnosed as suffering from severe stress. As well as my growing health problems, my son, Murray, was getting a hard time at school.

During my playing career, we had chosen to live quietly in Edinburgh, rather than on the club's doorstep. This was because, although I'm keen to stress that I have never at any time wished to stand aloof from the supporters, I felt it was important to protect my wife and son from the less pleasant aspects of being an Old Firm player. However, after I was appointed manager, it had quickly become apparent that it simply wasn't practical to live so far from the job.

Some nights I was lucky if I managed five hours sleep. If we had a midweek fixture at Dundee, for example, I would arrive home in Edinburgh at 1 a.m. and be back in my office at Ibrox at 8.30 a.m. I made a habit of being the first one in each morning so I could pull up any player who arrived late for training. I felt I had to set an example, but after a year of white-knuckle rides through the rush hour traffic between Edinburgh and Glasgow it all became too much. Arriving home late each evening in a state of utter exhaustion was no way to live, and after too many traffic jams and being involved in two car crashes – neither of which were my fault I might add – we decided to up sticks and move home to Lenzie in August 1979, where some of the boxes from the removal remain in our loft, unopened to this day.

That meant Murray also having to change schools and I regret that for a long time I didn't realise just how difficult the situation was for him. He was suddenly pushed into the firing line as the son of John Greig, the Rangers manager, and it was much later, when I spoke with Jim Baxter's sons, Alan and Stephen, who attended the same school, before I became fully aware of the level of hassle Murray was getting.

What was happening to my family wasn't fair and I also felt that these problems were impacting on my ability to do the job.

There was also a spell when some fans began protesting outside the ground. Frankly, that situation broke my heart. I felt I was responsible for the team's poor performances and lack of results and, given my relationship with the supporters, it hurt a great deal that they obviously felt I was failing them.

The combination of events – Murray's situation at school, results generally and my own state of health – led me to the conclusion that it was maybe time to leave and I approached the chairman, Rae Simpson, and suggested that it was perhaps time for a change. Rae, whom I had the utmost respect for and whose friendship I valued, said that he understood and informed me that he and the other directors planned to hold a board meeting at John Patton's home. He also warned me not to expect a positive outcome.

On the day of the meeting I supervised training as usual, but the situation felt a little unreal. In truth, I endured a horrible morning. After showering and dressing, I went to my office to await the outcome of the directors' deliberations, feeling as if I had placed myself in solitary confinement. The chairman eventually appeared to announce that no decision had been taken. Willie Waddell was on holiday in Malta and Rae explained that the board had not felt in a position to decide my fate without his say-so.

In the meantime, I was told to carry on. By now I had signed a three-year contract, which still had eighteen months to run. I asked the chairman if the board would be prepared to honour the remainder of my agreement, but I was told, 'No way,' and was advised that the directors would have to look at the situation on a game-to-game basis. However, I had a wife and son to support and I said, 'With the greatest respect, Mr Simpson, I have no wish to live week to week, looking over my shoulder all the time, after the service I have given this club.' I added that I had tried to do the honourable thing and leave with the board's blessing, so now I would make up my own mind when the time was right to go.

We had begun the season with a home draw against St Mirren and that was followed by defeats at the hands of Celtic, Hearts and Aberdeen, but I refused to hide. I have never run away from anything in my life and I wasn't about to start now. However, as sometimes happens when the chips are down, results suddenly began to improve. In fact, we looked to be in with a great chance of advancing beyond the second round of the Cup-Winners' Cup, when we led FC Porto, 2–0, in the first leg at Ibrox, with just three minutes remaining.

Prior to the tie I had visited Portugal to watch Porto in action against Benfica, who at the time were managed by Sven Goran Eriksson. Sven was kind enough to brief me on Porto, on the understanding that I said nothing to cause him embarrassment. Given that he was managing a Portuguese club and offering assistance to the 'enemy' his assistance wouldn't have gone down too well with the locals. Sven invited me to his home in Estoril and we have retained a friendship to this day. I still speak with him from time to time and I have nothing but the highest regard for the England manager.

As luck would have it, Porto wriggled off the hook when Peter McCloy, who was normally so reliable, dropped a clanger and they scored a late goal. I have never blamed Peter, because it was an uncharacteristic mistake and even goalkeepers are allowed them from time to time! I knew in my heart, though, that if we had travelled to Portugal for the return two goals to the good we would have been capable of winning the tie. A 2–1 scoreline was a different story, however. In the event, Porto won, 1–0, and progressed to the next stage at Rangers' expense, by dint of having scored an away goal, but by then I was gone.

The following Wednesday, after the first leg of the Porto tie, we had beaten Hearts to clinch our place in the League Cup semi-finals and I chose that moment to call time on my management career. Looking back, perhaps if Willie Waddell had continued to take a more active role in the running of the club, instead of electing to retire as managing director and vice-chairman in September 1979, my role as manager might have been a little less onerous. Deedle had treated me like a son and I probably spoke back to him in a manner no one else associated with Rangers would have dared to do, but there was genuine mutual respect. After such a short time in management I could have done with his continued presence and the benefit of his expertise to guide me for a bit longer. In fairness, Deedle remained in the background in a consultancy role and I was able to turn to him from time to time, but, regrettably, he wasn't around on a daily basis.

Basically, I was left in charge of the entire club. People may laugh when they look at what Rangers has become. The club employs a staff running into the hundreds and they oversee a vast business empire, but back in 1978 I was running the show almost single-handed. I had to attend to matters such as the head groundsman coming to me to report that one of his cleaning staff would have to be dismissed as she was claiming unemployment benefit while working for the club. Even sanctioning the renewal of the washing machines in the laundry came under my remit.

Willie Waddell had insisted from day one that I was not only the team manager, I was responsible for the smooth running of the entire club and he made sure that I knew exactly what made Rangers tick. I also had to attend the weekly board meetings. They were held on a Tuesday and lasted from 3.30 p.m. to 9.30 p.m. with only half an hour allocated to discussing team matters. Initially, I wasn't an expert on ground safety, but I sure as hell became one. I even became involved in doing the deal that led to former world lightweight champion, Jim Watt, defending his title against the American, Howard Davis, at Ibrox in June 1980.

Jim's promoter, Mickey Duff, wanted to hire the stadium and I was left to do the negotiating. Typical of Mickey, who knew how to turn a coin, he offered me £1 a head, but I reckoned I was being well and truly conned. 'What size of crowd do you anticipate?' I asked Mickey. 'In the region of 30,000,' he replied. 'Well, in that case,' I said, 'I want £35,000 – take or leave it.' When I reported to the board I was instructed to settle for £15,000, including expenses, but I stuck to my guns and Mickey agreed to pay £35,000. As it happened, only 11,000 turned up on a typically wet Glasgow summer's evening, so if I had accepted his initial offer the club would have ended up with a cheque for £11,000. Mickey tried to put me under pressure by claiming that the additional funds would have to come out of Jim's purse, but he was trying it on.

Jim beat Davis and we have subsequently become good friends. Not so long ago I asked Jim if he had suffered financially because of my demands, but he assured me that he hadn't, adding that, in fact, he had managed to extract a very good deal from Mickey. I was pleased about that, but can you imagine Sir Alex Ferguson or Arsene Wenger being asked to conclude a deal with a boxing promoter to stage a fight at Old Trafford or Highbury?

Was it any wonder that a year into the job I decided that the time had come to move home to the west? I was trying to rebuild a football team and cope with a million and one other things at the same time.

Having taken the decision to quit following the win over Hearts, I informed the chairman the next day and returned to the ground on the Friday morning to tell the players and the rest of the staff. It was 28 October 1983 and one of the worst days of my life. As I shook hands with each of the players in turn, I wondered what Jimmy Nicholl thought of me. One of my last acts as Rangers manager had been to sign him on a temporary contract from Toronto Blizzard and he must have wondered what sort of person I was to do that and then walk out the next day. My assistant, Tommy McLean, was put in temporary charge of the team until Jock Wallace, who had returned to Scottish football by then to manage Motherwell, was re-appointed as my successor a fortnight later.

In an effort to escape the fall-out from my resignation and the attention of the media, in particular, Janette, Murray and I spent the weekend with friends in Edinburgh. I had offers of other jobs – Hearts had expressed an interest several times and Morton wanted me as manager – but I accepted that I had effectively put myself out of the game. Where do you go in Scotland after Rangers? Anyway, I could never have managed a team in opposition to Rangers and England wasn't an option either.

I felt a deep sense of sadness that it had ended in such a way. Being manager of Rangers had its highs and lows, but I still considered that it had been a privilege to have managed the club I had served for so long. The fact was, from a football point of view I felt it was in the best interests of the club for me to resign. From a personal point of view, it was the correct decision, because I had to get out for the sake of my family and my health.

After it was all over, I reflected on the fact that in the course of nearly five and a half years I had broken up an ageing double treble team and reintroduced young players. I had effectively undertaken a massive clear-out, for someone else to come in and derive the benefits of my hard work, in this case Jock Wallace. I had a feeling of disappointment that I had perhaps been used to an extent, without anyone realising fully what I had achieved, but, strange as it may seem, I never felt in any way bitter or that it was completely over. A voice inside my head kept telling me that I would return to Ibrox, although I didn't have a clue in what capacity that might be.

I was offered money by various newspapers to write stories about the club and I had no difficulty refusing every one of them. Money has never been that important to me. It seemed far more important to me to leave with the same degree of dignity that I had displayed when accepting the role of manager of Rangers.

CHAPTER 21

GETTING INTO THE SWING

I played in front of 130,000 Old Firm fans at Hampden. I captained Scotland in front of a hate-filled crowd of screaming Italians in a crucial World Cup qualifying match in Naples. I also rubbed shoulders with Pele. But being watched by just two guys reduced me to a quivering wreck. Mind you, the pair in question were Gary Player and Arnold Palmer. I never had a problem handling six-figure crowds when I played football, because I reckoned I knew what I was doing, but swinging a golf club in such exalted company was a somewhat different matter. So how come I was fortunate enough to be able to mix with two of the greatest golfers of all time? Quite simply, I happened to be in the right place at the right time.

The road to Orlando, Florida, began on a cold October day at the Old Course Hotel in St Andrews, when I bumped into a Rangers fan with the right connections. He later became a director of the club, but the first time our paths crossed I hadn't a clue who I was speaking to. I was involved in organising corporate hospitality at the time and I had the task of greeting guests who had been invited to attend the Dunhill Cup. That involved being on duty at the front door of the hotel at 8 a.m. On the second day of the tournament, the Friday, I had just arrived when this fellow appeared wearing a tracksuit. He spoke to me and explained that he had been jogging and I expressed the wish that I had been able to join him.

I didn't spot him the following morning, but that evening I bumped into him in the hotel foyer and commented that I hadn't seen him out jogging. 'No, I left early to go to the Rangers-Hibs game at Ibrox,' he said. 'You should have mentioned you were a football fan,' I replied. 'I would have got you a pass for the directors' box.' 'Oh, I had one of those,' he said. 'Obviously, you're at a disadvantage. I know who you are. My name is Alastair Johnston.' 'So, you're Alastair Johnston,' I replied, somewhat taken aback. 'I've heard about you.'

I think Alastair appreciated the fact that I had offered to supply him with a pass for the game without knowing who he was, and that evening I spotted him sitting with someone in the lounge and he called me over. Alastair introduced me to his companion. 'This is Nat Rosasco, John. He's from America.' Nat was smoking a large cigar and it was pretty obvious from his demeanour that he was a businessman with considerable clout. It was also fairly obvious when Nat asked me if I played golf that he had some involvement with the game and I proceeded to relate a story concerning a member of my own club, Lenzie.

I said that just a few weeks before I had met a fellow by the name of Malcolm Campbell, who was editor of *Golf Monthly*, and he had offered to give me a golf club that had once belonged to Sandy Lyle. Malcolm had explained that Sandy had been unable to hit the ball straight using the club and that he had experienced a similar problem, so did I want the club? It was a new-style metal wood driver and I was happy to take the club off Malcolm's hands.

Nat asked me what make the club was and I replied that it had been manufactured by an American company, Northwestern. Alastair burst out laughing. 'John, Nat owns the company,' he revealed. Nat then invited me to visit the Northwestern stand in the tented village the next day, promising that one of his staff would find me a driver that kept the ball going in a straight line. I thanked Nat for the offer and immediately regretted opening my mouth, because I reckoned it was going to cost me the price of a new driver.

The following morning, once I had dealt with my corporate guests, I made my way to the tented village and found Nat and his UK sales manager waiting for me. There was a third person and he began loading all sorts of clubs into a big exhibition golf bag. When I asked what he was doing, I was told we were going to go to the practice ground to try out various clubs, until I found ones that suited me. As the three of us made our way to the practice area behind the Old Course Hotel, several spectators stopped me to ask for my autograph. Presumably, they thought that, because I had someone carrying a bag of clubs, I was one of the competitors.

I cringed at the sight of a huge crowd gathered round the practice area. Scotland were playing Ireland in that day's round of matches and Sam Torrance and Des Smyth were among the players practising. I knew Sam, who was to go on to achieve even greater fame as captain of Europe's 2002 Ryder Cup-winning team, and he asked, 'What the hell are you doing here?' When I told him, Sam said, 'Well, I've seen you play, so if you're going to start hitting ball I'm getting the hell out of here.' With that he upped and left, much to the amusement of the spectators. Eventually, I hit a few balls before expressing a preference for a particular type of blade. As it happened, they were the same style of clubs as the ones used by Gary Player, who was about to sign a multi-million dollar contract with Northwestern.

I was told that Nat was going to send me a set and I was asked to dine with him that evening. We seemed to hit it off straightaway and Nat invited me to visit his factory in Chicago, prior to spending a week golfing in Florida as his guest. Initially, I was reluctant to take him up on the offer, as it would mean spending a fortnight away from my business, but Janette insisted that it was an offer I simply couldn't refuse and the following January I was Chicago-bound.

When I arrived in the Windy City there was eight inches of snow on the ground, but the sight of Nat's factory made me forget all about the weather. The place is the size of Ibrox and a veritable Aladdin's Cave of golf equipment. I was told to help myself to any clubs I fancied. I was also invited to visit Soldiers Field, home of the NFL side, Chicago Bears. A friend of Nat's was the stadium manager and when he found out I was a footballer he produced a ball and invited me to try my luck. To be honest, I'm not a fan of the American version of football, but I agreed to the request because I never experienced any difficulty hitting a ball over the bar!

The highlight of the trip up to that point was being invited to attend an American-Italian fund-raising dinner. The aim was to raise funds to help build a children's home and there was no shortage of star names present. There must have been thirty people at the top table, including baseball legend Joe DiMaggio, Dan Marino, the famous NFL quarter-back, and boxer Rocky Graziano, the former world middle-weight champion. Various other stars from the worlds of baseball, ice hockey and the NFL had also turned up. Sitting in front of each of the top table guests was a special putter with a gold-plated head. It was Nat's idea of a small token of his appreciation!

I was sat at a table immediately in front of the dignitaries, but I completely misread the situation when the auction began and the compère asked, 'Who will give me twenty-five for this item?' My hand shot up – and was immediately hauled back down by one of the other guests. 'He's talking twenty-five thousand, John,' I was informed. I nearly had a fit. I thought he had meant twenty-five dollars without the three zeros.

After a week in Chicago I was flown to Orlando to play golf, but I hadn't reckoned on the five-star treatment that awaited me. I had expected to be transported by ordinary car, but the first thing Nat did was to inform his drivers that I was to be taken everywhere in his gold-coloured Rolls Royce. 'This guy has come all the way from Scotland and is a Member of the British Empire,' explained Nat. 'So he travels first class.' Mind you, I insisted on my clubs being transported to the course by van!

Nat had organised a Pro-Am tournament at Disney World. Mostly, the professionals taking part were among the lesser known ones, but I do recall that Judy Rankin, one of the leading American women players at the time, played in the event. At the post-tournament banquet, which was a lavish affair, Nat presented the professionals with $3,500 watches. Following the prize-giving, the MC announced that Nat wished to make a special presentation.

The next thing I heard being read out was details of my career and the fact that I had visited Buckingham Palace to be honoured by the Queen. I was then presented with a blue bag bearing my name in white lettering and containing a brand new set of clubs. The other bags that had been given as prizes had all been green and white which, as it happened, were the official company colours.

Even Gary Player's bag was green and white, so when I returned to the table, Gary asked why I was being given special treatment. He also expressed a preference for the colour of my bag, but Nat quickly put the great man in his place. Nat, who was sat at the same table, told Gary, 'Listen, you're just about to sign a multi-million dollar contract, but he's the only guy in the world who will have a blue and white bag.

John's biggest rivals play in green and white, so there's no way he can have a bag in those colours.'

But if I imagined that I was in some sort of wonderland, the best was yet to come. Alastair Johnston, who looked after the affairs of both Gary and Arnold Palmer in his capacity as a top executive with the Mark McCormack organisation, asked me if I fancied playing golf with the pair of them the following day. Alastair didn't need to ask me twice. Now I really did believe that I had died and gone straight to heaven.

Unfortunately, because Gary was held up giving press interviews, by the time we arrived at the course, Arnold had already teed off, but that still left Gary, Alastair and the lawyer, who had been involved in the official contract signing – and me, of course. It was agreed that I would partner Alastair against Gary and the lawyer. It was bad enough that I had to display my swing in front of Gary Player, but when Arnold walked off the ninth green as we stood on the first tee I almost died of fright. I had been introduced to Arnold on a previous occasion and he actually became a Rangers shareholder through Alastair's influence, but despite not knowing me well, Arnold apologised for starting without us. I imagined that he would then carry on with his game, but, horror of horrors, Arnold stood where he was, waiting for us to tee off.

I had once managed to trim my handicap to eight, but the minute and a half that I stood waiting to drive the ball was the most nerve-wracking ninety seconds of my life. Imagine trying to hit the ball with the eyes of two of the greatest golfers on the planet fixed on you? Eventually, when I finally plucked up the courage to swing at the ball I made contact – and sent it all of twenty yards into the rough! Gary, God bless him, told me to call my shot a 'mulligan', explaining that you were entitled to one of those a round. Mercifully, when I teed the ball up a second time it went flying straight down the fairway.

Despite my nightmare start, I must have played quite well, because

Alastair and I won the first nine holes. We were still ahead after five of the back nine holes and, standing on the fifteenth tee, Alastair informed the opposition that if we won that one we would be three up with three to play. Gary agreed, but as we made our way down the fairway in a buggy, he turned to me and said, 'John, did I ever tell you the story of the time I played Tony Lema in the World Match-Play Championship at Wentworth?'

He hadn't, of course. So he recited the tale of one of golf's most remarkable comebacks in any thirty-six-hole match. 'When I walked off the eighteenth I was six down and headed straight for the practice range,' he recalled. 'Tony headed straight for the bar with the press lads. Just as we were about to tee off in the afternoon round, Tony turned to me and said, "Never mind, Gary, with your record, you'll be invited back." I fell further behind when Tony won the first, but, suddenly, I began landing my shots close to the pin and I eventually beat him at the thirty-seventh.'

By this time we had reached the spot where my ball had landed, but I had been so engrossed in Gary's story that I had taken my mind off the game. I think that was probably Gary's intention, for he turned to me and said, 'I guess it's your shot, John.' One word to describe Gary's action in reciting his tale at that moment is psychology.

Alastair and I held our game together sufficiently to have the match won by the time we reached the eighteenth tee, but Gary is renowned as one of the game's greatest competitors and he wasn't quite ready to throw in the towel. 'I don't believe in double or quits,' he announced. 'Why don't we have a twenty-five dollar bet on the outcome of the last hole?' I was being given a stroke a hole and we won that one as well, but it's a measure of Gary's professionalism that he became angry with himself when his approach shot to the green at the last landed and then spun back down. He was so determined to get it right that he asked to be given his 'mulligan', so he could play the shot again and get it right at the second attempt.

When we got back to the clubhouse, Gary reached into his wallet and counted out twenty-five dollars. I told him to forget it, but he insisted that I take the money, adding that I had played well, but if he had won the hole he would have insisted on me paying up, as a bet is a bet. I still have one of those dollar bills. My only regret is that I didn't get him to sign it.

That was probably one of the greatest days of my sporting life. Not only did I have the unique opportunity of playing golf in the company of one of the world's greatest players for four hours, I was also given the benefit of Gary's expertise. Gary took time to show me how to play certain holes, including ones out of the bunker, so it was like being given a private lesson and I don't know anyone who can say that they've been coached by the winner of nine Majors.

It was such a pleasure to play with Gary that I wanted to try and repay him in some way for the marvellous experience and when Alastair Johnston arranged for me to take part in pro-am at Turnberry I had my opportunity. Gary does a great deal of charity work for underprivileged kids and even has a school for black children on his farm in South Africa. When I learned of this I arranged through Admiral, the sportswear company, to have a set of Rangers strips sent to Gary and I now have a photograph of these youngsters in bare feet wearing Rangers jerseys.

I am also indebted to Alastair Johnston, who made it possible for me to play golf with Gary. Alastair and I have become close and on another occasion I was fortunate enough to enjoy dinner with him and Arnold Palmer at the world famous Turnberry Hotel. That chance meeting at the Old Course Hotel led to a chain of events. I was able to introduce Jim McDonald – David Murray's right-hand man – to

Alastair, who, in turn, introduced Jim to Mark McCormack. Mark extended the link by introducing Jim to Dave King, who has since become a major shareholder in Rangers. I also arranged for Alastair, who comes from Whitecraigs on the outskirts of Glasgow, to put Lawrence Marlborough in touch with Arnold Palmer, to design a golf course for him in San Francisco.

No matter what else I achieve in my life, I doubt that I'll ever replicate the experience of playing a round of golf with an all-time legend of the game – but I'll go on hoping all the same.

CHAPTER 22

REVOLUTION

Graeme Souness is credited with kick-starting the Rangers revolution when he succeeded Jock Wallace as manager in April 1986, but the wheels had been set in motion by Lawrence Marlborough, six months earlier. Lawrence was the grandson of the former Rangers chairman, John Lawrence, and had become head of his grandfather's business empire of the same name. The building group had effectively taken control of the club the previous November and although Lawrence had resigned as a director of the club two years earlier, he continued to take a keen interest in the affairs of Rangers from his home in Lake Tahoe.

Although domiciled in the States, Lawrence returned to Glasgow on a regular basis and it was during one of these trips that he asked to meet with me. I had been working as a freelance business travel consultant from the offices of Dixon Travel in the Shawlands district on Glasgow's south side and I was responsible for making all Lawrence's arrangements, as well as those of the club.

A lot of people had probably imagined that I wouldn't be able to live without direct involvement in football, but as I have already made clear, I knew I could never become manager of another Scottish club and I had no intention of pursuing a job in England.

However, I still had to earn a wage and I didn't have a clue what I was going to do. The first week was fine, but then I had to ask myself, 'What the hell do I do now?' So I went into the travel business. Part of my new career also involved arranging corporate hospitality at various sporting events. It was something that interested me and I enjoyed the work.

By the time Lawrence Marlborough asked to see me, David Holmes was running the show at Rangers, after being appointed to the board. It was David Holmes who extended the invitation on behalf of Lawrence and I was only too glad to make myself available if he felt I could be of assistance. I had known Lawrence a long time, for he used to train with the part-time players when I joined the club and we had been close since we were teenagers.

Lawrence got straight to the point. 'How do you feel about me taking outright control of the club?' he asked. 'I am going to offer to buy Jack Gillespie's shares, which will give me over fifty per cent of Rangers' share capital.' I replied that I thought it was the best thing that could happen, because there was too much in-fighting going on at the time and the power struggle was having a detrimental effect on Rangers. So Lawrence picked up the phone and put in a call to Jack Gillespie. Jack was vice-chairman, but a deal was worked out whereby he sold 29,000 of his shares to John Lawrence Ltd.

That was the birth of the Rangers Revolution and I like to think I had a small part to play in it. Mind you, I could have had an even more direct role in the club's dramatic change of direction had I chosen to accept an offer from David Holmes of a directorship with responsibility for running the youth side. Very reluctantly I turned David Holmes down, though. For a start we couldn't agree a job description, because the manager at the time, Jock Wallace, didn't know a thing about it and I refused to take the job without his say-so, although his days were numbered. Graeme Souness had been earmarked by David Holmes to become player-manager. Graeme was coming to the end of his contract with the Italian club, Sampdoria, and David Holmes, who was by now chief executive, moved swiftly to tempt him with an offer he simply could not refuse.

Graeme is also an Edinburgh man and I had first encountered him when he was just a young teenager. He was the friend of the son of a close pal of mine and I recall our meeting when Graeme visited their home. When he told me he was hoping to make it as a player I think I said something like, 'Stick in. I hope you do well.' He told me many years later that he had never forgotten our first meeting or my encouragement. Later, when I was manager of Rangers, I met him on two or three occasions, when I attended games in Liverpool and we formed a bond. Possibly it had something to do with the pair of us coming from the same city, but, whatever the reason, Graeme was great with me and I am very fond of him.

David Holmes was astute enough to realise that Graeme would benefit from having an assistant with local knowledge. Graeme had no real experience of Scottish football, after spending his career in England and Italy, and it made complete sense to have a right-hand man who could bring that to the new managerial team. His choice of Walter Smith, who was assistant to Jim McLean at Dundee United, was inspired. Walter had served his apprenticeship under a man who was vastly experienced and who had enjoyed a phenomenal amount of success, in spite of being forced to work with a very limited budget. Graeme and Walter complimented each other and when Graeme rather surprisingly left in 1991 to become manager of Liverpool, Rangers already had the ideal successor in place. When David Murray told me he was appointing Walter to take over from Graeme I told him he couldn't have made a better choice. Walter went on to become an outstanding manager in his own right and part of the reason was continuity. Walter had worked closely with the players during Graeme's time in charge and had earned their respect – another reason why he was so successful.

But going back to the start of the new regime, I doubt that anyone other than Graeme could have persuaded players of the calibre of Terry Butcher, Chris Woods, Gary Stevens, Trevor Steven, Graham Roberts and Ray Wilkins to sign for Rangers. The manager was helped by the fact that English clubs were banned from playing in Europe at the time, so there was a big incentive for players like Butcher and Woods to come to Scotland. Only a few years previously there was no way I could have signed players of the standing of Butcher and Woods. Every first-team player was earning the same wage, but when I resigned as Rangers manager I had anticipated that a wind of change would blow through the club. Indeed, I felt it was inevitable and I remember warning the board that the wage structure would have to change. But, fair play to Graeme Souness, his choice of players was excellent. He completely transformed the face of Scottish football. I also admired the fact that when certain signings didn't quite work out as he had hoped, he sold these players on, very often at a profit, because of his efficient housekeeping.

Rangers were crowned champions in Graeme's second season in charge and it was a measure of the power base he put in place that the club only once failed to take the title over the next ten years, including the remarkable run of nine in a row.

Behind the scenes further changes took place when, in November 1988, David Murray assumed ownership of the club. Lawrence Marlborough decided to transfer control of the club because of increasing business commitments in the States and he felt that David was the ideal man to succeed him. David had established himself as a hugely successful businessman. He had suffered the grave misfortune to lose both legs in a car crash when he was only in his mid-twenties, but his disability seemed to serve to make him even more determined to succeed. It just so happened that David and Graeme Souness were close friends and their relationship was a major factor in the transfer of ownership. Graeme, in fact, became a director with a ten per cent share in the club, which served to increase his power base.

However, I don't think anyone could have foreseen the drama that unfolded in the summer of 1989. The signing of Maurice Johnston did not so much create waves as a Force 12 hurricane. Why? It was simple really – Johnston was a Roman Catholic and some Rangers fans voiced their strong disapproval. In fact, a lot were very unhappy, not only because of the long-established religious divide, but because Johnston was also a former Celtic player who had appeared to be on the point of rejoining the Parkhead club from French side Nantes. When Graeme learned that Johnston had not, in fact, finalised a deal with Celtic he was determined to get his man and literally pinched the striker from the clutches of our closest rivals.

A lot of managers would have steered clear of doing such a deal, given the certain outcry it would create, but Graeme was different from most. His determined nature and refusal to bow to outside pressures meant that he was able to both persuade Johnston that it was the right move for him and then cope with the inevitable backlash. As far as Graeme was concerned, football and religion are two very different subjects and it simply didn't matter to him that Johnston was a Catholic or that he had once been a Celtic player.

The fact that Graeme is an east-coaster undoubtedly helped. It's inevitable that those brought up in the west of Scotland are confronted with the Catholic-Protestant divide, but it has always been far less of an issue in the east of the country and growing up in Edinburgh I was hardly ever aware of a problem. It has never mattered to me what religion a person is. I take people at face value. However, I will admit that when you're in the public eye you sometimes have to be careful to suss out whether people want to be friends with you because of the person you are, or whether it's the position you occupy, for example manager of Rangers.

The signing of Mo Johnston sent shock waves through Scottish football and made a lot of fanatical Rangers fans very unhappy, but others were pleased, because they recognised that Johnston's presence would improve the team further. The world has changed a great deal and in 2005 we look at a lot of situations very differently. As recently as even sixteen years ago, though, there was far less tolerance and those Rangers fans who burned their scarves displayed a deep sense of hurt at what they considered to be an act of betrayal. However, Johnston soon won over the vast majority of the support. With the spotlight on him more than any of his team-mates, he had to produce quickly and he did. He played to his full potential during his time with Rangers and worked his socks off for the team.

Meantime, I was still self-employed. I had set up my own pro-am golf tournament in the Caribbean and I was also working for the BBC, having graduated from reporting games at places like Cappielow and Boghead to working as a big game analyst. I enjoyed the work and it kept me as close to the game as I felt I wanted to be. However, when David Murray approached me with an offer to return to Rangers I just couldn't say no and on 2 January 1990 I returned to Ibrox in a public relations role.

I had always had a feeling deep down that I would go back one day, in some capacity other than that of manager. That was why, when I quit in 1983, there was no way I would criticise the club. I tried to leave with dignity and that was probably one of the principal reasons why I was asked back. Apparently, there was also another reason. David Murray told me that on the evening of Sandy Jardine's testimonial dinner in Edinburgh he had approached me to ask for my autograph for his sons. When I said that I hoped I had been polite and duly obliged, David replied, 'If you hadn't been, you wouldn't be here now.' Who says good manners aren't important?

CHAPTER 23

A TIMELY WARNING

Like many sportsmen who have maintained a reasonable level of fitness and have been fortunate enough to enjoy good health, I imagined that I was indestructible. However, I was disabused of that notion on 22 January 1998, when I suffered a heart attack. I was just fifty-five years of age and had no prior warning. One minute I was working out in the Ibrox gym, the next I was wondering what the hell was happening to me.

I had been invited by Walter Smith to participate in a game of head-tennis and, after changing in the manager's office, I headed for the dressing room, but I was informed by Walter's assistant, Archie Knox, that I would have to join the queue of those wanting to take part. Consequently, I decided to go to the gym for a quick work-out, rather than hang around indefinitely waiting for my turn. I was working away when one of the players, Charlie Miller, turned to me and warned, 'You'd better watch what you're doing or you'll end up having a heart attack,' but I replied that I was OK because I was using only light weights.

Charlie's warning proved chillingly prophetic. Suddenly I began to feel uncomfortable and it was a feeling like none I had ever had before.

I wasn't in great pain, but I felt tightness across my back and chest and decided to walk down the tunnel in the hope that I would benefit from breathing in fresh air. I was in the habit of carrying indigestion tablets, but I had left my kit bag in Walter's office and I didn't want to just barge in as he was in the process of giving a player a dressing-down, so I headed for the doctor's office.

Donald Cruickshank took one look at me and told me to lie down on his couch. The first thing he did was give me a pill to slip under my tongue, before informing me that he wanted me to go to hospital for a check-up. I asked Donald to contact my wife, whom he had known for years, but urged him not to panic her. As it happened, when he eventually got round to calling Janette she wasn't at home. She later told me she had been out shopping to buy fish for my evening meal!

Donald's daughter worked as a radiologist at the Southern General Hospital and he phoned her for advice. By now I was starting to experience increasing pain across my back and shoulders. Fortunately, the ambulance to take me to the Southern General arrived within minutes and I was quickly strapped into a wheelchair by the paramedics. When we reached the front door I remember Peter Jacobs, who was on duty at reception, grimacing as I was bumped down the steps. I also recall looking up at the club crest above the main entrance and saying to myself, 'Christ, surely it can't end like this.' Nearly forty years earlier, when I first went to Ibrox, I had also looked up at the crest and the memory had remained with me.

As soon as I was put in the ambulance, one of the paramedics placed an oxygen mask on my face, explaining that sometimes that helped ease the pain. But when I heard the other paramedic – a female – ask her colleague for directions, my heart sank. I thought to myself, 'If she doesn't know where she's going, what chance do I have?' The lady must also have been new to the job of driving an ambulance, because the next thing I heard was the crunching noise of the gears crashing. Even now I can still hear the sound of her grinding her way through the gearbox and me praying that we would make it.

As soon as we arrived at the hospital I was taken to intensive care and seen by a doctor, who gave me an injection in my thigh and the pain instantly disappeared. It was explained to me that I would have to undergo a series of tests. Once the tests had been completed, the doctor informed me that I had indeed suffered a heart attack. However, he did not elaborate on his statement, other than to stress that the next forty-eight hours would be very important in terms of my recovery and it was imperative that I have complete rest.

The only other time that I had been in hospital was when I developed kidney stones. There was a humorous side to that experience, though. I sat bent over in agony as Janette was wheeling me along a corridor at 8.30 a.m. but that didn't stop one Rangers fan from asking for my autograph. It must have been obvious the state I was in, but the fact that I could hardly lift my arms didn't appear to cut any ice with the intrepid autograph-hunter. You really couldn't make it up at times.

Janette and my son, Murray, were the only people allowed to visit me, but there were plenty of others who tried to reach my bedside – the gentlemen of the press. In addition to the hospital switchboard being under the threat of meltdown, forcing them to employ extra telephonists to deal with the hundreds of calls enquiring after my wellbeing, the intensive care unit came under siege. The journalists tried every sort of ruse to con their way in. One guy claimed that he was my uncle from Aberdeen and photographers were peering through windows in the hope of catching a glimpse of my lying flat on my back, with all nature of monitors protruding from my chest. The antics of the press pack may have appeared comical to outsiders, but it was no joke and I felt sorry that my fellow patients were inconvenienced in such a way.

Eventually, I was moved to a private room next to the nurses' station. I guess the doctor and nurses must have been Rangers fans, because not only did they afford me privacy, they were also able to keep a close eye on me. In fact, the nurses were wonderful. A couple of them actually visited me regularly at home for quite a while afterwards and I will never forget their kindness.

When I eventually saw the scan of my heart there was no visible evidence that I had suffered a heart attack, but when you're lying in intensive care with monitors attached to various parts of your body the reality quickly sets in. One of the first things the doctor asked me was if I smoked and I replied that I had stopped. 'When?' he asked. 'Oh, about thirty-five minutes ago,' I said. I used to enjoy a cigar, but I haven't smoked since it was explained to me the damage it does to the heart.

I suppose what happened to me wasn't really all that surprising, given that there was a history of heart trouble in the family. My three brothers all died as a result of suffering heart attacks. Tam was only forty-eight and Alfie and Alex were in their early sixties when they passed away. Alex, who lived in Gloucestershire, was advised by a specialist at Papworth Hospital to ensure that the rest of us had regular check-ups after it was discovered that he had a problem with his blood and he was prescribed medication. I didn't see it as a problem at the time, because I was still playing football and did plenty of regular exercise. I think, too, because of the kind of person I was, playing with a stress fracture in my foot and the like, I probably imagined that nothing could bring me down. That was clearly not the case, but while I got a real fright, I never thought that my heart attack would prove fatal.

Mind you, I would have been in danger of suffering a relapse had Paul Gascoigne carried out his threat to pay me a visit. It was bad enough having Ally McCoist and Ian Durrant at my bedside. The pair of them arrived one afternoon after training and promptly tied a couple of 'L-plates' to the bottom of my bed. They also came armed with several packs of sweet cigarettes. I was able to laugh at their antics, but the revelation that Gazza was planning a visit instantly wiped the smile off my face. Gazza is notoriously hyperactive and I had this terrifying vision of him rampaging around a room just ten feet by ten feet pulling out wires and plugs and asking what purpose they served. There was nothing else for it but to ban Gazza – albeit that he meant well.

All the players were great and I received hundreds of get well cards and letters from people in the game and from supporters. I was also fortunate that hospitals hold no fears for me. I had spent most of my adult life visiting supporters in hospital, so I understood their workings and felt reasonably comfortable in my surroundings. But, having said that, I didn't want to spend longer than was absolutely necessary laid up in bed in the Southern General. In the event, I spent two weeks in hospital and I had to pass the treadmill test before I was released. That involved proving my fitness by walking on a treadmill, something I was confident of doing.

However, I wasn't prepared for what happened when I was taken by ambulance to a different part of the hospital for my 'work-out'. I was accompanied by a sister and a nurse and we were larking about to the extent that the lady in charge of the treadmill became increasingly flustered. Eventually, after she had shaved my chest and applied several monitors, she switched on the machine with me standing on it and I took off at a hundred miles per hour. I must have looked like Superman flying through the air as I hung on to the side bars with my legs stretched out behind me. I was none the worse for my experience, though. I passed the test with flying colours and left with the instruction that I was to stay indoors for a week before venturing out for a maximum of five minutes walking on the flat.

Everything was going to plan until the third day of my second week back home, when I slipped while putting on my slippers and injured my back. I had suffered from back problems previously and spent three days sleeping on the floor. Rather stupidly, once I was back on my feet, I reckoned I had to make up for lost time and instead of going for a five-minute walk I completely overdid things. When I returned a friend had come to visit me and I had to ask him to go because I was starting to feel dizzy.

Janette immediately telephoned the family doctor, who ordered me back into hospital. I told him that Janette would take me in her car, but I was informed that there was no way he could allow that. I was vain enough to insist, though, that when the ambulance arrived the last thing I wanted to see was flashing lights to attract the attention of the neighbours. I ended up spending the weekend in Stobhill Hospital.

A few weeks later I was seen by Frank Dunn, the heart specialist who had advised my former Celtic rival, Billy McNeill, to have bypass surgery just the year before. I had already been reassured that I had not suffered a second heart attack, but that I had simply overdone things, and Frank confirmed that diagnosis. He had been off on the weekend I was admitted to Stobhill and I chided him about the fact that he had been there to look after Billy, but had been posted missing when the other half of the Old Firm required his assistance. All joking apart, it was another timely warning, however, and I vowed there and then to stick to the script in terms of my rehabilitation. It was four months before I was able to return to work, by which time I was stir crazy, but at least I didn't have to face the drama of surgery.

While I could happily have done without the experience of a heart attack, the one good thing that came out of it was that six months later Billy and I were invited to open a new rehabilitation unit at Stobhill. They managed to spell my name wrong and were forced to erect a new commemorative plaque, but I was happy to do anything I could to assist the medical staff, who do such a marvellous job of saving lives, often under intense pressure. Most of us take good health for granted and it's only when something unpleasant happens that you realise the importance of those employed in the National Health Service. I will certainly always be grateful to those nurses and doctors who cared for me.

I continue to exercise fairly regularly, but nowadays I go at a more sedate pace and I no longer use weights. Instead I walk a lot. Until our granddaughter, Kaitlin, arrived on the scene last year, Janette and I used to power-walk for three miles, three times a week, but it's difficult to hurry along when you're pushing a pram.

CHAPTER 24
A DUTCH OF CLASS

Dick Advocaat changed my life. He almost turned me round full circle in my career and put fire back in my belly. I was recovering from my heart attack when the news broke in February 1998 that Dick was to replace Walter Smith as manager. By the time he actually arrived in Scotland, four months later, I was in the process of rehabilitation and working only a few hours a day.

In the interim, I had been asked by the chairman, David Murray, to look after Dick's assistant, Bert van Lingen, and his wife, Vera, and help them find a suitable home in the Glasgow area, so they could settle in quickly. Bert had obviously mentioned me to Dick and explained my background, so he was aware of who I was when the chairman's private jet eventually touched down in Edinburgh to deposit the new Rangers manager.

I was assigned the task of collecting Dick from the airport and on the return journey from Edinburgh Dick quizzed me about the club's training facilities. I explained that we had been using several sites, but the one that impressed me most was the Glasgow University training ground at Stepps, on the outskirts of the city. Dick asked if it would be possible for me to take him there straightaway, to look over the facility, and afterwards he asked me a series of questions, including how far it was from Ibrox. That was my first indication of just how thorough and meticulous Dick is when it comes to preparing his ground-work. We followed what I considered to be the quickest route from Stepps to Ibrox, also being careful to explain that the journey time was dependent on the volume of traffic at certain times in the day, and often that was considerable.

The following day I was supposed to take Dick house-hunting, but Dick was more interested in immersing himself in the job and he asked me where my office was in relation to his own. Dick had been given an office on the ground floor at Ibrox, while my office was situated next to the Thornton Suite on the next level, but Dick wanted me to move into an adjoining office. I didn't have a problem with that and promised that I would help in any way I could.

I had also accepted the task of helping Dick's wife, Dieuwke, find a suitable property, no mean task considering that Dick didn't fancy most of those his other half liked.

It turned into a real problem eventually. I have always taken the view that when a player signs for a club it is very important to ensure that his wife and family settle quickly. Once the family is happy with their surroundings it eases the pressure on the player. If he comes home from training and isn't playing well, the last thing he needs is for his wife to start nagging, because she is unhappy. That only serves to drag him down even further and exacerbates the problems. I felt the same thing applied to Dick, but initially he and Dieuwke settled for a luxury chalet on the bank of Loch Lomond and, while it is a magnificent setting, it can be dreich and dark almost all day long during the winter months. There is also very little do there. Prior to them moving into their chalet, I took Dick to see a number of properties, but he didn't like any of them and made me swear not to tell Dieuwke. Eventually, they chose a house in Newton Mearns and the problem was solved.

I also had to explain to Dick that I had been off work for several weeks following my heart attack and that I had booked a holiday in Jersey. He said that he understood, but added that when I returned from holiday he wanted me to work closely with him. So while Janette and I headed for Jersey, the team flew to Bergen in Norway for pre-season training. However, by the Friday of the first week of our planned fortnight's holiday, I received a telephone call from Martin Bain, now the club's director of football, informing me that Dick urgently required my presence in Norway.

According to Martin, Dick simply couldn't handle the Scottish press corps and he wanted someone the journalists knew to deal with the media. I agreed to return a week early and flew to Norway the following Monday. The first thing Dick said to me was that I would need to get the press off his back. He also explained that he was prepared to hold two media conferences a week, before and after a game, and four in the event of the team playing twice in the same week. Dick also wanted it made crystal clear that he would not do any one-to-one interviews. In other words, it was my job to act as a press liaison officer. It was also the start of what turned out to be a difficult relationship between the manager and the press. Dick took the view – rightly or wrongly – that his job was to put a winning team on the park, not satisfy the demands of the press and, in fairness, he never played favourites with any of the journalists.

The players were still training when I arrived in Bergen and, as I hadn't seen any of them since my heart attack, they came over to ask how I was keeping and to wish me good luck. Unbeknown to me, Dick was watching and could clearly see that I had a close relationship with them. Perhaps that helped make his mind up about me, for the following day he took me into his confidence and shocked me with the comment that he had only three decent players. He omitted to say which players he was referring to, but I suspect that Jorg Albertz and Barry Ferguson were two of the trio.

I felt it was a pity that so many had been allowed to leave following the break-up of the previous team; players like Andy Goram, Paul Gascoigne, Stuart McCall, Richard Gough, Ian Durrant, Ally McCoist, Brian Laudrup and Gordon Durie – almost an entire team. I am not saying that those players would have been the solution in the long term, but short term they could have provided some answers at least until Dick got himself properly organised. In the event, Dick's observation that, 'I need to buy players,' was spot on.

The notion that he would have to do so with great gusto was strengthened when Rangers found themselves three goals down to Shelbourne in Dick's first European game in charge. It was a UEFA Cup preliminary tie and the match was played at Tranmere's Prenton Park, due to concerns about possible crowd trouble if the game took place in the Irish Republic. It was also Gio van Bronckhorst's debut and, although the team fought back to win, 5–3, Dick must have wondered what the hell kind of club he had joined. In addition to van Bronckhorst, Dick had set about the transfer market with vigour and Arthur Numan, Andrei Kanchelskis, Lionel Charbonnier, Gabriel Amato and Rod Wallace were the other early arrivals.

It had also become obvious to me that Dick was a very demanding man. The only time I saw him was at training or to inform him that the press were waiting to see him. He didn't invite me into his office and he was not a social person, especially at the beginning. A lot of people – especially those in the media – had already made their minds up that Dick was cold and aloof, but while I could understand those sentiments to an extent, they did not paint an accurate picture of the man.

I often felt that people misunderstood him. Before a game, for example, he was so focused on the job to be done that he wasn't into casual chat, while afterwards he had to see his own players and then the media and after that it was time to get back on the team coach. Dick isn't inwardly what he appears to be on the surface. People forgot that he was the first foreign coach at the club and, in my experience, he never liked walking into a room full of people. In fact, he's a very private person and in many ways he is very shy – unless he's on the training ground, where he feels at home working with players.

It was a difficult time for me, trying to keep the press happy, but my personal situation began to change one day at training when I remarked to Dick that I had spotted a difference in Lorenzo Amoruso's attitude. I had observed that Lorenzo had been surly and uncommunicative during the morning training session, but that the Italian had undergone a change of attitude in the afternoon. 'You noticed, too,' commented Dick. It was small things like that that led to us building a relationship. Dick had obviously been briefed about me, but he had wanted to see for himself what my strengths were.

Eventually, we became very close, probably as close as anyone could ever get to Dick, who never had many friends. Thinking about it, probably the only people he was close to during his time at Rangers were the chairman, his assistant, Bert van Lingen, and me. We used to meet at the club's training complex at Murray Park at 8.15 a.m. for coffee and Dick would bounce ideas off Bert and me. I described it as a 'relaxed meeting of minds' and thoroughly enjoyed those sit-downs. Dick and Bert were so close it wasn't true. I think Dick looked upon Bert as a dear friend who had joined him on an adventure.

Dick was obsessed with football, to the point that he drove his wife mad at times. After being at the ground from first thing in the morning until 5 p.m., Dick would drive home, have dinner with Dieuwke and then lock himself away in another room and watch videos of game after game. Dick is a workaholic. He's also a perfectionist, who puts his heart and soul into the job and leaves no stone unturned. Consequently, he makes big demands on others.

Dieuwke is very different from Dick. She wanted to go out and enjoy herself socially and Janette and I enjoyed several evenings in their company. Dick doesn't drink or smoke, but the pair of them visited us from time to time and he was capable of being good fun. If Dick knew you and trusted you he was capable of relaxing, but invariably he had his guard up and I think that had much to do with the language barrier. Dick can communicate perfectly well in English, but he was never sure if he was using the correct words and was always scared that he would put his foot in it.

Dick also had a problem dealing with the laws of this country. When he was involved in a car smash outside the gates of Cameron House on Loch Lomond, he didn't think he was in the wrong, and on another occasion, when he was prosecuted for using his mobile phone while driving, he couldn't understand what all the fuss was about.

Dick's attention to detail also let him down from time to time. He would have his training schedule mapped out to the letter, but didn't take into account the possibility of a player being injured and throwing his plans into disarray. On more than one occasion I was forced to pick up my mobile and put a call into Jordanhill, where the reserves trained, and request that a player be whisked over to Stepps to make up the numbers.

The closer we became the more Dick talked about the players and tactics. He would instruct me to watch the defence or the midfield and then we would sit down after lunch and discuss what we had seen. I became increasingly more involved with that side of the club. For example, when Barry Ferguson was waiting to undergo surgery on a hernia, while the team was chasing the title, we discussed the need for a replacement for Barry and both of us hit on the American midfield player, Claudio Reyna. Claudio was with Wolfsburg in Germany at the time and he turned out to be an excellent signing for Rangers.

Our relationship continued to grow on the back of things like that and I think Dick trusted me to always give him an honest opinion, not what I thought he wanted to hear. Dick, in fact, rekindled the flame in me that had died when I had quit as manager. I was given the opportunity to get back into studying the way teams played and the tactical side of the game, which I have always had a passion for.

People never seem to tire of quoting that Dick spent £70 million on players and yet failed to achieve success in Europe, which the chairman had hoped he would bring to the club when he bankrolled the various deals, but Dick did not enjoy the best of luck.

Beating Parma in the European Cup in season 1999–2000 to qualify for the group stage of the Champions League was a marvellous achievement. Then there was the evening in Munich when the team produced one of the finest displays I have seen from a Rangers side abroad and should have murdered Bayern. Instead, the club suffered the misfortune of seeing Michael Mols sustain a horrific knee injury. Not only did we lose the game, but we lost Mols and that was a savage blow, because Dick had created a very good side, with experienced players like Rod Wallace and Arthur Numan. Mols had been signed from FC Utrecht for £4 million and his pace and ability to turn defenders had quickly established him as a key man, but he was never the same player after a freak challenge by the Bayern goalkeeper, Oliver Kahn, left the Dutchman with knee ligament damage.

Dick is an astute tactician who believes in players doing their job in a simple and disciplined fashion, but one thing no one can take away from Dick was his achievement in guiding Rangers to the SPL championship in his first season in charge. Winning the title at Celtic Park represented a massive feat, in my view. Rangers, in fact, completed the treble in season 1998–99 and retained the title twelve months later.

Dick claimed that I was the first to know of his decision to quit as manager, in December 2001, and accept the role of Dutch national coach for a second time. However, I suspect that he had already discussed the situation with David Murray, because he thought the world of the chairman. Dick explained that he felt he had done everything he could for Rangers and did not want to risk harming the club in any way. That was typical of the man.

A year before Dick left, I told him I was getting too old to be running after players and the press. I also made the point that the job I was currently doing for him would no longer exist when he left, because a Scottish manager coming in would know the ropes. Dick asked me what I wanted to do and I replied that I fancied the idea of working with young players and school kids. I felt that I had the credentials to be able to deal with parents and put their minds at rest and Dick thought it a great idea, although he insisted on me continuing to be present at first-team games. After Alex McLeish took over I continued to assist him for six months before taking a step back, but I am still involved with the youngsters at the club and that's thanks to Dick. Youth development is an important area of the club and I thoroughly enjoy being part of that.

I keep in close contact with Dick, and Janette and I remain friends with him and Dieuwke. When he was Dutch national coach he invited the pair of us over for a few days to watch Holland play the Czech Republic in a European Championship qualifying match and looked after us splendidly at the team's hotel. We continue to exchange phone calls and text messages and I will never forget his wonderful gesture when he presented me with the gift of an SPL championship medal inscribed to me. Dick walked into Ibrox one day and said, 'John, I have a gift for you. I want you to have this because you deserve it.' He then proceeded to hand over the medal with a mixture of shyness and the minimum of fuss. It was a very touching moment and confirmation, if any was needed, of the bond that had grown between us.

CHAPTER 25

FAMILY AFFAIRS

I t's not easy being the wife of a football player. Often the demands of the job mean that the husband has to come first and that leads to inevitable disruption of family life. However, I have been fortunate that the woman I first met at a dance in her home town of Bo'ness in August 1962 has always shown understanding. Janette has undoubtedly been my biggest supporter and without her help and guidance over the past forty years my life would have run far less smoothly.

I guess it was a case of love at first sight, for I asked Janette to marry me within a week of our meeting, but once she had agreed to become my wife, Janette had to put up with football disrupting our planned wedding day. Having become engaged on Janette's twenty-first birthday on 14 May 1965, we had planned to get hitched on 20 March 1967 – until a football match came between us and our nuptials. We had deliberately chosen a Monday to get wed so there was no direct clash with football, or at least so we thought, but the European Cup-Winners' Cup draw led to a dramatic change of plans.

Nowadays, the date of each round is announced well in advance, but the competition was less well organised thirty-eight years ago and we didn't discover that Rangers would be playing Real Zaragoza on 22 March, in the return leg of our third round tie until after our wedding arrangements had been made. Football won – not for the first time – and our wedding had to be put back a week, but, fortunately, as it was a weekday, the sudden change in arrangement didn't cause too many problems.

The hotel where the reception was being held, the Fox Covert at Corstorphine, was very understanding and so was the Minister, the Reverend Selby-Wright of the Cannongate Kirk on the Royal Mile in Edinburgh. The Reverend Selby-Wright was in actual fact Moderator of the General Assembly of the Church of Scotland. The Cannongate Kirk is also the Queen's church, because of its close proximity to Holyrood Palace. It just so happened that in addition to the Scotland football captain being a member of the Cannongate Kirk congregation, so, too, was the Scotland rugby captain, Pringle Fisher. I recall one Sunday morning the Reverend Selby-Wright inviting me back to his manse for a glass of sherry, explaining that Charles would be joining him and it would be a great thrill if he had an opportunity to meet the captains of the international football and rugby teams. 'Charles who?' I asked. Silly question! He was referring to HRH Prince Charles, but I declined the invitation as I had already had the good fortune to meet the heir to the throne.

When our wedding eventually did go ahead on 27 March, Rangers were through to the semi-finals of the European Cup-Winners' Cup, by dint of me having won the toss of a coin to decide the tie, after it had ended 2–2 on aggregate following extra time. Inevitably, many of the telegrams we received referred to my stroke of good fortune. Others contained less flattering references to Rangers' Scottish Cup defeat by little Berwick Rangers two months earlier.

Given the circumstances, we experienced very few problems,

despite the disruption to our original arrangements. The hymn sheets had already been printed so the date showed 20 March, but other than that, everything more or less fell into place. The only drama involved the late arrival of Janette's uncle, who was giving the bride away as her father had died when she was a youngster. He travelled from his home in Dunfermline and was delayed by a traffic jam on the Forth Road Bridge, but as someone remarked, he was only a few minutes late, while according to the hymn sheet we were a week late!

Our first home was in the Liberton district of Edinburgh, near Braidhills Golf Club. I had been asked on numerous occasions by the Rangers manager, Scot Symon, to move to the west, but I preferred the idea of living in Edinburgh, because I felt it would afford us greater privacy. Janette, who had been employed as a civil servant with the Department of Pensions and National Insurance prior to our marriage, gave up work. Most days I caught the 8.30 a.m. train from Waverley and returned home on the 1 p.m. from Queen Street and, as I was still a growing boy, I was ready to tuck into a three-course lunch when I arrived home, so I wasn't keen on my wife working.

However, after our son, Murray, was born on 20 June 1969, I opened a shop on the Royal Mile, specialising in the design and sale of club ties and Janette looked after the books. I employed a full-time manager, but it was still hard going, because people expected to see me behind the counter and my football commitments with Rangers and Scotland meant that the shop was a huge drain on my time and impacted on our family life. Eventually, it seemed like a good idea to chuck in the business and concentrate on football and family, but we were happy to continue living in Edinburgh and I spent the entire eighteen years of my playing career travelling back and forth to Glasgow. But as I have already explained, a year after becoming manager I was forced to concede defeat and move closer to the job – before the travelling killed me.

Murray was never going to be a footballer like his dad and, in many ways, I was pleased about that. Had he tried to make it as a footballer, I would have hated Murray to have had to labour under the burden of inevitable comparisons with his old man, because it's hard enough for youngsters growing up nowadays without them having to try to emulate the feats of their parents.

Many a time I have asked Janette for her advice when I have been offered a deal of some sort or been asked to perform a certain duty and she has cautioned me against going ahead with it. Invariably, a few weeks or months later, her intuition that it wasn't right for me has been proved correct.

Janette and I have been very happy together, but we don't share any sporting passions. She used to attend games when I was a player and she enjoyed being a spectator at that time, but she doesn't go to games nowadays. We are probably happiest with our own company and have never been the sort to go partying or nightclubbing. We have a small and select group of friends and we know how to enjoy ourselves in their company, but I have always felt that it's important for people to like us for what we are, rather than who we are.

Life has been pretty good to us, but it got a whole lot better with the arrival of our granddaughter, Kaitlin, on 10 March 2004. It was like winning the lottery. Having a grandchild has changed our lives. I was away from home a great deal of the time when Murray was a youngster and it was left to Janette to undertake a lot of the duties of the father. I suppose I missed him growing up to an extent and it wasn't easy for Janette, but she did a great job and we are both extremely proud of our son. Now that I have much more time to spend with Kaitlin I realise just want a wonderful job Janette did.

Murray didn't get married until he was thirty and we never heard him or our lovely daughter-in-law, Laura, discuss plans to have children, so when they broke the news to us that Laura was pregnant, it came as a wonderful surprise. I don't think Janette and I could have been more pleased.

When Laura went into labour I surprised myself at just how concerned I was that everything would work out and that Laura and the baby would be well. To be honest, I was probably more uptight than I ever felt prior to a football match. I had the distraction of football when Janette was expecting Murray, but probably having more time to think about the impending arrival of Kaitlin put me on edge.

On the day that Laura was due to have the baby, Murray kept phoning from the hospital, The Princess Royal in Glasgow, to keep us informed about what was happening. He also promised to give us a call the moment our grandchild was born, but eventually the waiting became unbearable and I got myself so worked up that I decided to drive to the hospital rather than wait for Murray's call. At one stage, I even considered going to reception to enquire after Laura. Fortunately, I managed to resist the temptation. I had arranged with Murray to pick him up at the hospital and when he phoned to give us the news that Kaitlin had arrived, Janette told him that she would need to contact me on my mobile. Murray asked where I was and when Janette told him that I was sitting outside the hospital he was completely taken aback. We are very fortunate that Murray and Laura live nearby, because it means we see a lot of Kaitlin. Janette looks after her a couple of days a week and one of our pleasures these days is pushing our granddaughter in her pram.

Not that I'm ready for retirement – far from it. I still lead an active life and my work with Rangers keeps me busy. When I returned to the club in January 1990, I initially had no specific role. I think I was invited back because of my relationship with the media and the supporters and I suppose the chairman considered that I was ideally suited to work in public relations.

I immediately made it clear to Graeme Souness that I wasn't interested in becoming involved on the football side, largely because I didn't want people pointing fingers at me. I would have hated to have been accused of wanting to meddle in team affairs, because I was a former manager, so there was a very fine line to be walked. Mind you, Graeme involved me anyway, probably more than I wanted, and later, when Walter Smith became manager, he, too, kept me involved, although not to the same extent. However, I saw myself more as a conduit between the club and the supporters and I launched the Teddy Bear Club, for the benefit of the younger fans. The club mascot, 'Broxi Bear', which is an anagram of Ibrox, was spawned from that idea. I also introduced stadium tours, because I feel that every supporter has the right to walk through the front door and see what happens behind the scenes.

I was eventually given the title of public rangers executive, but, to begin with, I didn't deal with the press on match days. That was Alistair Hood's job, but as he was operations director and often had to deal with matters pertaining to ground safety or crowd control, the press came into my domain, even more so when Dick Advocaat became manager and made it clear that he wanted as little to do with the media as possible.

Part of my remit was to act as a liaison between the club and the fans and I was deeply honoured, thirteen years ago, when I was elected president of NARSA, which stands for the North American Rangers Supporters' Association. When I attended my first NARSA annual general meeting in Toronto there were just seven member clubs. Now there are forty-five spread throughout America and Canada. I have since attended several NARSA meetings, including two in Las Vegas, and I hope to be present at next year's AGM in San Francisco, a city I have visited previously and liked.

Three years ago I was also appointed chairman of the Rangers Charity Trust, but the greatest honour to be bestowed on me by the club was my appointment as a director in December 2003. I didn't have the least inkling of what was about to happen when the then chairman, John McClelland, asked to see me in his hotel room prior to our November Champions League tie with Manchester United at Old Trafford. John informed me that he had been speaking with David Murray and that they were keen to make me a director. It was a bolt from the blue and a real surprise, but a very pleasant one all the same. It also meant a lot when Lawrence Marlborough, who had sought my opinion before buying control of the club in the 1980s, was one of the first to telephone and congratulate me on my appointment.

The role of director has changed out of all recognition since I was a young player. Then, if a director of Rangers Football Club walked into a room he had an aura about him. They were the money men and shared control of the club. Nowadays, the club is run by working directors. I hold shares in Rangers, but I am by no means a leading shareholder, although given that football is the business we're in, I can offer my experiences as a player and manager and my football knowledge, which is very important. Over the years, Rangers have tended to have a former player on the board. Alan Morton, George Brown and Willie Waddell served as directors at various times and they were people that the fans recognised and could relate to. I think it's the same in my case. I am a supporter myself and I see myself as a representative of the fans. It's not just a job to me. I am an ambassador for the club. I attend all first-team games and represent the club. More often than not I hear people refer to me not simply as 'John Greig', but 'John Greig of the

Rangers' and I take that as a huge compliment. I also make no apology for the fact that I regard being a director as a massive honour.

I was also deeply flattered when I was elected to the Scotland Sporting Hall of Fame in Edinburgh on St Andrew's Day 2002 and the Hampden Hall of Fame last year. I have certainly come a long way since the days forty-five years ago when I travelled to training by public transport. I used to catch a corporation bus along with Jim Baxter, Ralph Brand and Jimmy Millar for the journey from Queen Street Station to Ibrox and I have to laugh when I recall our mode of transport. Can you imagine David Beckham or Zinédine Zidane catching the bus to training? Not likely. If the Ferrari fails to start they have a second one parked in the garage as back-up! Mind you, our bus journeys were often undertaken in complete silence. It depended on what sort of mood Baxter and Brand were in as to whether they even bothered to talk to Jimmy Millar and I.

Meanwhile, I have no difficulty recalling the last time I travelled by corporation bus. Janette and I had booked dinner at one of our favourite restaurants, La Lanterna in Glasgow's Hope Street, and after dropping my wife off I went in search of a parking place. I was forced to park the car a couple of streets away and I was making my way back to the restaurant when a bus came round the corner and stopped. 'Where are you headed, Greigy?' asked the driver. There were no passengers aboard and when I told him he instructed me to hop on. It didn't bother him that he ended up driving the wrong way up a one-way street. Being John Greig of the Rangers definitely has certain advantages!

CHAPTER 26

BACK TO THE FUTURE

T he thought of retirement scares me. The prospect of playing golf every day appealed to me at one time, but not any more. I'm sure I would soon tire of that. Anyway, I don't think my body would stand up to the demands of eighteen holes, seven days a week. Mind you, I haven't had a real job for the past forty-five years. I have been very fortunate to do something I love and I consider myself to be one of the lucky few who are able to say that.

One thing is for sure, though, when the time comes they won't have to drag me screaming from my office at Murray Park. I promise that I'll go quietly, albeit reluctantly. I won't continue to work for Rangers unless I feel that I still have a contribution to make. I would never want to become a hindrance or an embarrassment to the club that has been my life since I was a teenager, so I won't overstay my welcome. However, as long as the chairman, David Murray, feels I'm capable of continuing to serve a purpose and I'm enjoying what I am doing, I'll carry on for a few more years yet – health permitting.

I have one distinct advantage over most others in my age group in that I work with youngsters and that helps keep me young, mentally at least. It's amazing how their enthusiasm rubs off on you. It's infectious and I get a huge lift when I don't see a kid for a few months and then discover how much he has developed in the intervening period. These lads make me feel wanted and sometimes my wife, Janette, has to remind me to grow up and start acting my age. I recall how Sandy Jardine and I used to share the view that one of the best jobs in football was coaching the young players at a top club. It is unbelievably rewarding watching them develop into top class players and making the grade.

I also attend all the first-team games. I suppose I do so in an ambassadorial sense in my role as a director. The game has changed a great deal over the past forty-odd years and now when I walk into most boardrooms the majority of those present are businessmen. There isn't the same number of football people around any more. It's a little different when the team plays abroad. Those involved with clubs on the continent appear to be more enlightened about the football side of the business. I can often see when I am introduced to someone and my background is explained to them that their face lights up. They invariably display a level of respect and want to talk to me about the game in general and I enjoy that aspect. After all, football has been my life. When I am asked whether I get bored with it all I reply, how could I possibly become bored with something I enjoy so much?

Irrespective of the day when it ends for me at Rangers, you will never hear me say a single word against the club. How could I possibly? Rangers have given me years of pleasure and sheer enjoyment in various capacities. Maybe when it does end though – a few weeks after the realisation hits me – I'll ask myself what was it all about? It is sometimes difficult to comprehend what my life has been, but I am immensely proud of what I have achieved. In quieter moments I reflect on this wee boy from Prestonfield getting a skelp across the back of his head from his old man for scuffing his shoes playing football and realise that I haven't done so badly for myself. Most of what I have achieved and the benefits my family and I have enjoyed have come through football.

One of the benefits of retirement will be the opportunity to spend more time with Kaitlin, our granddaughter. I try to make as much time as possible to spend with her, but it's different from your own child in that you hand her back to her parents at the end of the day. Mind you, I must confess that when Janette and I go on holiday we miss the wee one terribly. Not that I am a great holiday person. Ten days is usually more than sufficient before I become home sick and develop itchy feet.

Having more free time will also allow me to indulge my other sporting passion, boxing. I have been a fan since I was a kid listening to Sugar Ray Robinson and Randolph Turpin slugging it out for the world middleweight title. I also became friendly with Ken Buchanan, who was a member of the same boys' club in Edinburgh. Kenny went on to become world lightweight champion and I performed the opening ceremony at his hotel in the capital. Kenny, who was a great champion, invited Willie Henderson and me to watch his British title fight with Maurice Cullen in London in 1968, when he stopped the Englishman in the eleventh round. Kenny and his former wife, Carol, used to visit our home in Edinburgh and it was a measure of his dedication that whenever Janette asked him what he would like to eat he invariably replied, 'A cup of tea and a water biscuit.'

Walter McGowan was another favourite of mine. Walter trained at Ibrox when he was world flyweight champion and regularly joined in bounce games with the rest of us. Walter's father and trainer, Joe Gans, was some character. I recall when Scotland played Italy in our World Cup qualifier in 1965, Joe wandering the streets of Naples with a battered old bag stuffed with millions of lira. Mind you, no one in his right mind would have dared to tackle wee Joe. Walter had fought and lost to Salvatore Burruni a couple of nights before in a European title bout and Joe had demanded payment in readies. He didn't trust the locals and refused payment in the form of a cheque.

I never boxed myself. The only boxing I did was with my feet, but I have always enjoyed watching the big fights and I actually considered arranging a trip to Las Vegas for a world title bout when I worked in the travel and hospitality business. I was a huge fan of Sugar Ray Leonard and of the great middleweight division of his era, which included the likes of Marvin Hagler, Thomas Hearns and Roberto Duran.

Believe it or not, I have always been a keen gardener. Imagine the Rangers captain with green fingers? Seriously, though, I enjoyed the escapism of pottering about in my garden, but since suffering my heart attack I have had to cut back on the heavy stuff and confine myself to putting plants in pots, much to the amusement of my fellow director, Campbell Ogilvie, who always gives me a bit of stick when we travel to games together.

As I have said, apart from the huge enjoyment I derive from being with Kaitlin, my work with the youngsters at Rangers, overseeing their training, gives me my greatest pleasure nowadays. I am involved mainly with players from school-leaving age up to first-team level and I am at Murray Park on certain evenings watching the various teams, from the under-tens to the under-sixteens. I offer opinions on the development of these lads and I try to ensure that I stay in touch with all the players. I also feel that it is important for me to speak with their parents to let them know what Rangers is all about.

No matter what the future holds, I doubt very much that I will ever lose my passion for football. That is why I am concerned at the current state of the game. Having spent my entire career in Scotland, I have a lot to thank this country for and, therefore, I would love to see our domestic game regain the status it once enjoyed in Europe when Rangers, Celtic, Aberdeen and Dundee United were contesting – and winning – European finals. There is no doubt that the game has sunk to the lowest level I can recall, particularly at international level, but I believe the talent is still out there and that it simply needs to be moulded and a bit of pride restored.

I think Walter Smith will eventually manage to turn the situation round as far as the Scotland team is concerned. Walter was appointed national team coach at a time when the players and the supporters were at their lowest ebb, but already we have seen positive signs of a revival. I believe, with the proper backing, Walter will succeed in lifting the nation's spirits, but it isn't going to happen overnight.

The reason for my optimism is that I have the opportunity to see young players develop and progress into the first-team squad at Rangers, as well as watching those who come to Murray Park to play games at various levels, and I have no hesitation in saying that there is still a lot of individual talent in the Scottish game. No matter what the prophets of doom say to the contrary, the product has not reached its sell-by date.

If only we could replicate the games of street football that were once such a common sight. Nowadays, any kids playing in the street run the risk of being knocked down by a motor car, but when I was a youngster it was our way of life. Our parents always knew they could find us in the street or down at the local park kicking a ball. I am also a great believer that everything in life goes in cycles. The situation will turn again and it won't take that long.

Of course, football, in keeping with most sports, has to compete with a growing number of pursuits and interests that weren't available to people of my generation. I have never owned a bicycle in my life and I wouldn't even know how to operate a computer, but with so many counter-attractions there are simply not as many youngsters playing football these days – and that's a problem.

Digressing for just a moment, I have been surprised that football has not had the impact in the States that I thought it would. I had imagined that the parents of American youngsters would welcome the fact that they don't have to spend a fortune on equipment to enable their kids to participate in the sport. All that is required is a ball, whereas most American sports are expensive, because of the gear that is required. One of the reasons why so many working class kids made it in this country is because football is a cheap sport to play. Times change, though, and youngsters in our more affluent society expect to be offered decent facilities and a higher level of coaching and if we provide both, standards will gradually rise again.

One of the consequences of falling standards among our own young players was the influx of foreign imports, but I am not one of those who bemoaned that, for I believe it was a good thing for our game, in as much as it provided a lesson for Scottish youngsters. They quickly realised that they would have to attain the same high technical standards to become great players themselves, but it's not just about skill. I believe it would be wrong for any one to try to remove the competitive spirit from our youngsters.

Take Brian Laudrup as an example. Brian was blessed with unbeliev-able skill, but one of the things I have often said to our players is that I have never seen youngsters in another country with more competitive spirit or a greater will to win. None can match their energy, work rate and ability to keep on running for ninety minutes. On the other hand, I do see a lot of younger players in other countries who have a far higher level of technical ability. I preach to our players that they must practise their skills, so that they reach the same level, in the belief that they will eventually become even more effective than their foreign counterparts.

Regrettably, there appears to be a misconception abroad that the Scottish game is vastly inferior to other countries. I have spoken with a lot of foreign players and they tell me that their friends raised their eyebrows when they heard that they were coming to play in Scotland. Significantly, though, when these same players returned home they were quick to point out to their countrymen just how difficult they had found it to adjust to the pace and passion of our game. The physical nature of Scottish football invariably takes them by surprise. The ferocity of tackles and the fact that these players don't have time to stand off opponents and play passes is a shock to the system and most agree that they have to work harder to be successful in the SPL.

Old Firm games are a mind-boggling experience for players coming from abroad. Their eyes pop out of their heads the first time they experience the intensity, speed and physical nature of a Rangers-Celtic match. They can't believe just how hard they have to work, because the pace of the game never dips. Old Firm games are fast and furious from the first minute until the last and some simply cannot cope with the demands. Personally, I enjoyed the competitive nature of these games, though not always the aftermath, when I occasionally witnessed a post-match bust-up while travelling home to Edinburgh.

Because Celtic are Rangers' biggest rivals I always looked forward to playing against them. Apart from the satisfaction to be derived from a victory, the outcome of Old Firm games invariably had a large say in the destination of the championship. On the downside, though, defeat left you with an awful feeling. When I was a player and Rangers lost to Celtic I locked myself away for the remainder of the weekend, because I felt so deflated. Old Firm occasions are still massive, but I don't believe that these games are quite as big as they once were. Part of the reason for my saying that is the fact that the teams play four times a season in the SPL. There is a far greater familiarity, whereas when I began my career and for many years afterwards, Rangers and Celtic met twice a season in the league. The gap between games was also much longer, so the build-up to Old Firm games tended to be more concentrated.

Prior to the formation of the Premier League in season 1975–76, it was possible for the teams to meet four times in the course of one season, if we were drawn together in the cup competitions. Nowadays, the Old Firm can square up to one other half a dozen times. Consequently, less rests on the outcome of one game. If you lose the first one there is still time to play catch-up. The teams and the fans also don't have to wait quite so long for a second bite at the cherry. It is also difficult for the respective managers to do something hugely different, because the players know each other's styles so well.

Other factors have contributed to altering the face of Old Firm games. Prior to the capacity at Ibrox and Parkhead being drastically reduced, it was not uncommon for crowds of 80,000 and 90,000 to attend these games, with the support divided roughly fifty-fifty. Now the home support heavily outnumbers that of the opposition, but I doubt that the rivalry between the fans will ever lessen in terms of its sheer intensity. A lot of those not associated with either club say it is just another game, but they don't realise just what winning and losing means to the supporters. Depending on the outcome, many find it difficult to go to work the next day to face their colleagues if their team has lost and they are part of a mixed work force. Is it any wonder that it has been said that the most satisfying outcome of an Old Firm game is a draw, because then both sets of fans go home reasonably satisfied?

The foreign players have also had a bearing on Old Firm rivalry on the pitch. Half of them now look to play football and that is it. They have also brought their own unique style into the game, but there was definitely a time when careers were made and ruined in the course of one Old Firm game, because of a certain incident.

The fans are also more inclined to let players get away with certain things that would normally result in a reprimand. For example, if a player boots the ball upfield in an Old Firm game he is seen to be clearing his lines and is applauded for denying the opposition. However, if he does the same thing the following week you will hear muttering among the fans, because that individual has failed to be more constructive.

Mind you, I fear that finance has taken over the game to such an extent that it is increasingly difficult for Rangers and Celtic to survive in the Scottish game. When you consider what Rangers and Celtic receive from TV revenue compared to the top clubs in England, it doesn't require a degree in rocket science to work out that we are seriously disadvantaged when we enter the European arena. Rangers and Celtic are effectively playing a different ball game in terms of financial resources.

Let's be honest, in many ways football has only itself to blame when you consider that the top clubs attracted far larger crowds in the 1950s and 1960s, at a time when players were on a standard wage and that revenue clearly wasn't reinvested as it should have been. Quite frankly, the top players were often not paid their true worth, but the pendulum has swung too far in the opposite direction. I don't begrudge any footballer a top salary commensurate with his talents and his worth to his club, but some of the wage scales in what is still basically a working class game are obscene compared to what the average fan earns. To be perfectly blunt, the situation is out of control and needs to be addressed.

The reality, as things stand, is that from a financial point of view Rangers and Celtic must look to England and I think it would be very difficult for the majority of the clubs in the Premiership to accept the

Old Firm for immediate membership. That isn't going to happen, in my view. Rangers and Celtic would probably have to start off in the Championship and take their chance, but I shudder to think of the possible consequences if they weren't promoted straightaway. Probably the best hope is that Rupert Murdoch decides to change the menu and include Rangers and Celtic on the bill of fayre. Sky calls the shots and pay-for-view TV is certainly a huge carrot when you consider the limited number of tickets available to away fans.

Much as I don't think it will happen, should Rangers and Celtic ever leave to play in England, I would be very concerned about the fate of Scottish football. One possible solution would be for the Old Firm to field a second team in the SPL. That would help bolster the game north of the border, because the fans would continue to support a second team. One thing is for sure, we need to have something to excite the fans and attract sponsors if we are going to have a strong Scottish game in the future.

I also feel that the number of organisations running our game needs to be streamlined. We are a small country, yet we have three separate bodies administering the game. Is there really a need for the SFA, the SPL and the Scottish League? I believe we should have one major body governing Scottish football. Dick Advocaat used to laugh at the set-up and ask, 'Which set of rules are we playing to this week?'

League reconstruction is another hobby horse with me. It simply doesn't make economic sense for the smaller clubs to be asked to travel long distances to fulfil a fixture in front of just a few hundreds fans. Regional leagues would reduce that unnecessary financial burden.

I also believe that UEFA and FIFA ought to concern themselves less with the introduction of petty rules, such as implementing a ten-yard radius around the corner flag to prevent players from encroaching, and look at ways to assist referees in dealing with players who cheat. Nothing annoys me more than watching a player take a dive or feigning injury. I would welcome the introduction of a zero tolerance initiative, whereby any player deemed to have cheated in an effort to con the referee received an automatic red card. That would have an instant effect on the cheats. When I came into the game, players were reluctant to go down after a heavy tackle, because they didn't want anyone to know that they had been hurt, because that gave their opponent the upper hand, but nowadays you see players diving all over the place. Everything is done to assist the players, but little seems to be done to help the referees, who are on a hiding to nothing.

Since the controversy surrounding Geoff Hurst's goal in the 1966 World Cup final, the football authorities have been talking about the idea of installing cameras to determine whether the ball has crossed the line – and they are still talking! Referees, meanwhile, continue to be slaughtered by TV evidence. They have to make instant judgements based on what they have seen, without the benefit of high-tech equipment. They are only human and are bound to make mistakes, but the majority of them are honest guys. No one is going to tell me that referees are in it for the money.

I am also opposed to the suggestion that non-Scots should be brought in to referee Old Firm games. That's nonsense, in my view, because the guys refereeing every week in the SPL know the players and are far better equipped to handle situations that would be foreign to outsiders. Basically, all that is required to assist our referees is for those running the game to display a little more common sense.

Still on the subject of referees, I find it ridiculous that they are forced to retire at the age of forty-nine and are forced to come off the FIFA list four years earlier. The situation has become even more farcical with the introduction of a plan to reduce the retirement age to forty-seven within the next two years. The best referees tend to be the most experienced ones, so why does the game want to discard them at a certain age?

Hugh Dallas is a classic example. Hugh was fourth official at the 2002 World Cup final, but he chose to quit at the end of last season rather than eventually be pushed. By the time a referee reaches his forties, if he's not a class one official then he isn't going to be a major loss to the game, but if a referee is considered good enough to be on the FIFA list he must have achieved a high level of competence and consistency. In my opinion, the game needs these guys to continue until they can no longer meet the physical demands or they begin experiencing difficulties with their eyesight. Even then, what is to stop them passing on their expertise to younger referees at a lower level by assisting them to run games? A footballer's body tells him when it's time to quit. You begin missing the ball, because your timing becomes a fraction slower, but your ability to read the game remains unimpaired.

While the Scottish game is still some way short of a major revival, there are encouraging signs that more indigenous talent is coming through the ranks and Hibs are one of the clubs which have brought a freshness to the domestic scene. Hibs have given young players their head and encouraged them to play football. The problem for these youngsters at Easter Road will be in coping with challenges to their growing reputations after making such a big impact in season 2004–05, but, hopefully, Hibs will continue to prosper, along with the likes of Aberdeen and Hearts. Dundee United, too, have the potential to have a bigger say in domestic affairs.

Having three or four teams mount a more sustained challenge to the Old Firm would make the SPL a much more competitive league and would also lead to a general rise in standards. But while Hibs were deserving of great praise for finishing third in the 2004–05 championship, the worrying fact is that they were a long way behind

Rangers and Celtic. A thirty-two and thirty-one points differential tells its own story.

Obviously, from a personal point of view, Rangers being crowned champions was tremendous, but it was perhaps the most bizarre season in living memory. Rangers and Celtic kept handing the title to one another and it almost seemed as if neither team wanted to win it until the last two minutes of the season. No one in their right mind could have prophesied the drama that unfolded at Easter Road and Fir Park, with Rangers beating Hibs and Celtic surrendering a one-goal lead as Motherwell struck twice in the dying moments. If you had suggested to any Rangers fan that the team would concede eleven points to Dundee United and Inverness Caledonian Thistle and still be crowned champions they would have suggested that you were crackers – but football wouldn't be the great game it is if it were ever wholly predictable.

STATISTICS

John Greig, born Edinburgh, 11 September 1942.

Career: United Crossroads Boys' Club, Edina Hearts, Whitburn, Rangers August 1960. Debut 2 September 1961 Scottish League Cup v Airdrie (scored). Retired May 1978 and appointed Rangers Manager, resigned October 1983. Worked in travel industry and broadcasting. Became Rangers PR Executive January 1990.

Honours:

5 Scottish League Championship, 6 Scottish Cup, 4 Scottish League Cup, European Cup-Winners' Cup 1972. Scottish Player of the Year 1966, 1976. Awarded MBE 1977. Won 44 Scottish International caps, 14 Scottish League appearances, 2 Under-23 Internationals. 857 first team appearances for Rangers, 136 goals. As a manager 2 Scottish Cups, 2 Scottish League Cups.

Season	League		Scottish Cup		Scottish League Cup		European	
RANGERS								
1961–62	11	7	1	-	2	1	1*	-
1962–63	27	5	7	-	5	5	2#	-
1963–64	34	4	6	2	10	-	2*	-
1964–65	34	4	3	-	7	-	7*	1
1965–66	32	7	7	-	10	1	-	-
1966–67	32	2	1	-	8	1	9#	-
1967–68	32	11	4	2	6	-	6+	1
1968–69	33	6	5	1	6	-	9+	2
1969–70	30	7	3	2	6	-	4#	-
1970–71	26	8	7	-	8	1	2+	-
1971–72	28	8	6	1	6	-	8#	-
1972–73	30	7	6	-	10	3	2~	-
1973–74	32	6	1	-	10	2	4#	2
1974–75	22	1	-	-	1	-	-	-
1975–76	36	2	5	-	10	1	4*	-
1976–77	30	-	5	-	11	1	2*	-
1977–78	29	2	5	1	5	1	2#	1
Total	498	87	72	9	121	17	64	7

*   European Cup
+   Fairs Cup
#   Cup-Winners' Cup
~   Super Cup

Other matches

Glasgow Cup 20 (3 goals); various cup and tournament games 82 (13 goals).

INTERNATIONAL MATCHES

Scotland

1964 v England, West Germany, Wales, Finland, Northern Ireland.

1965 v England, Spain, Poland, Finland (1 goal), Northern Ireland, Poland, Italy (1), Wales (1), Italy.

1966 v England, Holland, Portugal, Brazil, Wales, Northern Ireland.

1967 v England, Northern Ireland, Wales.

1968 v England, Holland, Denmark, Austria, Cyprus.

1969 v West Germany, Wales, Northern Ireland, England, Cyprus, Republic of Ireland, West Germany, Austria.

1970 v Wales, England, Denmark.

1971 v Belgium, Wales (sub), Northern Ireland, England.

1975 v Denmark.

SCOTTISH LEAGUE

1963 v Irish League

1964 v Football League, League of Ireland.

1965 v Football League, Irish League.

1966 v Football League.

1967 v Irish League (1 goal), Football League.

1968 v League of Ireland, Football League.

1969 v Football League, Irish League.

1970 v Football League.

1976 v Football League (sub).

UNDER-23

1963 v Wales.

1964 v England.

INDEX

More Non-fiction from Headline

1966 AND ALL THAT

GEOFF HURST

'Stands out from the standard ghosted
autobiographies . . . the period detail gives it
huge charm' Simon Barnes, *The Times*

Geoff Hurst's unique hat-trick in the 1966 World
Cup final catapulted him to international
superstardom and changed his life forever. Now,
in this updated edition of his long-awaited and
bestselling autobiography, he recalls England's
greatest sporting moment, and reveals the inside
story of what it was like playing with and against
some of the finest footballers in history –
Pele, Moore, Beckenbauer and Charlton.

His assessment of today's superstars, packed with
insight from one of the game's true legends,
must be read, as England look to the future
with an exciting young squad.

NON-FICTION / AUTOBIOGRAPHY 0 7472 4187 2

Now you can buy any of these other bestselling
sports titles from your bookshop or
direct from the publisher.

FREE P&P AND UK DELIVERY
(Overseas and Ireland £3.50 per book)

The Autobiography	Gareth Edwards	£7.99
The Autobiography	John Barnes	£6.99
Crossing the Line	Charlie Brooks	£7.99
Ultra Nippon	Jonathan Birchall	£7.99
Barmy Army	Dougie Brimson	£6.99
Vinnie	Vinnie Jones	£6.99
Formula One Uncovered	Derick Allsop	£7.99
Manchester United Ruined My Life	Colin Shindler	£5.99
God Save the Team	Eddy Brimson	£6.99
Dark Trade	Donald McRae	£7.99
A Lot of Hard Yakka	Simon Hughes	£6.99
Left Foot Forward	Garry Nelson	£6.99

TO ORDER SIMPLY CALL THIS NUMBER

01235 400 414

or visit our website: www.madaboutbooks.com

Prices and availability subject to change without notice.